THE FLAVOR OF
California

Fresh Vegetarian Cuisine from the Golden State

MARLENA SPIELER

HarperCollins*West*
A Division of HarperCollinsPublishers

FRONT COVER: *Grilled Old and New World Vegetables*

FIRST HARPERCOLLINS HARDCOVER EDITION PUBLISHED IN 1994

This book was previously published in a different format in the United Kingdom by Thorsons, an imprint of HarperCollins*Publishers*.

Library of Congress Cataloging-in-Publication Data

Spieler, Marlena.
    The flavor of California : fresh vegetarian cuisine
    from the Golden State / Marlena Spieler.
        p. cm.
    Includes index.
    ISBN 0-06-258517-7
    1. Vegetarian cookery. 2. Cookery,
    American–Californian style. 3. Cookery, International. I.
    Title.
    TX837.S69   93-5431
    641.5'636–dc20   CIP

- -
94 95 96 97 98 XXX 10 9 8 7 6 5 4 3 2 1

Photography by Petrina Tinslay
Food prepared for photography by Elise Pascoe
Styling by Elise Pascoe

Contents

Acknowledgments

TO LEAH AND ALAN, WITH OLIVE OIL, GARLIC, CHILI PEPPERS, AND LOVE.

Thank you to:

- enthusiastic and attentive editor Siobhàn O'Connor in Australia, Sarah Sutton and Jane Middleton in the UK, and Joann Moschella at HarperWest, USA.

- Bachi for her love of cooking and feeding, and joy of life.

- friends in tasting: Amanda and Tim Hamilton-Hemeter — for friendship and reviving doses of warmth at their Sonoma County vineyard; Gretchen Spieler; Hélène and Robin Simpson and family; Rachel and Jim Wight and family; Fred and Mary Barclay; Christine Smith; Paula Levine; India and Josephine Aspin; Paul Richardson and Nacho Trives; Tricia Robinson; Alfredo, the gargoyle man; Esther Novack and John Chendo; and Jerome and Sheila Freeman.

- *San Francisco Chronicle* food editor Michael Bauer and senior book editor Janice Gallegher, who have taught, and continue to teach me, so much.

- My cat, Freud, a continual source of inspiration who eats his way through every fresh pot herb I bring into the house. He is the only cat I know who smells of garlic.

FURTHER ACKNOWLEDGMENTS

Stylist Elise Pascoe and the publishers wish to thank the following contributors for generously supplying props for photography:

Accoutrement Cook Shops
Barbara's Storehouse
Connoisseur Collection
David Jones (Australia) Pty Limited
Freedom Furniture
Gempo Giftware Australia
Hale Imports Pty Limited
Jacobus
Kambrook Distributors
Piper-Bishop
Studio Haus
The Bay Tree

In particular, they wish to acknowledge Monique Williams Artisan for hand-painted ceramics and Sean Tinslay for painted backgrounds.

Preface

I grew up with oranges growing outside my window, and these were picked to make freshly squeezed orange juice every morning. We had salads every evening, artichokes, avocados, asparagus, garden tomatoes, and lots of Mexican food. From my kitchen window I have watched Californian food evolve and change dramatically, becoming more and more of its essential self: fresh, zesty, full-flavored.

Modern Californian cuisine, especially vegetable cookery, is exciting, vibrant, and sensually delicious. It is simple-to-prepare and healthy everyday eating, yet is also perfect for entertaining — the bright colors and savory, rambunctious flavors stimulate the senses and help spark conversation. It combines the freshest fruits and vegetables with classical French technique, ethnic ingredients, a merging of gourmet with natural foods, an awareness of both contemporary style and health consciousness, and an appreciation of well-grown vegetables.

As food in California has absorbed the flavors of a wide variety of cuisines, so has much of the world in turn been influenced by Californian cuisine.

A Californian-style vegetarian diet, like the so-called 'Mediterranean' diet — lots of salads, fruit, grains, and olive oil — not only tastes delicious, it is a way of eating for health that nutritionists everywhere are recommending.

Though I am not a strict vegetarian, I am passionate about fresh vegetables and partial to animals who are alive rather than on my plate. I tend to agree with Nobel Prize writer Isaac Bashevis Singer. When asked if he was a vegetarian for health reasons, he replied, 'Yes. The health of the animal.'

Whatever your reasons for eating no or less meat may be, I hope you find this collection of robust vegetarian dishes as much of a pleasure to prepare and enjoy as I have had creating and compiling them.

SETTING THE SCENE:
THE MARIN COUNTY FARMERS' MARKET

The sunshine has a golden, honey-colored glow on the hilltop as I stroll from one vegetable and fruit stall to the next. A lazy bee settles on the pile of wild strawberries in front of me; I fill a bag gently with the delicate berries, trying not to crush them. On the next stall are blackberries and raspberries, both golden and red; the tomatoes are heaped in what seem like a rainbow of colors, from apple green to bright yellow, neon orange, and ruby red; the flavors cover a whole spectrum, too, from sweet to tart, tangy to juicy, and so richly varied are they that they redefine the meaning of the word 'tomato'.

Straw baskets hold fat artichokes on long stalks, ripe peaches with sweet flowery smells, purple plums nearly bursting with their tangy juices; they all go into my bag, along with a loaf of crisp and crusty bread that tastes of olive oil and a cache of wild spring greens and herbs that had been picked a mere hour or two before.

The air smells sweet and gentle in the late morning, and in an hour or so the food will all be on the table — a portrait of freshness for a sun-drenched summer lunch.

In our kitchen, the shopping is transformed into the following menu: multicolored tomatoes topped with fresh basil and rosemary, steamed artichokes with fresh tarragon aïoli, a salad of wild greens and herbs with crumbled local goat cheese, and crusty bread to soak up all the lusty juices. A bottle of chilled Chardonnay alongside and, for dessert, deep bowls of sweet berries, peaches, and plums, topped with scoops of locally churned ice cream.

This is Californian cuisine at its best: a veritable feast of simplicity.

Introduction

California has a fascinating cuisine and vegetarianism figures prominently for a variety of reasons, including ethnic influences, worldwide immigration, the natural foods movement, and devotion to the body beautiful.

Fruits and vegetables grow lushly and easily — the 'Golden State' produces 50 percent of America's fresh food on 3 percent of its farmland. Then there is the lifestyle: Californians, as a group, are health- and fitness-conscious. In fact, Californian vegetarian food is not limited to those who eschew meat; it is such superb, exciting, and fresh food that the absence of meat is hardly noticed and so it is eaten by everyone.

Like Mediterranean food, it is an olive oil-based cuisine rather than a butter-based one. Indeed, at most restaurants in northern California, the crusty loaf of bread that comes to the table with your meal will be accompanied by a saucer of fragrant olive oil rather than butter. Fresh herbs figure prominently, too, especially basil and coriander. Garlic is nearly everywhere, either rubbed on rough, toasted bread, *bruschetta*-style; chopped and sautéed; stir-fried into all manner of dishes; roasted whole and eaten as it comes; or used as the base for myriad sauces.

Seasonings reflect the ethnic makeup of the area: Chinese, Southeast Asian, Hispanic, Italian, Jewish/Russian, and so on. Cross-cultural dishes are the rule rather than the exception and so Italian pasta might be topped with an East–West coriander pesto, Chinese pot-stickers filled with Brazilian black beans, French-style goat cheese with Latin American chilies, Moroccan chermoula spooned onto bread, Russian pierogi filled with puréed vegetables, Californian style . . . somehow it all works. The food that comes to the table is exuberant, unexpected, and delicious.

HISTORY AND INFLUENCES

Californian cuisine as such may be a recent phenomenon, but people living on the West Coast have always eaten differently from the rest of the country. Even in the fifties, while those in the Midwest were eating canned vegetables, Californians were feasting on guacamole, artichokes, tacos, and chow mein.

To understand Californian vegetarian cookery, one must look at California's cultural and culinary history. East- and West-Coast culinary styles have differed markedly from the very beginning. When the first tribes of Native Americans are believed to have walked across Alaska's frozen Bering Straits down to what is now known as California, the staple diet for most of the Californian tribes was acorn porridge. Life revolved around its making: gathering, storing, grinding, and cooking the acorns, even the weaving of the baskets to cook them in. First, the acorns were pounded into a mealy flour, then the flour was leached of its bitter tannins and cooked to a mush. The cooking was done in tightly woven baskets, by plopping white-hot rocks into the water and acorn meal. The resulting porridge was eaten with whatever could be gathered — wild onions, berries, pine nuts, fish, and wild game. Often the mealy mixture was patted into cakes and baked on rocks in the hot sun.

In the southern desert regions, the Yuma and Mojave tribes ate their own distinctive diet: corn, pumpkins, beans, and squash, which they cultivated.

Until the Gold Rush, both Coast's culinary styles grew separately from each other and from the rest of the country. On the Atlantic side, the food was Anglo-European, adapted to the native products of the New World.

In 1769, the Spanish missionaries from Nueva España (now Mexico) began to colonize the forestry wilderness that is now California. They did it via a chain of missions that extended from San Diego in the south to Sonoma in the north. The padres brought with them olives, artichokes, garlic, vine cuttings, dates, nuts, and over 20 varieties of chili peppers — the crops that have formed the basis of modern Californian agriculture.

Over time, the Spanish and Native American influences melded together and evolved, resulting in a distinctive style of cooking: fresh cheeses, cured olives, olive oil, fruit preserves, fire-grilled foods, plus the exotic ingredients that arrived via the traders — among them coffee, sugar, and ginger root. This early Californian cuisine included mild red chili stews topped with egg, *champurrado* (a sweet drink based on puréed corn), *buñuelos* (crisp, sweet pastries), green chilies cooked with tomatoes and onions, and tortillas to scoop up the savory, spicy stew.

Mexican rule secularized the missions in the early 1800s. Land was then granted to individuals and these cowboy settlements were in the form of huge farms or ranchos. Their style of frontier/adobe elegance influenced what is now modern California and their cowboy fare was seasoned with chilies, served with great pots of simmering beans and soft tortillas.

The food in what was still a rather quiet corner of the world remained a Native American–Spanish hybrid until one day in 1848, when James Marshall found a shiny, golden pebble at John Sutter's mill in the tiny Sierra village of Coloma. Gold! Everything changed. California was to be transformed — and so was its style of cookery.

Within weeks, California was teeming with fortune hunters from France, Italy, Germany, Spain, Switzerland, Portugal, Armenia, Ireland, Japan, and China, among others. Gold — enough to make a difference — was discovered by few. The rest plied their *original* trades, being farmers, dairy men, fishermen, winemakers, cheesemakers, even *chocolatiers* (Domingo Ghiradelli came from Argentina to find fortune in the foothills and stayed on to found Ghiradelli Chocolate) in their new country.

San Francisco and Sacramento became boom towns, supplying the mining camps. Luxurious restaurants catered to the few who hit it rich; dingy, shabby cafes served crude 'grub' to the rest. California's canning and preserving industry grew out of a need to bring long-keeping foods to the austere mining camps.

As immigrants arrived and settled, they brought with them the ethnic foods of their homelands — a phenomenon that continues to this day — sending home for seeds and cuttings of favorite fruits and vegetables, which formed the basis of California's rich and varied agriculture.

The advent of the railways in the late 1800s connected the West Coast to the East via a land route, easing the movement of travelers to the far coast, with their cargoes of vegetables and fruit. Many of the workers from China who were brought in to build the railways stayed behind once their work was completed and opened restaurants, adding a distinctive Oriental taste to the Native American–Spanish multicultural hybrid that was already developing.

Californian country fare — that of the farm hands, ranchers and workers' boarding houses — was what most were eating in the turn-of-the-century years. However, the newly prosperous state boasted a wealth of grand hotels. Chefs prepared highly refined and elegant menus featuring specialties that may have had their origins in haute Euro-style, but that also incorporated the Californian produce and relaxed style.

Car culture no doubt had its roots in California — roadside diners, absurd architectural creations such as giant oranges or booths that served orange drinks, drive-in restaurants where waitresses wore roller skates, and so on, all publicized by the industry that has been perhaps most important in settling Southern California: Hollywood.

In the late 1960s, Californian food began to mature from a ragtag collection of unconnected flavors to a fully-fledged cuisine in its own right with its own hallmark flavors. Young people who flocked to the West Coast as the open-minded land of opportunity brought with them their curiosity, enthusiasm, and tastes culled from worldwide travels (the jet age had arrived). A greater variety of ethnic foods became available and exotic far-flung flavors, and all manner of dried beans, lentils, and grains, oils, and seasonings broadened the fare of omnivores and vegetarians alike.

The sixties' natural foods and hippie movement left its mark on Californian cuisine, with its emphasis on tofu, seeds, nuts, and beans. And with the gourmet blossoming of the seventies and eighties, a certain marriage of natural foods and gourmet took place. Even omnivores were veering towards delicious saucy and grain-based mixtures that made meat irrelevant.

Restaurants changed, from heavy traditional American fare to ethnic, French, and Italian food, rich with fresh, local vegetables. Though they were not *called* vegetarian restaurants, vegetables were often featured, with love and care. The enthusiasm for French, Italian, or other foreign authenticity turned from imported items to locally produced ones. French goat cheese gave way to Sonoma goat cheese, Dijon mustard to Mendocino mustard, Persian pistachio nuts were replaced by Central Valley pistachios, Roquefort and Stilton by Maytag blue, Italian sun-dried tomatoes by Central Valley ones, Mediterranean olive oils by Californian ones, and so forth. Californian wines, of course, create their own standards.

It is the carefully grown and utterly delicious garden produce that makes it all work.

The birth of the organic gardening movement in the sixties fused with eighties-style gourmet dining so that, by the nineties, home and restaurant cooks were all heading towards the garden for the most flavorful salads, herbs, tiny vegetables, and orchard fruits. (One of my favorite restaurants, now gone, picked the salad leaves as the diners sat at their table.)

The decades of the 1960s to 1990s saw a revolution in breads as well. While the San Francisco Bay Area has long had a tradition of sourdough French bread from the Basque settlers, it was not until the 1960s that our bread revolution took effect. A wide variety of ethnic and natural breads — from *ciabatta* to pita, sprouted wheat and millet to herb-scented *fougasse*, whole-wheat (wholemeal) raisin to oatbran–hazelnut — ousted ordinary sliced white.

The result of this history is a cuisine that is ever-changing, with layers of ethnic flavors based on the indigenous foods of the early Native American – Spanish beginnings and later immigrants. Waves of immigration continue to add to these layers of flavors: Mexican–Hispanic, Chinese, Southeast Asian, Middle Eastern, Italian, Eritrean, Ethiopian, Russian, Indian, Iranian to name just a few. With such a brightly flavored fresh cuisine, Californians seldom just eat. Meals tend to be a celebration, in the way that eating in the Mediterranean often is.

Here, in *The Flavor of California*, I offer a collection of Californian vegetarian cuisine: some classics, some adapted, and many original dishes from my own Californian kitchen — their only claim to authenticity being that they bear the typical Californian hallmarks of innovation, freshness, and strong, bright flavor. So take advantage of the abundance of fresh ingredients available today and enjoy the results.

Important Notes

All cup measurements given in this book are for both US and metric cups. The small difference in size between these measures has been absorbed, and will not affect the recipes. Imperial and metric measurements are given after cup measurements. Where fluid ounces and millilitres only are given, the fluid ounce measurement is for both US and imperial measures.

Tablespoon and teaspoon measurements are treated as universal. As with cups, the difference in tablespoon measures between countries has been absorbed, and will not affect the recipes.

Listed below are the weight and measure equivalents that have been used as standard throughout this book. A table of cup and spoon measures is also given for readers' information:

WEIGHTS

US/Imperial	Metric
4 oz. ($\frac{1}{4}$ lb.)	125 g
8 oz. ($\frac{1}{2}$ lb.)	250 g ($\frac{1}{4}$ kg)
16 oz. (1 lb.)	500 g ($\frac{1}{2}$ kg)
32 oz. (2 lbs.)	1000 g (1 kg)
48 oz. (3 lbs.)	1500 g (1$\frac{1}{2}$ kg)

EQUIVALENT CUP AND SPOON MEASURES

(all countries use the same teaspoon measure)

	United States	United Kingdom
1 cup	240 ml (7 fl. oz.)	250 ml (8 fl. oz.)
1 tablespoon	15 ml ($\frac{1}{2}$ fl. oz.)	15 ml ($\frac{1}{2}$ fl. oz.)

	Australia	New Zealand
1 cup	250 ml	250 ml
1 tablespoon	20 ml	15 ml

MEASURES

	US/Imperial	Metric
1 cup	8 fl. oz.	250 ml
$\frac{1}{2}$ cup	4 fl. oz.	125 ml
$\frac{1}{4}$ cup	2 fl. oz.	60 ml

OVEN TEMPERATURES

Oven temperatures are given in both Fahrenheit and Celsius. The following table is a guide to equivalent gas marks. However, to find the correct setting for your own oven, please refer to the manufacturer's instruction manual for your own oven. The following conversion chart should be used as a guide only. Gas mark calibrations vary from old to new models, and from manufacturer to manufacturer. The following guide to selecting temperature settings has been prepared by British Gas.

OVEN TEMPERATURES AND GAS MARKS

Fahrenheit	Celsius	Gas Mark	Heat
225°F	110°C	$\frac{1}{4}$ (S)	very cool
250°F	120°C	$\frac{1}{2}$ (S)	very cool
275°F	140°C	1	cool
300°F	150°C	2	cool
325°F	160°C	3	moderate
350°F	180°C	4	moderate
375°F	190°C	5	fairly hot
400°F	200°C	6	fairly hot
425°F	220°C	7	hot
450°F	230°C	8	very hot
475°F	240°C	9	very hot
500°F	260°C	10	very, very hot

Note: The gas mark S is a special setting available on some ovens used for cooking slowly, e.g. meringues.

Salads

*T*he curious custom of serving salad first is said to have originated in the boarding house restaurants of the post–Gold Rush days. The meal was served family style from big platters, on long tables that seated 12 to 20 diners, and huge bowls of greens were brought to the table for the hungry lodgers to fill up on.

Today salad is not just a first course. Long before it was chic in the rest of the country, lunch in California often meant a full-meal salad. Whether as a solitary midday meal at home in between chores, eaten at the desk in the office, or in an elegant restaurant, it was chock-a-block with crunchy, fresh, and hearty bits, all tossed with a platter of greens. On sunny, 85-degree-plus days, a meal like this refreshes while it nourishes.

Salad dressing traditions developed from humble beginnings with simple greens being tossed with oil and vinegar French–Italian-style, but over the past several decades the variety of dressings has increased substantially. They may be highly seasoned vinaigrettes or thick and creamy dressings based on mayonnaise and sour cream or yogurt, with the addition of herbs, spices, and pungent cheeses such as blue or goat.

Our ethnic influences as well contribute to our salad cuisine: Italian and French salad traditions; Mexican crisp toppings for tacos and the like; crunchy crisp–tender vegetables in the Japanese/Chinese manner; and the platters of spicy raw vegetables that the Thai and Vietnamese immigrants love.

The simple fact is that ingredients in California are readily available and relatively cheap. Happily this is now the case in many other parts of the world as well.

The Californian culinary revolution of the last 20 years has had a massive influence on the variety of greens available. Instead of the de rigueur iceberg lettuce and tomato wedge of my childhood, even the most common supermarket offers the most amazing mesclun mixtures (Continental leaves), often pairing traditional European ingredients, such as arugula (rocket), mâche (lamb's lettuce, corn salad), and radicchio, with Oriental ones such as mizuna and Latin American ones such as amaranth. These light, leafy blends are so filled with changing, seasonal lettuces, herbs, and greens that forking one's way through them is like nibbling through wild greens in the garden.

Warm salads have entered our repertoire, as have salads based on pasta, cheese, grilled vegetables (see 'Grilled foods', pp. 75–85), and dressings that have massive flavors, but are lighter and leaner than the thick and creamy ones, seasoned with fresh herbs, spices, olives, garlic, and chilies.

A huge range of oils is available that includes olive (of course), sesame, hazelnut, walnut, and chili. Vinegar, too, comes in all sorts of wonderful flavors, such as raspberry, pear, red wine, garlic- or herb-flavored, and these share the salad bowl with citrus juices. Indeed, there are times when the word 'salad' is so all-encompassing that the borders between salad and other dishes blur, so much so that it makes one wonder exactly what it is that makes a salad a salad.

For a selection of other salads and salady dishes, see 'Appetizers' (pp. 17–23) and 'Side dishes' (pp. 99–109).

SONOMA SALAD OF GRILLED GOAT CHEESE, CARAMELIZED PECANS, AND SPINACH
Serves 4

This is my version of a simple appetizer courtesy of Sonoma chef Charles Saunders. It is a sprightly little salad and a delicious starter: sweet, crisp, toasted nuts, tangy, warm goat cheese, and fresh, leafy spinach.

> ½ cup (2 oz., 60 g) pecans or walnuts
> 2 tablespoons sugar
> stale baguette or other French bread, thinly sliced
> olive oil, as required
> 4 slices goat cheese or 4 tiny individual goat cheeses
> 1 lb. (500 g) fresh spinach leaves, washed, blanched until bright green and just tender, drained or squeezed dry, and coarsely chopped
> ¼ cup (2 fl. oz., 60 ml) extra virgin olive oil, or to taste
> 2 teaspoons balsamic vinegar, or to taste

To caramelize the pecans or walnuts, heat the nuts in a hot, ungreased pan over a medium heat or on a baking sheet in a 400°F (200°C) oven until they are half-toasted (about 10 minutes).

Remove the nuts from the heat and sprinkle with the sugar, then return to the heat to finish toasting. They are ready when the sugar has lightly caramelized (about another 7 minutes or so in the oven; about half that in an ungreased pan over a medium heat).

Meanwhile, to make toasted croûtes, brush the bread slices with the olive oil and put them on a baking sheet. Bake in a 400°F (200°C) oven until they are dry and lightly golden brown.

At the same time, place the little cheeses or slices on a baking sheet and brush them with olive oil. Grill in the oven until lightly browned, hot, and melting.

Arrange the spinach on four plates, then place a hot cheese next to each portion of spinach. Scatter the plates with the caramelized nuts, garnish with the olive oil-toasted croûtes, and dress the spinach and cheese with the extra virgin olive oil and balsamic vinegar. Eat immediately.

PREVIOUS PAGE: *Californian Classic (top left), Late-Summer Salad (center right), and Sonoma Salad of Grilled Goat Cheese, Caramelized Pecans, and Spinach*

CALIFORNIAN CLASSIC: WARM GOAT CHEESE SALAD WITH SUN-DRIED TOMATOES AND BASIL

Serves 4

Warm goat cheese salad is as much a classic of the Californian kitchen as it is in France. Marinating the goat cheese first permeates the cheese with the flavors of the marinade: garlic, thyme, olive oil, and vinegar. The marinated cheese rounds are then coated with breadcrumbs, drizzled with olive oil, and grilled or baked until crisp on the outside and quiveringly soft in the center. Served on a bed of fresh greens, which the heat of the cheese slightly wilts, and garnished with tangy sun-dried tomatoes and sweet basil, it is one of the most delicious dishes imaginable.

Serve it with fresh bread such as *ciabatta* to scoop up the bits of lettuce and basil, and on which to spread some of the delicious melting cheese.

6 oz. (185 g) goat cheese, cut into 4 or 8 slices
2 garlic cloves, finely chopped
½–1 teaspoon fresh or ¼–½ teaspoon dried thyme, crumbled
2 tablespoons extra virgin olive oil
1–2 teaspoons red wine vinegar or raspberry vinegar
½ cup (2 oz., 60 g), approximately, dried breadcrumbs
7 oz. (225 g) assorted salad leaves: lollo rosso, frisée (curly endive), radicchio, arugula (rocket), mâche (lamb's lettuce, corn salad), watercress, etc.
1 oz. (30 g) sun-dried tomatoes, cut into strips
8–12 tiny black olives (niçoise or kalamata)
4 large sprigs fresh basil or handful of the leaves, torn up
3 tablespoons extra virgin olive oil and 1 tablespoon red wine vinegar, shaken together as dressing
freshly ground black pepper, to taste

Put the goat cheese slices on a plate or in a heatproof glass, enameled or stainless steel baking dish.

Coat each slice with the garlic, thyme, extra virgin olive oil, and vinegar. Leave to marinate for at least 5 minutes, preferably longer (up to 2 hours). Preheat the oven to 450°F (230°C).

Coat each marinated cheese slice with the breadcrumbs and place them in a baking dish or on a baking sheet, leaving a little space between each cheese slice as they spread as they bake. Drizzle any leftover marinade over each crumb-coated cheese and bake in the preheated oven for about 5 minutes, or just long enough for each cheese to melt slightly and turn golden brown with darker spots in places.

Arrange the salad leaves on four plates. When the cheese slices are ready, remove them from the oven and place one or two of them atop each salad. Quickly garnish with the sun-dried tomatoes, olives, and sprigs of basil. Drizzle the extra virgin olive oil and red wine vinegar dressing over the cheese and salad. Season with black pepper and serve.

LATE-SUMMER SALAD: GARLICKY TOMATOES WITH GOAT CHEESE, BLACK OLIVES, AND FRESH SWEET HERBS OR PESTO

Serves 4–6

Come August, the tomatoes begin to ripen in the languid hot weather of the Great Central Valley. The scent of the leaves gives off an intoxicating aroma as you wander through the garden, picking tomatoes for the evening's meal.

While vine-ripened tomatoes are always best, if supermarket tomatoes are all that's available, try my mother's trick: line the unripe tomatoes along the windowsill in full sunlight. Within a few days of bright sun, the tomatoes will be nearly as ripe as if they had lived their lives fully on the vine.

10–12 small to medium sweet, ripe tomatoes, sliced
2 garlic cloves, finely chopped
4 oz. (125 g) fresh soft goat cheese (preferably flavored with chives, herbs, or garlic), chopped into bite-sized pieces
10–12 black olives (such as niçoise)
handful of fresh herbs (basil, oregano, parsley, etc.) as desired or a few spoonfuls of pesto
4 tablespoons extra virgin olive oil
1½ tablespoons red wine vinegar

Arrange the tomatoes on a platter and sprinkle them with the garlic.

Place pieces of the cheese atop the tomatoes in a pleasing array, then top with the olives and herbs or pesto. Dress with the extra virgin olive oil and vinegar, then serve, accompanied by crusty bread.

SCARLET SALAD HIDDEN UNDER A BED OF HOME-MADE GARLIC CROUTONS

Serves 4

It looks like a bowlful of bread chunks, but when you spoon into it you unearth a cache of scarlet-colored beets (beetroot) and tomatoes. Fresh rosemary and sweet garden mint enhance this tangy salad and, as the salad sits, the croûtons absorb the marinade. The perfect thing for eating on a terrace on a warm summer evening.

GARLIC CROUTONS
4–6 slices crusty bread, cut into large cubes
2–3 tablespoons olive oil
1–2 garlic cloves, finely chopped
salt and freshly ground black pepper, to taste

SCARLET SALAD
8 ripe tomatoes, quartered
3 small to medium fresh beets (beetroots), quartered or diced
3 tablespoons olive oil
1 tablespoon red wine vinegar, or more to taste
2 garlic cloves, finely chopped
1–2 teaspoons chopped fresh rosemary
1 tablespoon chopped fresh mint, or to taste
salt and freshly ground black pepper, to taste

Prepare the Garlic Croûtons by tossing the bread cubes in the olive oil, then baking them in a 375°F (190°C) oven for 20 minutes or so, until they are lightly golden brown and quite crisp–dry. Remove from the oven and season with the garlic, and salt and pepper. Leave to cool.

Combine the tomatoes with the beets, olive oil, vinegar, garlic, rosemary, mint, salt, and pepper. Spoon into four bowls and top with a layer of the croûtons. Let the salad sit for about 15 minutes before serving.

BELOW: *Scarlet Salad Hidden under a Bed of Home-made Garlic Croûtons*

Mediterranean Island Salad of Chopped Herbs, Olives, Feta, and Fresh Vegetables

Serves 4

The Mediterranean ingredients of olives, feta cheese, garlic, and fresh herbs were brought to California by the waves of Spanish, Italian, Basque, French, Portuguese, and Greek immigrants. These savory ingredients fit the Californian lifestyle and climate as well as they do their native Mediterranean. In California, however, unshackled by traditional culinary restraints, we put these foods together in a wide variety of ways. And if one ingredient is not available, another one is, and it may taste even better than the original. This is how our distinctive cooking style evolves.

In this recipe, I combine an assortment of sun-drenched ingredients into a little salad perfect for summer. Other combinations of fresh herbs may be used in place of the ones given in the recipe: try dill, scallions (spring onions), and coriander; coriander and mint; basil, mint, and thinly sliced spinach; tarragon, sorrel, thyme, and a few leaves of romaine (cos) lettuce, thinly sliced — experiment with whatever the market offers. Each pungent herb (and combination of herbs) chosen gives this simple salad a totally different character: arugula (rocket) and chervil taste of Provence; coriander and mint, vaguely of North Africa; basil and mint or marjoram of Italy.

Serve this salad accompanied by naan or *ciabatta* bread, and enjoy it as an appetizer-type salad or as part of a picnic, followed by a cozy Californian Cassoulet (pp. 92–3).

3 arugula (rocket) leaves
1–2 tablespoons coarsely chopped chervil
2 tablespoons coarsely chopped chives
1 garlic clove, finely chopped
2 tablespoons chopped parsley
½ cucumber, diced
2 ripe tomatoes, diced
2–3 oz. (60–90 g) feta cheese, diced
10 kalamata or other black Mediterranean-type olives, pitted and sliced
2 tablespoons extra virgin olive oil
2 teaspoons balsamic vinegar
freshly ground black pepper, to taste

Combine all the ingredients well, and serve as soon as possible to enjoy this salad at its best.

Variation

Add a spicy bite by tossing ½–1 hot green chili pepper (such as serrano or jalapeño) into the salad. Refreshing on a hot, sultry afternoon.

Salad of Lettuce, Orange, and Onion with Ruby Orange and Rosemary Vinaigrette

Serves 4

This salad is at its best when oranges are in season, especially when the rare ruby oranges make their appearance in the winter/spring market. Fresh rosemary offers a fragrant, sweet herbal flavor to this simple but delicious salad.

Ruby oranges, renamed rather more sedately as they were originally called blood oranges (*sanguine* in French), have a distinctive flavor as well as color. In the Mediterranean they are often very sweet, but in California they are usually quite sharp. If the ruby oranges that you find are sweet rather than tart, add some lemon juice or vinegar to the salad.

1 round lettuce, washed, dried, and torn into bite-sized pieces
2 small oranges, peeled and sliced
1 onion (preferably a sweet, red onion), thinly sliced
1–2 teaspoons coarsely chopped fresh rosemary
1 ruby (blood) orange, halved
2–3 tablespoons olive oil
salt and freshly ground black pepper, to taste

Arrange the lettuce on four plates, then top with the slices of orange and onion.

Sprinkle with the rosemary, then squeeze the juice from the ruby orange over each salad, drizzle with the olive oil, and season with salt and pepper. Serve immediately.

Variation

ORANGE AND SWEET BASIL OR FRESH MINT: You may need an extra orange for this variation. Omit the onion and replace the rest of the ingredients with about 2 tablespoons of thinly sliced fresh basil leaves, just a tablespoon of extra virgin olive oil, plus ½ teaspoon or so to taste of red wine vinegar, and a few unsprayed orange blossoms or other edible flowers (optional — if using, see p. 6). Simply combine all the ingredients (except the flowers) and chill until serving. Serve as a side dish, garnished with the blossoms or other flowers, if using.

EDIBLE FLOWERS

Generally speaking, flowers from bulbs can be toxic so, no matter how attractive tulips, daffodils, or lily of the valley flowers look, leave them *off* your plate. Most herbs and many vegetables have beautiful flowers, and these are often delicious: choose from purple thyme, blue borage, lavender and chive flowers, deep purple violets, yellow cucumber flowers, white-petaled pepper flowers, the flowers from scarlet runner beans, saffron-hued marigold petals, the sunny yellow of pumpkin and squash flowers, the carnival colors of nasturtium flowers, and, of course, roses of every color and fragrance. Check that any flowers you intend using have not been sprayed with toxic chemicals and always make sure that you have correctly identified the plant. If in doubt, don't use.

Flowers can add charm to other dishes besides salads. Float them in soup, freeze them in ice cubes, use them to discreetly garnish a pot of sweet, herbed butter, and small bits sprinkled on a sauce or sauced entrée or large, colorful flowers flamboyantly strewn atop a platter of highly spiced foods look delightful. One of the most charming flower presentations is also the simplest: tiny petals scattered carelessly atop a linen-covered table. No stems, no vase, just the simplicity of the gaily colored little petals.

MESCLUN SALAD AND EDIBLE FLOWERS WITH NICOISE OLIVES AND WEDGES OF TENDER EGG
Serves 4

Mesclun is the Provençal mixture of tiny fragrant greens and herbs so beloved in this region that shimmers in the hot Mediterranean sun and is parched by the merciless gusts of the mistral winds. The word *mesclun* itself comes from the Provençal dialect, from the word 'mescla', which means to mix. A similar salad is served in Italy, known as *misticanza*, or mixture.

Mesclun is truly a product of the garden: tiny sprigs of herbs, the tiny thinnings of vegetables — carrots, spinach, leeks, handfuls of baby lettuces, mâche (lamb's lettuce, corn salad), arugula (rocket), chervil, young dandelion greens — all will often appear in a French mixture, while Italian ones will often include tiny chicory or *frisée* (curly endive) or thin strips of red radicchio. Californian *mesclun* will also include delicious un-European greens, such as amaranth.

The charm of these salads lies in the fact that no two bites are the same and the mixtures will differ each time you buy them. The contrast of flavors, colors, and textures of the greens is beguiling.

Edible flowers are often dotted over such salads and, while their flavor often falls short of their colorful charm, their textures add interest — smoothness and a slight velvety fuzziness. With their popularity today, it is tempting to think that they are a recent phenomenon. The truth is that edible flowers were favored on the West Coast long ago: first by the Aztecs and Mayans in the region that is now Mexico and, more recently, orange blossoms were especially popular in Los Angeles during the early movie days when the town was first growing.

This is a classic salad served in endless variations in cafés throughout California. There may or may not be wedges of egg or olives, but there is always the fresh greens, the bright flowers, the silky cloak of good olive oil, and a dash of fruity balsamic vinegar.

4 big handfuls of mesclun *mixture*
3 tablespoons chopped chives or green parts of scallions
   (spring onions)
1–3 tablespoons fresh chervil, basil, tarragon, and/or other
   fresh herbs (optional)
2–3 tablespoons balsamic vinegar
1–2 teaspoons Dijon-type mustard
⅓ cup (3 fl. oz., 90 ml) extra virgin olive oil
salt and freshly ground black pepper, to taste
12 or so edible flowers, unsprayed (see below)
3 hard-boiled eggs, cut into wedges or 8 hard-boiled
   quails' eggs, halved
16–24 niçoise olives

Combine the *mesclun* with the chives or scallions, and fresh herbs, if using.

In a small bowl, whisk together the balsamic vinegar and mustard, then whisk in the extra virgin olive oil until well combined. Season with salt and pepper.

Toss the *mesclun* mixture with the dressing, then arrange it on four individual chilled plates or on one large platter.

Garnish with the flowers, egg wedges or halves, and olives. Serve immediately, accompanied by either crusty country bread or thin garlic-rubbed toasts.

POTATO AND ARTICHOKE SALAD WITH WATERCRESS MAYONNAISE
Serves 4

Tender potatoes and artichokes sit in an emerald-colored mayonnaise sauce, which gets not only its hue, but also its nippy character from the addition of lots of finely chopped watercress.

Delicious with potatoes and artichokes, the sauce is also good with other foods: serve it coating halved hard-boiled eggs as given under *Variation* as a twist on the French classic, *oeufs mayonnaise*, or as a party dip for raw vegetables such as cucumber and carrot sticks, red sweet pepper (capsicum) strips, or broccoli florets.

1 garlic clove, chopped
2 oz. (60 g) watercress leaves, coarsely chopped
½ teaspoon dried tarragon, or to taste
½ cup (4 fl. oz., 125 ml) mayonnaise
2 tablespoons butter, melted
juice of ½ lemon
salt, to taste
tiny pinch of cayenne pepper
12–16 small, waxy potatoes
2 large or 4 small to medium fresh artichokes
1 teaspoon all-purpose (plain) flour

In a blender or food processor, whirl the garlic, watercress, and tarragon until a finely chopped mixture results. With the machine on, pour in the mayonnaise through the top. When well mixed, slowly add the melted butter. When it has been absorbed, add the lemon juice, then season with the salt and cayenne pepper. Chill until ready to serve.

Boil or steam potatoes until just tender. When cool enough to handle, cut into quarters.

Prepare artichokes by snapping back the thistle-like leaves. They will break right off. Trim rough edges and peel stems with a paring knife. Cut artichokes into quarters lengthwise, then cut out the inside 'choke'.

Add flour to a saucepan of water. Boil artichokes in this until just tender, about 5–8 minutes. Drain.

Serve potato wedges and artichoke quarters at room temperature or cooler, covered with some of the sauce.

Variations
Serve the potatoes and artichokes diced, bound with the green mayonnaise.

OEUFS MAYONNAISE AUX HERBES: Serve the above watercress mayonnaise coating tender, just cooked hard-boiled eggs. Enjoy this dish as a starter or part of an antipasto-style lunch.

CHINESE LEAF WITH SCALLIONS, CUCUMBER, CORIANDER, AND EAST–WEST DRESSING

Serves 4

Chinese salads, based on lettuce or Chinese leaves, have been extremely popular in California since the early eighties. Sometimes they are heaped with other ingredients that turn the salad into a full meal, sometimes merely a garnish of chopped peanuts or crisp, crunchy fried noodles.

½ teaspoon mustard powder, dissolved in ½ teaspoon water
1 tablespoon soy sauce
3 tablespoons cider vinegar
2–3 tablespoons hoisin sauce
½ teaspoon Chinese five-spice powder, or to taste
2 teaspoons sugar
3 tablespoons sesame oil
¼ cup (2 fl. oz., 60 ml) vegetable oil
1 big head of Chinese leaf or Napa cabbage or Chinese cabbage, including the stalks and core, thinly sliced
6 scallions (spring onions), thinly sliced
½ cucumber, cut into julienne
2–3 tablespoons fresh coriander sprigs

Mix the mustard, soy sauce, cider vinegar, hoisin sauce, five-spice powder, and sugar together until smooth. Whisk in the sesame and vegetable oils, and blend until they are well combined.

Arrange the Chinese leaf or cabbage, scallions, cucumber, and coriander on a platter or in a salad bowl.

Toss with the spicy dressing and serve.

TABBOULEH

Serves 4

This salad of uncooked bulghur wheat (burghul) is seasoned generously with scallions (spring onions), mint, and parsley, and soaked with just enough olive oil and lemon juice to enliven the hearty wheat.

Like hummus, tabbouleh has become a 'naturalized citizen' of Californian cuisine. Like hummus, too, it lends itself to endless permutations. I have eaten it with grated carrots, chickpeas (garbanzos), sun-dried tomatoes, chilies, fresh coriander, and so on, but I still think it is best when it keeps close to its ethnic origins. Serving it on a bed of vine leaves is particularly nice: fresh from the garden and raw they look lovely, but if you'd like to nibble the leaves along with the tabbouleh, be sure to choose only the young tender ones and blanch them first. If not, bottled ones, drained and rinsed, are fine. Chickpeas are a good addition as they add nutty nuggets of texture, as well as boosting the protein content of the salad to main-course status. I always like serving yogurt alongside, too — it lightens the grain-based salad deliciously.

2 cups (12 oz., 370 g) medium-ground bulghur wheat (burghul)
1 bunch of scallions (spring onions), green parts included, thinly sliced
1½ oz. (50 g) parsley, chopped
1 bunch or ½ oz. (15 g) fresh or 2–3 tablespoons dried mint, chopped
½ cup (4 fl. oz., 125 ml) extra virgin olive oil, or to taste
juice of 2–3 lemons or ⅓ cup (3 fl. oz., 90 ml) bottled lemon juice, or to taste
¼ cucumber, finely diced
salt and freshly ground black pepper, to taste

TO SERVE

romaine (cos) lettuce leaves or vine leaves (see above), sufficient to line a platter
10–15 black Mediterranean olives
1 lemon, cut into wedges
sprigs of fresh mint and/or parsley
1 cup (8 fl. oz., 250 ml) plain yogurt

Soak the bulghur in cold water for 15–30 minutes. How long the bulghur takes to soften depends upon the grind of the wheat: you want the grains to give more resistance than *al dente* pasta, but not be hard inside their centers.

Drain the soaked bulghur in a sieve.

Mix the drained bulghur with the scallions, pressing and squeezing the wheat and scallions together with your hands to release the aroma of the scallions so that it permeates the cracked wheat.

Add the parsley, mint, extra virgin olive oil, lemon juice, cucumber, and salt and pepper. Mix well. Chill for at least 30 minutes so that the flavors have a chance to meld together.

Serve on a platter lined with the romaine lettuce or vine leaves, garnished with the olives, lemon wedges, sprigs of mint and/or parsley all around, and with the yogurt in a bowl.

PAGE 6: *Mesclun Salad and Edible Flowers with Niçoise Olives and Wedges of Tender Egg*

OPPOSITE: *Chinese Leaf with Scallions, Cucumber, Coriander, and East–West Dressing*

Helene's Midsummer Night Salad Bowl

Serves 4

My friend Hélène Simpson has a passion for salads that reflects her Provençal childhood. Meals at her house always include a bowl of vividly fresh vegetables. Whatever is freshest in the market, Hélène heaps lovingly into a big bowl, and dresses with a Gallic glistening of olive oil and a splash of red wine vinegar.

The garnish of marinated artichoke hearts is common to both California and the Mediterranean. In California, artichoke hearts are ubiquitous — sold in little jars and used in everything from salads to sandwiches, snacks, and the like, even puréed into sauces such as a very tangy mayonnaise. A lovely appetizer is a plate of artichokes paired with diced goat or ewe cheese, and golden-yellow tomatoes, garnished with fresh herbs such as marjoram, thyme, or basil.

This salad makes a sprightly first course or accompaniment for a savory tomato and eggplant (aubergine) dish served with crusty bread or chewy *focaccia* (see p. 134).

½–1 cucumber, thinly sliced
6–8 tomatoes, sliced
1 garlic clove, finely chopped or crushed
6–8 oil-cured black olives
6–8 green olives
½ onion, chopped or thinly sliced
2–3 tablespoons coarsely chopped fresh coriander or
*   sweet basil*
olive oil and red wine vinegar, to taste
10–15 marinated artichoke hearts, drained

Toss the cucumber with the tomatoes, garlic, black and green olives, onion, and coriander or basil. Spoon into a salad bowl.

Dress with the olive oil and vinegar, then garnish with the artichoke hearts.

Summer Salad of Yellow Sweet Peppers, Tangy Cheese, and Sweet Basil

Serves 4 as an appetizer, first course, or side salad

Pepper salads are usually prepared with roasted and peeled sweet peppers (capsicums) and, although they are delicious, in a rich, silken, and slightly smoky way, it is a nice change to enjoy the peppers sweet and crunchy fresh from the garden.

While this recipe calls for Roquefort, most blue cheeses will be equally good: Gorgonzola, Danablu (Danish blue), even Stilton. Goat cheeses are a delicious choice, too, pairing deliciously with the sweet basil and fresh, crisp sweet peppers.

3 medium yellow sweet peppers (capsicums)
4 oz. (125 g) Roquefort cheese, crumbled or cut into small
*   chunks*
3 tablespoons olive oil (preferably extra virgin)
1 tablespoon red wine vinegar
handful of fresh sweet basil, torn or coarsely sliced

Remove the stems and seeds from the sweet peppers, then slice them into rings ⅛ in. (5 mm) or so thick.

Arrange the peppers on a platter or plate, and sprinkle the cheese over them. Chill until you are ready to serve.

When ready, dress the salad with the olive oil and vinegar, and sprinkle the basil over the top.

OPPOSITE: *Hélène's Midsummer Night Salad Bowl*

WARM SALAD OF RED CABBAGE, WATERCRESS, AND TOASTED WALNUTS OR PECANS

Serves 4

Red cabbage lends itself so well to warm salads: it holds its shape when coated with the warm vinaigrette and red cabbage wilted is just as nice as red cabbage crunchy. When dressing with a warm vinaigrette, some of the cabbage warms and wilts while some stays cold and crunchy, and this contrast of textures delights.

½ medium red cabbage, thinly sliced
1–2 oz. (30–60 g) watercress leaves
several thin slices red onion, pulled apart into rings
2 oz. (60 g) shelled walnuts or pecans
2 tablespoons vegetable oil
2 tablespoons orange juice
¼ teaspoon grated or finely chopped orange rind
1 golden shallot, finely chopped
1 tablespoon red wine vinegar

Arrange the cabbage and watercress on a plate or platter, then top with the onion rings.

Quickly sauté the walnut or pecan halves in a hot pan with a teaspoon or so of the oil. When they have lightly browned, remove the nuts from the pan and spoon them onto the platter.

Add the orange juice and rind to the hot pan and cook over a high heat until the liquid has reduced to a nearly syrupy glaze. Remove the pan from the heat, then add the golden shallot, remaining oil, and red wine vinegar.

Return the pan to the heat briefly, then pour the shallot mixture evenly over the salad. Serve immediately.

PEAR, CHICORY, STILTON, AND SMOKY BITS

Serves 4

Sweet pear, slightly bitter chicory, pungent Stilton or other blue cheese, and bits of smoky soybean protein make a hearty, satisfying salad that is particularly good as an appetizer.

Pears, especially the small sweet Bartlett, are grown throughout the Central Valley — trees planted along the Sacramento River over 100 years ago still produce abundant crops. The original Bartlett was a small, yellow, wild pear, discovered in England by a schoolmaster called Stair. The fruit was then named after him — Stair-pear. It was later planted in the Massachusetts Bay colony and, when the land was passed on to a certain Enoch Bartlett, the Stair-pear became the Bartlett.

½–1 oz. (15–30 g) watercress
2 ripe but firm pears (preferably Bartlett), sprinkled with lemon juice to prevent discoloration
2 small to medium heads of chicory
4 oz. (125 g) Stilton or other blue cheese

DRESSING
3 tablespoons bland vegetable oil
1 tablespoon balsamic or fruit vinegar, such as pear

GARNISH
2 tablespoons smoky bacon-flavor soybean protein bits (optional)

Arrange the watercress, pears, and chicory on four plates, then sprinkle the cheese over them.

Next make the dressing. Mix the oil and vinegar together in a bowl with a fork or whisk until well combined, then pour evenly over the salad.

Serve immediately, sprinkled with the smoky bacon-flavor soybean.

OPPOSITE: *Warm Salad of Red Cabbage, Watercress, and Toasted Walnuts or Pecans*
BELOW: *Pear, Chicory, Stilton, and Smoky Bits*

SUSHI RICE WITH ASSORTED VEGETABLE TOPPINGS

Serves 4

Short-grain rice is seasoned in the sushi way, that is, by dressing it with a sweet vinegar and fanning the rice as it cools to encourage it to glisten.

Served on a bed of watercress, and decorated with a selection of vegetable toppings, this dish is accompanied by a tiny bowl of savory dipping sauce to season every bite of the fresh vegetables to perfection.

1¼ cups (8 oz., 250 g) short-grain white rice

2 cups (16 fl. oz., 500 ml) cold water

1 tablespoon sweet rice wine or sherry

1 teaspoon salt

¼ cup (2 fl. oz., 60 ml) rice vinegar

2 teaspoons sugar

1 scallion (spring onion), including the green part, thinly sliced

2 tablespoons finely diced cucumber

2 teaspoons thinly sliced pickled ginger root (available from Asian food stores)

1 bunch of watercress, washed and dried

DIPPING SAUCE

½ cup (4 fl. oz., 125 ml) soy sauce

2 teaspoons sesame oil

1 teaspoon sugar

1 tablespoon rice vinegar

GARNISH

2 medium-sized carrots, thinly sliced diagonally

2 scallions (spring onions), cut into julienne

½–1 cucumber, thinly sliced

2 teaspoons toasted black or white sesame seeds (optional)

Rinse the rice well under running water and leave it to drain for 30 minutes. Put the rice, cold water, wine or sherry, and ½ teaspoon of the salt into a pan. Bring to the boil and simmer, covered, until the rice is just tender and the liquid has been absorbed (about 12–15 minutes). Remove the rice from the heat and let it cool slightly, then pour it into a bowl.

In a clean saucepan, combine the rice vinegar, sugar, and remaining salt. Bring to the boil, remove from the heat, then slowly pour this hot vinegar mixture over the rice. Toss the rice with a fork, then fan with a piece of cardboard or heavy paper until it

glistens (about 5 minutes). When the rice has cooled, add the scallions, cucumber, and pickled ginger root.

Combine all the Dipping Sauce ingredients well.

Serve the seasoned rice on a bed of the watercress, with the vegetable garnishes arranged attractively and the Dipping Sauce in a small bowl.

Warm Salad of Garlic Roast Potatoes and Crisp Mediterranean Vegetables on a Bed of Lemon-spiked Greens

Serves 4

The contrast of hot roast potatoes with the fresh and crisp raw vegetables, all punctuated with coriander, onion, olive oil, and lemon juice, is deliciously satisfying and refreshing.

1½ lbs. (750 g) waxy potatoes, peeled and cut into halves or quarters

2–4 tablespoons olive oil, for roasting the potatoes

1 head of garlic, cloves separated, unpeeled

salt and freshly ground black pepper, to taste

1 green sweet pepper (capsicum), deseeded and diced

1 cucumber, diced

1 onion, chopped

½ oz. (15 g) fresh coriander leaves

10 or so black olives (such as kalamata), stoned and diced (optional)

1 teaspoon olive oil and 1 teaspoon lemon juice, or to taste, for dressing

3 garlic cloves, chopped

1 head of frisée (curly endive) or other lettuce of choice (mesclun, arugula (rocket), mâche (lamb's lettuce, corn salad), romaine (cos), etc.)

Put the potato chunks into a pan, cover with water, and bring to the boil. Cook them until they are barely tender, then pour off the water and set potatoes aside to cool slightly. Now toss the cooked potatoes with 3 tablespoons of the olive oil, the garlic cloves, and salt and pepper. Spread in a baking dish and roast in a 400°F (200°C) oven for 30–40 minutes, turning the potatoes several times, until they are golden brown and the garlic cloves are tender.

Meanwhile, combine the sweet pepper, cucumber, onion, coriander, and olives (if using) in a bowl. Dress with some of the olive oil and lemon.

When the potatoes are ready, remove them from the oven and toss with the chopped garlic. Arrange the *frisée* or other lettuce on a platter, dress with the remaining olive oil and lemon mixture, then top with the hot potatoes. Garnish with spoonfuls of the dressed vegetable salad. Serve immediately.

OPPOSITE: *Sushi Rice with Assorted Vegetable Toppings*

BELOW: *Warm Salad of Garlic Roast Potatoes and Mediterranean Vegetables on a Bed of Lemon-spiked Greens*

Appetizers

Small portions of strongly flavored dishes suit California as much as they suit the Mediterranean; the platters of savory foods, often in bite-sized amounts, lend themselves easily to the convivial and informal entertaining that typifies the Californian lifestyle. Parties and gatherings often center on a table boasting a large array of such delicacies, to be nibbled on as finger food or to be gathered onto little plates for a more formal meal. Even proper sit-down meals usually begin with a buffet of appetizers.

You will find other dishes that are perfect as appetizers scattered throughout the rest of the book, especially in the 'Side dishes' chapter (see pp. 99–109). Indeed, like the Spanish tapas, any strongly seasoned dish served in small portions makes a wonderful appetizer, Californian-style.

At home, formal starters, served once the diners are sitting, are less usual — with the exception of the green salad, which is California's traditional starter. In contemporary restaurants, however, with European influence, the habit of the starter is gaining momentum. Dishes to cover all contingencies follow.

SMOKED TOFU AND SUN-DRIED TOMATOES IN OLIVE OIL

Serves 4

Smoked tofu is firm and smoky-flavored, much like smoked mozzarella cheese, and is delicious served in similar ways. In this simple plateful, all that is needed is a slick of olive oil, a few sun-dried tomatoes, and a dusting of coarsely ground black pepper. It is a delicious and easy-to-make first course.

4 oz. (125 g) smoked tofu, cut into 4 slices
8 sun-dried tomatoes, cut into strips
small handful of arugula (rocket) leaves
3–6 tablespoons extra virgin olive oil
freshly ground black pepper, to taste

Place a tofu slice on each plate and garnish with the sun-dried tomato and arugula leaves.

Drizzle each plate with the olive oil, grind black pepper over the top, and serve, accompanied by crusty country bread, such as *ciabatta* or Greek/Turkish quilted bread.

OPPOSITE: *Black Olives and Roasted Green Sweet Peppers in Cumin Oil with Crusty Bread (top left), Smoked Tofu and Sun-dried Tomatoes in Olive Oil (center right), and Sweet–Tart Multicolored Sweet Peppers Baked with Olive Oil and Vinegar*

BLACK OLIVES AND ROASTED GREEN SWEET PEPPERS IN CUMIN OIL WITH CRUSTY BREAD

Serves 4

This dish came about accidentally: a puddle of olive oil and several olives remained behind on a plate, post-salad, and I could not resist wiping them up with a chunk of crusty, cumin-sprinkled bread.

The slightly smoky scent of roasted green sweet peppers (capsicums) is a lovely adjunct, but the olives with their spiced oil, all sopped up with the bread, are delicious even without the peppers.

Do not worry about the quantities, they are simply a guideline. For seconds, simply have an extra sweet pepper or two ready and waiting, open the jar of olives, pour a little more oil onto each plate, and season as you wish.

Olives have been grown in California since the days of the padres and missions. They were offered as a delicacy and sign of Californian hospitality to travelers staying at the missions, as well as years later in the up-market hotels and railway dining cars. In 1910, a process for making very mild black olives called 'California ripe' was discovered that led to the popularizing of the savory, oily fruit. While a ripe, black olive is probably better than no olive at all, it pales insipidly beside the more flavorful specimens of the Mediterranean. An exception to this rule is one of my favorite sandwiches, which uses any kind of chopped black olives, chopped hard-boiled egg, and scallions (spring onions), all bound together with mayonnaise on a slice of whole-wheat (wholemeal) bread, then topped with a handful of alfalfa sprouts and another slice of bread. Sometimes Spanish olives are treated in a similar manner, and may also be used in this sandwich.

In recent years, cured olives have been staging a comeback in California, as small companies turn their backs on mass production and concentrate instead on producing hand-crafted olives of great flavor.

2 green sweet peppers (capsicums)
4 tablespoons extra virgin olive oil
ground cumin, to taste (about ⅛–¼ teaspoon per person)
several drops of lemon juice per person
a drop or two of hot pepper sauce (such as Tabasco) per person, to taste
16–20 oil-cured black olives
4 thick slices crusty bread

Roast the sweet peppers over an open fire, under a broiler (grill), or directly over a gas burner until they are evenly charred. Place them in a bowl, or in a plastic or paper bag, seal tightly, and leave for 20–30 minutes.

Peel the peppers. (Doing this under running water will result in more skin coming off, but the water tends to wash away the smoky flavor.) Remove the stems and seeds, then slice into thin strips and set these aside.

Onto each plate, pour a tablespoon of the olive oil. Sprinkle with the cumin, lemon juice, and hot pepper sauce. Add a little of the thinly sliced peppers and 4 or 5 olives per plate, then serve, accompanied by the crusty bread.

SWEET-TART MULTICOLORED SWEET PEPPERS BAKED WITH OLIVE OIL AND VINEGAR

Serves 4–6

This dish is one of disarming simplicity. A dash of honey or sugar added to the baked sweet peppers (capsicums) enhances their sweetness, resulting in an almost *agrodolce* or sweet–sour effect.

Serve at room temperature, with little chunks of bread as an appetizer, on their own, or with goat cheese seasoned with garlic, parsley, chives, and herbs for something a little more substantial.

2 medium red sweet peppers (capsicums), deseeded and cut into bite-sized pieces
2 medium green sweet peppers (capsicums), deseeded and cut into bite-sized pieces
2 medium yellow or orange sweet peppers (capsicums), deseeded and cut into bite-sized pieces
6–8 garlic cloves, chopped
¼ cup (2 fl. oz., 60 ml) extra virgin olive oil
2 tablespoons red wine vinegar, or to taste
1 tablespoon sugar or honey, or to taste
½ cup (4 fl. oz., 125 ml) tomato purée (passata) or diced fresh or diced canned tomatoes
salt and freshly ground black pepper, to taste
¼ teaspoon crumbled dried oregano leaves or thyme
1–2 tablespoons chopped fresh parsley or sweet basil

Put the sweet peppers in a shallow baking dish and toss with the garlic, extra virgin olive oil, half the vinegar, the sugar or honey, tomato purée or chopped tomatoes, salt and pepper, and oregano or thyme.

Bake them in a fairly hot 400°F (200°C) oven for 40–50 minutes, tossing every so often so that the peppers bake and brown in spots, their sugars lightly caramelizing. Remove the peppers from the oven and toss with the remaining vinegar.

Let them cool to room temperature and serve as an appetizer, sprinkled with the fresh parsley or basil.

ARTICHOKE AND SWEET PEPPERS WITH CAPER MAYONNAISE
Serves 4

Artichokes are quintessential Californian fare. When I was a child, I used to delight in seeing the expressions on my relatives' faces when they visited from far-away places. They would look at the thistley vegetables with something akin to alarm, an expression that turned to utter pleasure as they learned to pull off the prehistoric-looking leaves and dip them into a savory mayonnaise or warm, melted butter.

While in the Mediterranean artichokes are often prepared with the leaves removed then simmered in savory sauces, in California they are most often cooked whole, with sauces for dipping the leaves into. This recipe is a combination of both methods: the whole cooked vegetables are halved, then baked with a bit of oil and balsamic vinegar, garlic, and a shower of roasted sweet pepper (capsicum) strands, and served with a caper mayonnaise for dipping. It is delicious to pull off the leaves and get the flavorings from the peppers and the baking sauce, as well as the dipping mayonnaise.

2 large or 4 small to medium artichokes
1 yellow sweet pepper (capsicum), deseeded and sliced into strands
1 red sweet pepper (capsicum), deseeded and sliced into strands
2 tablespoons olive oil
1 tablespoon balsamic vinegar
2 garlic cloves, chopped
salt and freshly ground black pepper, to taste

CAPER MAYONNAISE
1 tablespoon capers
4 tablespoons mayonnaise

Clean the artichokes and peel the stems. Cut each into half lengthwise, then boil or steam them until they are just tender (add a dash of lemon juice or flour to the water to prevent them discoloring).

Drain and leave the artichokes to cool.

Meanwhile, toss the sweet peppers with the olive oil, vinegar, salt and pepper, and garlic in a baking dish, then bake them in a hot 425°F (220°C) oven for 15–20 minutes.

Add the artichoke halves to this pepper mixture and toss them in the pan juices, then bake together for about 10 minutes, or long enough for the artichokes to heat through and combine flavors with the peppers and juices.

Remove from the oven and adjust seasoning. Leave to cool to room temperature.

Now make the dipping mayonnaise. Mix the capers and mayonnaise together, then spoon equal amounts of the mixture onto each of the plates, add the artichokes, with the pepper strands on top, and serve.

CALIFORNIAN CHEESES

Cheese in California is seldom served as a dessert course. Rather, it usually makes its appearance as an appetizer or informal nibble. Glasses of wine are often accompanied by platters of cheeses, various wholegrain crackers, and, perhaps, a selection of raw vegetables or fruit.

California has a tradition of cheesemaking that, like so much of the agriculture and cuisine, dates back to the Spanish missionaries. The first cheeses were very simple, Spanish-type cheeses: *queso blanco* (white cheese) and *queso del pais* (country-style cheese). The post–Gold Rush development ushered in the production of California's first (and still best-loved) cheese: Monterey Jack. Captain David Jacks, who gave this cheese its name, was a Scottish immigrant, a failed '49er, but a very successful landowner who oversaw vast holdings in the Monterey region. His cows produced such abundant milk that the Spanish workers on the land began making massive quantities of a tangy, mild cheese that Captain Jacks soon began marketing. These days in America there is not only original Monterey Jack, but a similar Sonoma Jack, both available in their *au naturel* state as well as flavored with various seasonings, such as garlic, onion and herb, and hot chilies. Jack cheese may also be aged to a Parmesan-like intensity and dryness, delicious for grating onto pasta for a Californian accent.

California produces other cheeses as well: creamy, soft Teleme; Camembert; fresh Italian cheeses, such as mozzarella and ricotta; and a wide variety of goat cheeses. Maytag blue is a deliciously sharp blue made by a family that also produces excellent beer, and there is even a fledgling production of ewe's milk cheeses.

MARINATED FRESH MOZZARELLA

Serves 4

Fresh mozzarella is a relatively new cheese in California, but now it is as easily available in most supermarkets as it is in Europe. At first, the milky balls of tender cheese were imported in their familiar bag of brine, but lately local cheesemakers have been crafting their own.

2 balls of fresh mozzarella, each 2–3 in. (5–7.5 cm) in diameter
3 garlic cloves, chopped
1 teaspoon chopped fresh rosemary or 2 tablespoons chopped fresh basil
salt, to taste
⅛ teaspoon red pepper flakes, or to taste
½ cup (4 fl. oz., 125 ml) extra virgin olive oil

Dice the cheese into bite-sized cubes.

Combine them with the remaining ingredients and leave to marinate for at least 2 hours. Serve with crusty bread and/or arugula (rocket) or other greens to garnish.

RED AND YELLOW SWEET PEPPERS STUFFED WITH RICOTTA CHEESE, SERVED WITH TOMATO AND MUSTARD VINAIGRETTE

Serves 6, more as canapés

Roasted sweet peppers (capsicums), their flavorful flesh filled with fragrant herbed cheese, make luscious appetizers — as delicious to the eyes as to the tongue.

While they smell enticing as they bake and look lovely as they come out of the oven, do not lose your self-discipline — wait until the peppers have cooled before serving or eating. Not only are they even better chilled, but the tangy Tomato and Mustard Vinaigrette and olive garnish balance the richness of the morsels of cheese-stuffed peppers.

3 yellow sweet peppers (capsicums)
3 red sweet peppers (capsicums)
18 oz. (560 g) ricotta cheese
¾ cup (3 oz., 90 g) freshly grated Parmesan cheese
3 garlic cloves, chopped
1 teaspoon fresh thyme or rosemary or mixed Italian herbs
2 eggs, lightly beaten
salt and freshly ground black pepper, to taste

DRESSING
2 cloves garlic, finely chopped
1 teaspoon Dijon-type mustard
1 teaspoon tomato paste (purée)
1 tablespoon red wine vinegar
3 tablespoons extra virgin olive oil
2–3 oz. (60–90 g) fresh basil leaves, coarsely chopped
salt and freshly ground black pepper, to taste

GARNISH
6–10 niçoise or kalamata olives
handful of unsprayed nasturtium flowers

Roast the sweet peppers, removing their stems and seeds, but leaving them otherwise whole.

Combine the ricotta with the Parmesan, garlic, thyme or rosemary or Italian herbs, and eggs. Season with the salt and pepper, to taste.

Stuff the cheese filling carefully but firmly into each pepper, filling it until it is plump. Place the stuffed peppers in a shallow baking dish.

Bake in a 325°F (170°C) oven for about 20 minutes, or until the cheese seems somewhat firm to the touch. Remove the peppers from the oven and leave to cool, then chill overnight.

Make the dressing. Combine the garlic with the mustard, tomato paste, vinegar, and olive oil. Just before serving add the basil, salt, and pepper.

Cut each pepper into several slices. Spoon a little of the dressing onto each plate and top with several slices of the chilled stuffed peppers, taking care that each portion contains both red and yellow ones. Garnish with the olives and nasturtium flowers, and serve immediately.

OPPOSITE: *Red and Yellow Sweet Peppers Stuffed with Ricotta Cheese, Served with Tomato and Mustard Vinaigrette*

GREEN OLIVES WITH RED SWEET PEPPERS AND GARLIC IN A PAPRIKA MARINADE WITH CORIANDER LEAVES AND TOASTED CUMIN

Serves 6 with other appetizers

Served either warm or cool, home-spiced olives are distinctively delicious. Ordinary supermarket olives, spiced with your own seasonings and herbs, can vary wildly according to your whims and desires: lemon puréed herbs, olive oil, lemon or vinegar, seasonings such as fennel, paprika, thyme, or rosemary.

The following spiced olives are heady and spicy, delicious with bread accompanied by a garlicky yogurt dip such as some variation of tzatziki.

½ red sweet pepper (capsicum), diced
4–6 garlic cloves, chopped
3 tablespoons olive oil
1 fresh green chili pepper, or more to taste, chopped
1 jar of green olives (about 6–8 oz. (185–250 g)),
  drained, reserving 2 to 3 tablespoons of the brine
juice of 1–2 lemons
½ teaspoon toasted and ground cumin seeds (see p. 144)
2 tablespoons finely chopped fresh coriander leaves

Sauté the sweet pepper and garlic in the olive oil, then add the chili and olives.

Heat through over a medium–high heat then add the reserved brine, lemon juice, and cumin seeds. Remove the pan from the heat. Stir in the coriander, then pour the mixture onto a plate and leave to cool.

Serve either warm or cool, with fresh, crusty bread.

CRUNCHY FRIED TOFU SNACKS

Makes about 11 oz. (340 g)

Bite-sized squares of tofu, dusted in cornstarch (cornflour), fried until golden and crisp, taste quite nutty and have a delightful texture — crunchy outside, soft and tender inside. Though one finds commercially prepared fried tofu, its consistency is quite different, airy yet chewy and rather oily. It is good for slitting and stuffing, or cutting up and stewing, but not nearly as fresh and satisfying as these for sheer nibbling enjoyment.

Though these crunchy morsels are just fine served with no fanfare whatsoever, I sometimes serve them with a bowl of the simplest salsa for dipping. Try diced tomato with fresh chili, onion, garlic, and coriander.

11 oz. (340 g) firm tofu, cut into bite-sized squares
several tablespoons cornstarch (cornflour)
oil for frying

Toss the tofu in the cornstarch, patting it on so that it sticks well. Shake off any excess.

Heat the oil (about 1 in. (2.5 cm) in depth) and place the cornstarch-coated tofu into it (a wok works best for this as you get a deep small puddle of oil that is easy to keep hot).

Fry the tofu over a medium–high heat. You will find that they take a surprisingly long time to go golden and crisp. Turn them once or twice so that they cook evenly, then remove them from the oil and drain on paper towels or absorbent kitchen paper.

OPPOSITE: *Green Olives with Red Sweet Peppers and Garlic in a Paprika Marinade with Coriander Leaves and Toasted Cumin (top) and Crunchy Fried Tofu Snacks (bottom)*

Spreads & Dips

MEXICAN-SPICED PEPITA SPREAD SERVED WITH SPINACH AND CRUSTY BREAD

Serves 4

Toasted pepitas or pumpkin seeds, ground then puréed with spicy seasonings, are a staple food of the Yucatán Peninsula of Mexico. Like so many of the specialties from south of the border, Yucatán food has been embraced in California. Pepita mixtures, or, more authentically, pipián, vary wildly in flavor and consistency. Some are as soupy as a dip, others firm and quite stiff. They are as healthful as they are delicious, packed with the nutritional vitality of seeds.

Cold, cooked spinach is a clean yet earthy contrast to the richness and spiciness of the pepita mixture. Serve it with crusty, sesame-seed-topped bread to spread it all on.

6 oz. (185 g) shelled pepitas (pumpkin seeds)
1–2 fresh green chili pepper(s), deseeded and diced,
    or to taste
2 garlic cloves, chopped
3–5 scallions (spring onions), thinly sliced
½–¾ teaspoon ground cumin
3 large, fresh tomatoes, peeled, deseeded, and diced,
    or 5 canned ones, chopped
juice of ½–1 lime
salt and freshly ground black pepper, to taste
3 tablespoons tomato purée (passata) or tomato juice
8 oz. (250 g) fresh or frozen spinach, cooked, cooled,
    and drained or squeezed dry

Toast the pepitas in an ungreased skillet or frying pan over a medium-high heat. Cook for 5–10 minutes, shaking and turning as they sputter, pop, and turn golden brown. Or you may place them on a baking sheet in a 350°F (180°C) oven for about 20 minutes.

When the pepitas have cooled, grind them coarsely in a blender, grinder, or food processor. Add the remaining ingredients, except the spinach, and whirl until a smoothish mixture results. Taste to check that the seasoning is as you like it and chill to meld the flavors.

Serve the spread alongside the spinach, with slices of crusty bread for dipping and spreading.

OPPOSITE: *Mexican-spiced Pepita Spread Served with Spinach and Crusty Bread*

GUACAMOLE — SPICY AVOCADO SPREAD/SAUCE/DIP

Serves 6—8

Mexican in origin, variations of this rich, green, sauce-like concoction have been prepared throughout most of Latin America for a very long time. In the West of the USA and in many other parts of the world, guacamole is eaten as a party dip, as a topping for Mexican-style specialties, or as a dressing for sandwiches, salads, tacos, soups, almost anything.

For a good guacamole, choose good avocados. Look for even coloring, avoiding ones with bruises or dark areas that indicate hard or fibrous spots or discolored, off-flavored flesh. A ripe avocado should be firm, yet with a certain delicacy that hints at a buttery texture. The best place to feel the fruit is at its neck. Press it there gently and if it gives, despite a certain resistance, it is likely to be just right. Once cut into, an unripe avocado will ripen no further.

A good way to reduce the likelihood of bruises occurring before your carefully chosen avocados arrive home is to ripen the fruit yourself. Purchase them when they are still hard and let them ripen in a dark place (such as a store cupboard) at a temperature of between 55 and 70 degrees Fahrenheit, or 13 and 21 degrees Celsius. Occasionally, though, you will find that the odd avocado will refuse to soften and grow ripe.

The Haas avocado — thick black-skinned and oily-fleshed, with a fine savory flavor — is, to my mind, the tastiest variety and superior to the disturbingly sweet, watery, thin green-skinned Fuerte, usually imported from Florida. California produces 80 percent of the total crop of avocados for the USA and the Haas is the most commonly grown variety on the West Coast. It is the best for guacamole.

While there are approximately 99 varieties of avocado, only a few are grown commercially. Of these, I especially like the tiny, thumb-sized avocados, with their smooth, silken flesh. Although, to assemble enough of them for a good guacamole is not only difficult, but a waste of time and effort. Better to eat them as they come, one by one, scraping your teeth against the tender skin to extract all the pale green, buttery flesh.

There are endless permutations on the basic guacamole mixture. Some recipes add diced, hard-boiled eggs, chopped white or red onions, scallions (spring onions), a tiny bit of mayonnaise, a bit of cooked, diced zucchini (courgette), tomatillos (Mexican green tomatoes), and so on. I am fondest of the following recipe, which is particularly tangy. Not only has it been a favorite with my cooking class students and catering clients over the years, it conjures up images of midnight feasts with my family — a big bowl of tortilla chips and guacamole disappearing into our mouths as we sit on the couch, blanket up to our chins, watching late-night movies.

If eating guacamole as a dip, be sure to use really good-quality tortilla chips: ones that are brittle–crisp, taste richly of corn, and are neither overly fatty nor salty. Restaurant-style tortilla chips are often best.

Controversy reigns as to the best way to keep guacamole green and prevent it turning gray. Some place a pit (stone) from one of the avocados in the mixture, but I favor placing a piece of plastic wrap (cling film) over the top, letting the wrap rest directly on the surface of the guacamole, thus eliminating the exposure to air that turns it dark gray. If unsuccessful in the endeavor, don't worry, simply stir the discolored top into the guacamole and the sauce will take on its attractive green color again. Actually, you will find that this recipe, with its dose of acids in the form of the lemon or lime, and the tomatoes, does not discolor easily.

4 avocados (preferably black-skinned Haas)
juice of 2 lemons or limes
2 garlic cloves, chopped (optional)
½ onion, finely chopped
4 small or 2 large tomatoes, chopped or diced
2 tablespoons chopped fresh coriander
½–1 fresh green chili pepper, chopped, or to taste
¼ teaspoon ground cumin
pinch of mild Mexican chili powder, or to taste
salt, to taste

Cut each avocado in half and scoop out the flesh, discarding any dark or fibrous areas.

Coarsely mash the avocado flesh with a fork, and mix in the lemon or lime juice.

Gradually add the remaining ingredients, mixing well, and season with salt.

Warm Refried Beans with Melted Cheese and Vegetable Toppings

Serves 4

Almost like a dip or fondue, warm, creamy refried beans, topped with melting cheese, are delicious dipped into with soft corn tortillas or crusty bread. Fresh vegetables add a delicious accent, as do dabs of as spicy a salsa as you can bear, all smoothed over with snowy white sour cream or Greek yogurt.

refried beans (either recipe, p. 108, or 2 medium cans,
   gently heated with a little added water)
6 oz. (185 g) cheese that melts easily, grated
½ teaspoon cumin seeds
3–4 ripe tomatoes, diced
½ red or white onion, chopped
2 fresh green chili peppers, chopped
2 tablespoons chopped fresh coriander
½ cup (4 fl. oz., 125 ml) sour cream or Greek yogurt
salsa, as desired (see p. 138)
soft, warm, fresh flour tortillas or naan or crusty bread

Spoon the reheated beans into a casserole dish and top with the cheese, then sprinkle the cumin seeds over the top.

Combine the tomatoes, onion, chilies, and coriander. Set aside.

Heat the cheese-topped beans in a hot 425°F (220°C) oven or under the broiler (grill) until the cheese has melted.

Serve immediately, topped with the tomato, chili, and coriander relish, and spoonfuls of the sour cream or Greek yogurt. Offer salsa on the side and break off pieces of the tortillas or bread for dipping.

Variation

Instead of serving the hot, cheese-topped beans with bread, serve it with crunchy blue corn tortilla chips, the chips surrounding the beans, stuck in at various points so that the dish takes on a porcupine-like appearance.

BELOW: *Warm Refried Beans with Melted Cheese and Vegetable Toppings*

Cumin-scented Hummus with Diced Cucumber and Tomatoes, Fresh Mint, and Coriander Leaves

Serves 4–6

Hummus has, in recent years, become as Californian as it is Middle Eastern. In California, however, basic hummus is just the beginning. Other flavorings and toppings often embellish the robust dish. Here, diced cucumber, tomato, and leaves of fresh mint and coriander give it a fresh flavor and outlook. It is delicious scooped up on crusty bread or dipped into with little individual pita breads.

3 garlic cloves, finely chopped
15–16 oz. (475–500 g) cooked dried or canned chickpeas (garbanzos)
3 tablespoons sesame tahini
¼ cup (2 fl. oz., 60 ml) lemon juice, or to taste
¼–½ teaspoon ground cumin, to taste
pinch of curry powder
salt and freshly ground black pepper, to taste
¼ cucumber, diced
2 small or 1 large ripe tomato(es), diced
handful of fresh mint, coarsely chopped
handful of fresh coriander leaves, coarsely chopped

Whirl the garlic in a blender or food processor, then add the chickpeas, tahini, and lemon juice. Whirl until smooth. Season with the cumin, curry powder, salt, and pepper, then check that the seasoning is to your taste and adjust if necessary.

Spoon the hummus into a serving bowl and arrange the cucumber, tomatoes, mint, and coriander over the top in a pleasing pattern. Serve immediately.

Pate Forestiere

Serves 4–6

Baked in an earthenware terrine, marbled with spinach, studded with mushrooms, and topped with several bay leaves, this rustic, sliceable pâté is at home anywhere. It is amazing, bordering on sorcery, how such an unappetizing-looking bean as the soy can be transformed into such a wonderfully flavorful pâté.

Serve it in its own terrine and accompany it with crusty bread or crisp crackers, oil-cured black olives or sour tarragon-scented cornichons, and a garnish of greens such as *frisée* (curly endive), arugula (rocket), watercress, or whatever you fancy at the time.

Basic Soybean Mixture

4½ oz. (140 g) uncooked soybeans (12 oz. (375 g) when cooked)
1 garlic clove, chopped
1–2 tablespoons olive or vegetable oil
1 cup (8 fl. oz., 250 ml) vegetable stock (see pp. 37–8)
up to ¾ cup (6 fl. oz., 185 ml) water, as needed, to achieve a smooth texture

The Pate

1 onion, coarsely chopped
2 garlic cloves, coarsely chopped
2 tablespoons unsalted butter or low-fat spread (add a little extra oil if using low-fat spread)
1 lb. (500 g) mushrooms, diced or coarsely chopped
½–1 teaspoon soy sauce
1–2 tablespoons brandy
4 oz. (125 g) soy mince or textured vegetable protein (TVP) (preferably beef flavor)
7 oz. (225 g), approximately, raw or frozen spinach
4 heaped tablespoons whole-wheat (wholemeal) breadcrumbs
2 eggs, lightly beaten
2 bouillon (stock) cubes, crumbled
freshly ground black pepper, to taste
½ teaspoon fresh or large pinch dried thyme
½ teaspoon fresh or large pinch dried marjoram
½ teaspoon fresh or large pinch dried rosemary
6 bay leaves

First, make the basic soybean mixture. Put the soybeans into a saucepan and generously cover with water. Bring to the boil, then remove the pan from the heat, cover, and leave to soak for an hour. Drain, add fresh water, bring to the boil, and simmer over a medium-low heat until the beans are tender (they will be slightly rubbery and squeaky when cooked). Leave them to cool in the water.

Grind (mince) the cooked, cooled soybeans in a blender or food processor (they will probably not break down to a smooth consistency at this point, so just get the mixture as smooth as possible).

Lightly sauté the chopped garlic in a small amount of the oil. Add the soybean purée and cook with the garlic for a few minutes, just lightly sautéing the mixture. Then add the stock and cook until the beans have absorbed most of the stock. Return the mixture to the blender or food processor and purée. Add a little water, if necessary, to achieve a smooth texture.

Now make the pâté. Sauté the onion and garlic in the butter or low-fat spread until they have lightly browned. Add the mushrooms and sauté over a

medium to high heat, letting the mushrooms brown. Add the soy sauce and continue sautéing and browning. Then add the brandy and continue to cook for a few minutes longer until the liquid has evaporated. The mushroom mixture should now be highly flavored, very brown, and quite dry.

Combine the sautéed mushroom and puréed soybean mixtures in the blender or food processor, allowing chunks of mushrooms to remain to give the pâté texture and nuggets of pure mushroom flavor.

Rehydrate the soy mince or textured vegetable protein by cooking it with the spinach in a pan with a tiny amount of water. When the spinach leaves are bright green and the soy mince has softened, remove the pan from the heat and drain off the liquid.

Mix the drained spinach and soy mince with the puréed soybean and mushroom mixture, then add the breadcrumbs, eggs, bouillon cubes, pepper, and herbs (except the bay leaves), mixing well so that the bouillon cubes dissolve and combine with the other ingredients.

Pour the mixture into a terrine or loaf pan, or glazed, round casserole dish and smooth the top. Press the bay leaves into the top of the mixture and drizzle the oil over the top.

Bake, covered, in a 325°–350°F (170°–180°C) oven for about an hour, or until the top has browned, is sizzling, and the pâté has puffed up a bit.

Remove the pâté from the oven, leave it to cool slightly and remove the lid. Place a piece of foil or a plate on top of the pâté and put a heavy weight (such as a large can of beans) on top. This gives the terrine the characteristic dense texture of pâté.

When cooled, cover and chill until ready to serve. Lasts 4–5 days covered in the refrigerator.

Bonus

SOY NUTS: Make a double batch of the basic soybean mixture as given above and drain. Use half for the pâté and half for the following crunchy, toasty little nibbling nuts.

Take the 12 oz. (375 g) cooked, drained soybeans, season with a little salt, and spread in the bottom of a shallow baking dish. Bake in a 400°F (200°C) oven for 30–45 minutes, tossing them occasionally, or until the beans have turned an even golden to nut brown, and are toasted and crunchy. Leave them to cool and enjoy as a snack or an alternative to croûtons.

ABOVE: *Pâté Forestière*

Garlic and Lemon Creamy Pureed White Bean Sauce with Toasted Cumin Eggplant Slices, Tender Green Beans, and Pita Bread

Serves 4

Smooth and creamy, this cousin of hummus is little more than cooked butter (lima) beans seasoned with lots of garlic and olive oil, then puréed with lemon juice. Served with a dusting of mild red chili powder, it makes a delicious dip for the pan-browned eggplant (aubergine) slices with toasted cumin seeds and fresh crisp–tender green beans, plus the pita bread for dipping.

Enjoy this on a lazy summer afternoon.

3 garlic cloves, chopped
4 tablespoons extra virgin olive oil
15 oz. (475 g) cooked dried or canned cannelini beans, drained
juice of 2–3 lemons, or to taste
salt and freshly ground black pepper, to taste

Garnish

pinch of mild Mexican chili powder
1 small to medium eggplant (aubergine), unpeeled (unless skin is tough), thinly sliced lengthwise, then cut into smaller pieces
1–2 tablespoons olive oil, or as needed
½ teaspoon or more toasted, lightly crushed cumin seeds (see p. 144)
salt, to taste
2 pita breads, cut into wedges
8 oz. (250 g) crisp–tender whole green or string beans, cold (either fresh ones, cooked then chilled or frozen ones, defrosted but still cold)

Purée the garlic with the olive oil in a food processor or blender, then add the beans and whirl until a smooth mixture results. Add the lemon juice, continue whirling, then season with salt and pepper.

Spoon into the serving bowl, dust with the mild chili powder, then set aside to chill.

Meanwhile, prepare the eggplant. In a tiny amount of olive oil, in several batches, brown the eggplant, then remove to a plate and sprinkle with the cumin seeds and salt. Leave to cool to room temperature.

When they are ready, arrange the eggplant and the pita wedges on a plate together with the green beans, accompanied by the bowl of the bean sauce for everyone to dip into.

Variation

WHITE BEAN PATE WITH CUMIN AND CITRUS VINAIGRETTE WITH SLICED CUCUMBERS: Decrease the amount of olive oil and lemon juice in the dipping sauce so that it is the consistency of hummus or a spreadable pâté. Serve the spread on individual plates, each portion garnished with a drizzle of Cumin and Citrus Vinaigrette (see p. 139) and surrounded by thick slices of cucumber for dipping.

Radicchio with Garlic Fava Beans and Pecorino

Serves 4

This simple appetizer was inspired by an item on the menu at Joyce Goldstein's Square One Restaurant in San Francisco. In simple and very chic surroundings, nestled alongside a financial district green park, Joyce serves up some of the gutsiest food I have ever tasted — robust, rustic dishes with decidedly Mediterranean influences (along with Eastern and Hispanic ones).

The slightly bitter radicchio is a delicious foil for the garlicky, earthy beans and the sweet basil and mint. Pecorino cheese adds a smooth enrichment.

3 garlic cloves, chopped
2 tablespoons olive oil
4 oz. (125 g) fresh shelled, peeled, and blanched or frozen fava (broad) beans
salt and freshly ground black pepper, to taste
1 small head of radicchio, cut into strips
olive oil and balsamic or champagne vinegar, to taste
3 oz. (90 g) pecorino or Parmesan or dry Asiago cheese, cut into thin slices or shreds
1 tablespoon fresh basil, thinly sliced
1 tablespoon fresh mint, thinly sliced

Lightly sauté the garlic in the olive oil, then add the fava beans and cook until well coated with the fragrant oil and warmed through (this will take a little longer if using frozen beans). Season with salt and pepper.

Arrange the radicchio on four plates, then top with the warm fava beans. Sprinkle the olive oil and balsamic or champagne vinegar over the top, and garnish with the cheese, basil, and mint. Serve immediately.

OPPOSITE: *Radicchio with Garlic Fava Beans and Pecorino*

TOMATO AND YOGURT MOUSSE WITH TOASTED CUMIN SEEDS OR FRESH SWEET BASIL

Serves 4

This mousse is at once tangy and creamy, and filled to bursting with intense tomato flavor. It is delicious as it is or served as an accompanying sauce for a Mediterranean vegetable terrine of layered eggplant (aubergine), zucchini (courgette), and red sweet pepper (capsicum). Here a spoonful of mousse is served accompanied by a little mound of vinaigrette-dressed *mesclun* greens or *frisée* (curly endive), and a handful of something plain and starchy to contrast with all the flavor and richness — either crisp, thinly sliced toasted baguette or plain boiled rigatoni or similar tubular pasta.

Having tried the recipe in two batches using toasted cumin seeds for one and fresh sweet basil for the other, I know both are sensational! The cumin is a provocative foil for the creamy tomato, while the basil is a lyrical echo of sweetness and green fragrance. I could not make up my mind which was best so I have included both.

2 small or 1 medium onion(s), chopped

3 garlic cloves, coarsely chopped

3 tablespoons olive oil

2 lbs. (1 kg) fresh, ripe tomatoes, skinned, deseeded, cored, and diced

¾ teaspoon sugar or honey

salt and white pepper, to taste

about 5 tablespoons tomato paste (purée)

3 tablespoons Greek yogurt or other rich yogurt

½ cup (4 fl. oz., 125 ml) whipping (double) cream

¼–½ teaspoon toasted cumin seeds, lightly crushed (see p. 144) or 1 tablespoon fresh sweet basil, cut into thin strips (see above)

ACCOMPANIMENTS

handful of mesclun or frisée (curly endive), coarsely cut up, dressed in a little olive oil and vinegar

12 very thin slices of baguette, crisply toasted, or about 6 oz. (185 g) cooked rigatoni pasta, cooled to room temperature

Lightly sauté the onion and garlic in the olive oil until they have softened slightly.

Add the tomatoes and sugar or honey, and cook over a medium to low heat, seasoning with salt and white pepper.

When the mixture is thick and not much liquid remains, add the tomato paste, stirring it in well. Remove the pan from the heat and leave it to cool.

Purée the tomato mixture with the Greek yogurt until it is smooth, then chill.

Meanwhile, whip the cream. If it is already very thick, though, just stir it well until it is very smooth. Fold the cream into the tomato and yogurt mixture, and chill for at least 2 hours.

Just before serving, season the mousse by either mixing in the cumin seeds or sprinkling with the basil. Serve a spoonful of the mousse on each plate, accompanied by a small mound of the greens and either the toasts or the plain cold pasta.

OPPOSITE: *Tomato and Yogurt Mousse with Toasted Cumin Seeds or Fresh Sweet Basil*

CALIFORNIAN CROSTINI
Serves 4–6

Crostini are tiny, Italian, broiled (grilled) open sandwiches served as appetizers or antipasti in various regions of Italy. In California, *crostini* are apt to be topped with any of a wide variety of savory, if untraditional, toppings.

The following is my favorite, combining the flavors of tomato, garlic, olives, basil, and cheese, all melted into a delectable, somewhat pizza-like tidbit. Serve as part of a selection of appetizers with raw fennel and diced beets (beetroot) in an olive oil vinaigrette, Sweet–Tart Multicolored Sweet Peppers Baked with Olive Oil and Vinegar (see pp. 18–19), a plate of ripe figs on a bed of arugula (rocket), all sprinkled with Gorgonzola and macadamia nuts.

12 oz. (375 g) fontina or Asiago or other melting cheese, coarsely chopped

2 oz. (60 g) fresh basil leaves, coarsely chopped

4–6 ripe tomatoes, chopped and drained of excess juice

2–3 garlic cloves, finely chopped

4 tablespoons pitted and coarsely chopped black kalamata olives

1 baguette, cut into ⅛–¼-in. (4–6-mm) slices

Preheat the broiler (grill) to hot.

Mix the cheese with the basil, tomatoes, garlic, and olives. Arrange the baguette slices on a baking sheet. Top each slice with about a tablespoon of the cheese mixture.

Broil (grill) until the cheese mixture is bubbling and golden-brown-flecked (take care, as *crostini* can burn in a split second). Serve immediately.

Variation

BAKED PANINO OF TOMATOES, SWEET PEPPERS, CHEESE, OLIVES, AND BASIL: A crusty French roll drenched with vinaigrette, stuffed with its savory filling, then baked until crisp-crusted on the outside, the cheese melted on the inside.

For four sandwiches, split 4 crusty rolls. Make a dressing from the following: ½ cup (4 fl. oz., 125 ml) each of olive oil and red wine vinegar, 3 crushed garlic cloves, freshly ground black pepper, crushed dried oregano, and 1 roasted red sweet pepper (capsicum), peeled and diced. Spoon some dressing on the cut surface of each half of the rolls, then spread the cheese mixture given above over the dressing. Close up the rolls and put them in a baking dish. Bake in a 425°F (220°C) oven for 15 minutes. Serve immediately.

TARTINES OF BLUE CASTELLO OR GORGONZOLA, PINE NUTS, AND BASIL

Serves 4

Creamy blue cheese atop crusty country bread, sprinkled with pine nuts and basil, makes a delicious appetizer or picnic dish, especially when toted out to the country on a fine day. Relax on the sweet grass, inhale its scent, feel the warmth of the sunlight, and open a bottle of a nice dry white wine to go with it all. Exact amounts are not needed — use your own judgment and personal tastes to guide you.

> *1 baguette, sliced*
> *Blue Castello or Gorgonzola or other creamy, pungent blue cheese*
> *pine nuts, for sprinkling*
> *handful of fresh sweet basil leaves*

Arrange the slices of baguette on a platter or plates, and spread with the cheese. Sprinkle the pine nuts over and top with the basil leaves. Serve and eat immediately.

BRUSCHETTA A LA CALIFORNIA WITH TOMATO, HERB, AND GARLIC RELISH AND FRESH FENNEL AND BLACK OLIVE RELISH

Serves 4–6

Fresh vegetables — diced and combined with the garlic, herbs, and olives, and dressed generously with olive oil and vinegar — make a refreshing starter, accompanied by crusty bread for dipping. The simplest version of this dish is a rustic meal of grilled country bread rubbed with a cut clove of garlic and ripe, sweet tomatoes and, then sprinkled with olive oil and a little thinly sliced basil. In California, it has been transformed into an elegant appetizer with such a wide range of toppings it is hard to recognize it as the Mediterranean classic. Yet, there is always the constant of grilled bread, the rub of garlic, and the balm of olive oil.

> *1 loaf crusty Italian or French bread, cut into thick slices*
> *3–5 garlic cloves, peeled and left whole*

TOMATO, HERB, AND GARLIC RELISH
> *2–3 ripe tomatoes, diced*
> *3 tablespoons chopped fresh parsley or basil or arugula (rocket) or herb of your choice*
> *3 garlic cloves, finely chopped*
> *3 tablespoons extra virgin olive oil*

> *1 tablespoon balsamic vinegar*
> *pinch of red pepper flakes*

FRESH FENNEL AND BLACK OLIVE RELISH
> *1 small or ½ medium fresh Florence fennel (finocchio) bulb, including a few of the feathery leaves, diced or coarsely chopped*
> *15–20 black Mediterranean-style olives (such as kalamata), pitted and diced, or coarsely chopped*
> *3 tablespoons extra virgin olive oil*
> *2 teaspoons balsamic vinegar*

Place the bread slices on a baking sheet and toast in a 350°F (180°C) oven. When cool enough to handle, rub each slice with a cut clove of garlic (the coarse texture of the toast 'grates' the garlic). Set aside.

Prepare each relish by combining all of the ingredients required for each one in separate bowls.

Serve the toasts immediately, each topped with several spoonfuls of the relishes.

WHOLE-WHEAT BRUSCHETTA WITH SUN-DRIED TOMATO PESTO

Serves 4

Whole-wheat (wholemeal) bread — rustic and tasting of wheat — toasted then rubbed with garlic and spread with sun-dried tomato pesto makes a lusty, robust appetizer. The perfect setting is a wooden table set out on a terrace or grassy patch beneath a tree casting dappled shadows. This combination of tradition (*bruschetta* and pesto) and innovation (whole-wheat bread and sun-dried tomatoes in the pesto) is what Californian cuisine is all about.

> *8 thick slices whole-wheat (wholemeal) country-style bread*
> *4 garlic cloves, or to taste*
> *4–6 tablespoons sun-dried tomato pesto (store-bought or home-made, see p. 141), or to taste*

Toast the bread over an open fire, under the broiler (grill), or in the oven (see above) until lightly browned on both sides. Cut the garlic and rub the cut side against the toasted bread (the rough texture of the bread acts as a mini-grater, extracting the full flavor of the garlic). Spread the toasts with the pesto and serve immediately.

OPPOSITE: *(clockwise from top) Tartines of Blue Castello or Gorgonzola, Pine Nuts, and Basil; Californian Crostini; Bruschetta à la California with Tomato, Herb, and Garlic Relish, and with Fresh Fennel and Black Olive Relish (center)*

Soups & Bisques

In California, soup might begin a meal, but it is just as likely to be the meal. Indeed, 'soup and salad' is a phrase synonymous with 'lunch' or 'light supper'.

The Californian repertoire of clear, light broths is limited, especially vegetarian ones, but we have a wealth of full-bodied soups, ablaze with vibrant, lively flavors, culled from the freshness of the garden, filled out with the heartiness of grains and legumes, scented with the garlic, herbs, chilies, and other aromatics we cherish. Our soups, too — even more than other dishes — reflect our multicultural cuisine. Asian, Mexican, and Mediterranean flavors predominate, combined not in traditional ways, but in whatever way tastes best. Gazpacho might be uncharacteristically spicy, with a splash of vodka or tequila, ravioli might float in a lemon-grass-scented broth, pesto might be stirred into creamy potato soup, and yogurt into a hearty bean potage.

VEGETABLE STOCK

When a recipe calls for vegetable stock, you can use a vegetarian bouillon (stock) cube mixed with water. If the soup is rich with other ingredients, this will be fine.

Most soups, however, taste best prepared with a home-made stock. As pure vegetable stocks are often pale in flavor — plus they seem so wasteful, requiring huge amounts of vegetables that are just simmered then thrown away. I have devised several stocks based on a combination of some vegetables and several bouillon cubes. The bouillon cubes take the place of salt, as they are salty anyway, and they have the added

OPPOSITE: Mission Viejo *Spicy Potage of Barley and Vegetables Seasoned with Refried Beans and Peanut Butter (top), Berkeley Barley and Split Pea Soup with Coriander, Chili, and Lemon Seasoning (bottom right), and Calasia Broth (bottom left)*

flavor of hydrolyzed vegetable protein. While I try to use home-made everything, I find bouillon cubes are extremely useful in these circumstances.

A very informal broth may be made by saving all the tiny bits of vegetables as you cook, storing them in a plastic bag in your freezer. Once a week you can take them out and simmer up a quick stock. The ends of carrots, bits of red sweet pepper (capsicum), stems of spinach or chard (silver beet), greens of scallions (spring onions) — all can be used for this purpose. Simply place them (thawed) in a pot of water, add a bouillon cube or two, season with onion, leek, and/or garlic, and bring to the boil. Simmer until tender. Strain and use as desired (the stock freezes brilliantly).

GARLIC AND BAY LEAF BROTH
Makes about 4 cups (1$\frac{3}{4}$ imp. pints, 1 litre)

This makes an unexpectedly gentle and subtly-scented broth, despite the prodigious amount of garlic used. As it cooks, the garlic takes on a mild, almost sweet quality.

You can use this as a basis for any vegetable soup — I suggest Berkeley Barley and Split Pea Soup with Coriander, Chili, and Lemon Seasoning (see p. 39), or Tortelloni in Broth with Broccoli and Herbs (see p. 44).

1$\frac{1}{2}$ quarts (2$\frac{1}{2}$ imp. pints, 1.5 litres) water
2–3 bouillon (stock) cubes
2 heads of garlic, broken into cloves and unpeeled
6 bay leaves

Put all the ingredients into a heavy-based saucepan and bring to the boil. Reduce the heat, cover, and simmer until the garlic is very soft and tender (about 45 minutes).

Leave it to cool, then strain the stock through a sieve, and discard the garlic skins and bay leaves left behind. Use as desired.

GRANDMOTHER'S BROTH
Makes about 4 cups (1$\frac{3}{4}$ imp. pints, 1 litre)

Every Sunday my grandmother made a big potful of this comforting broth, and I have followed suit, preparing it for family occasions.

The broth may be enjoyed as is, simply served with a big spoonful of tiny pasta or *pastina*. I adore the rice-shaped *orzo* or pepper-shaped *acini de pepe*, vermicelli, and the little noodle alphabets. It also makes a good base for almost any other soup.

3 carrots, thickly sliced
2 stalks celery, thickly sliced
1 onion, cut into wedges
handful of fresh parsley, coarsely chopped
pinch of dried dill weed or several sprigs of fresh dill (optional)
1 parsnip, cut into chunks (optional)
1$\frac{1}{2}$ quarts (2$\frac{1}{2}$ imp. pints, 1.5 litres) water
3 golden-colored bouillon (stock) cubes or bouillon cubes of choice

Put all the ingredients into a large pot and bring to the boil. Reduce the heat, cover, and simmer until the vegetables are very tender (about 45 minutes).

SOUPS

LEMON AND LEEK SOUP WITH FRESH CORIANDER LEAVES
Serves 4

Cookery books refer to leeks as 'poor man's asparagus' and in Europe that is certainly the case; the irony is that, in California, asparagus is almost always cheaper than the humble leek!

Despite California's passion for the *Allium* family, until recently, leeks have been the least well known. Appearing to Californian cooks to be overgrown scallions (spring onions), many, for the longest time, had no idea what to do with them. The passion for fresh vegetables of all types that has flourished more recently has changed all that — today, leeks are easily found in most American markets.

The following soup combines the flavors from the cuisines of California's large Armenian, Greek, and Iranian communities in its lemony egg enrichment, leeks, and fresh coriander.

1$\frac{1}{2}$ tablespoons butter
1$\frac{1}{2}$ tablespoons all-purpose (plain) flour
3–4 medium leeks, well-cleaned and cut into $\frac{1}{2}$-in. (1.5-cm) thick slices
3 cups (24 fl. oz., 750 ml) vegetable broth (see pp. 37–8)
1 large egg, lightly beaten
juice of 2 large lemons
pinch of ground cinnamon
salt and freshly ground black pepper, to taste
dash of vinegar, if needed

GARNISH
2 tablespoons or so fresh coriander

Melt the butter over a medium-high heat and, when it is just foamy, sprinkle in the flour. Stir in and let it turn lightly golden, then stir the leeks into the mixture and cook for a few moments.

Off the heat, stir in the broth, a little at a time, until it is all added. Cook the mixture over a medium heat, stirring every so often until any lumps have disappeared and the soup has thickened a little.

Beat the egg and lemon juice together. Remove the soup from the heat and ladle a few spoonfuls of the hot soup into the egg and lemon mixture, stirring it well so that the egg forms an emulsion rather than scrambling. When they are well combined, add a ladle more soup and stir well, then pour the egg- and lemon-enriched mixture back into the hot pot. Return the pan to a low to medium heat, and stir until smooth and thickened a little more. Add the cinnamon, salt, and pepper, then taste to check the seasoning. Add the dash of vinegar if the soup needs a little extra sharpness. Serve immediately, each portion garnished with the coriander.

BERKELEY BARLEY AND SPLIT PEA SOUP WITH CORIANDER, CHILI, AND LEMON SEASONING
Serves 4

A hearty, warming soup, enlivened by the addition of a spicy–tart coriander salsa paste. This unusual preparation of the two ordinary ingredients of barley and split peas makes this recipe all the more pleasing.

Serve with wholegrain (wholemeal granary) bread, butter, and a plate of radishes, scallions (spring onions), and black olives, along with some pickled chili peppers if you like them.

8 oz. (250 g) pearl barley
2 oz. (60 g) split peas
4 cups (1¾ imp. pints, 1 litre) vegetable broth
   (see pp. 37–8)
½ teaspoon ground cumin
3 garlic cloves, coarsely chopped
2 tablespoons olive oil
3–4 tablespoons Coriander and Lemon Salsa (see p. 102)
lemon juice, to taste
salt and freshly ground black pepper, to taste

Put the pearl barley, split peas, broth, and cumin into a saucepan. Bring to the boil, then reduce the heat, cover, and simmer until the barley and split peas are tender (about 40 minutes).

In a separate pan, heat the garlic in the olive oil until the garlic aroma is released — do not let the garlic brown. Add the mixture to the barley and split pea mixture, together with the Coriander and Lemon Salsa.

Taste to check the seasoning, then adjust with the lemon juice, salt, and pepper. Serve immediately.

CALASIA BROTH
Serves 4

Eastern ingredients such as chili peppers, coriander, coconut milk, and lemon grass have worked their way into contemporary Californian food, so it is not unusual to find such flavors paired with Western techniques and ingredients.

Accordingly, this broth is given a lovely, elusive perfume from the lemon grass simmering in it. Lemon grass is also known as citronella, and its essential oils are used in perfume, bathing mixtures, and as a natural insect repellent. It has a strong scent, so resist the temptation to add more than given in the recipe.

1 stalk fresh lemon grass, outer skin removed, cut into small
   pieces, or 1 to 2 teaspoons dried or ⅛ teaspoon dried
   and powdered lemon grass
4 cups (1¾ imp. pints, 1 litre) vegetable stock of choice
   (see pp. 37–8)
2 carrots, finely diced
4 oz. (125 g) fine soup pasta

GARNISH
2 tablespoons fresh mint (ordinary or apple mint, etc.),
   thinly sliced

Combine the lemon grass and stock in a pan. Bring to the boil, then reduce the heat so it simmers gently. Cook for about 15 minutes, then remove the lemon grass from the broth.

Add the carrot to the broth and bring to the boil, cooking until the carrot is tender (about 5 minutes).

Cook the pasta until it is *al dente*, then drain it.

Mix the pasta into the broth, and serve garnished with the mint.

CREAMY, LEMONY TABBOULEH SOUP

Serves 4

This soup came into being because once I had a bowl of tabbouleh languishing in the back of my refrigerator and I hate to waste good food. The soup is creamy and tangy, being enriched by lemon juice and beaten egg, Greek style. It is a surprisingly delicious soup — well worth preparing extra tabbouleh when you are making it so that you have leftovers with which to make it, though you can, of course, make tabbouleh especially for it or use store-bought tabbouleh from a Middle Eastern delicatessen. (Tabbouleh also makes a delicious addition to savory waffles — see p. 112).

> 2–3 *garlic cloves, chopped*
> 1 *teaspoon olive oil*
> 1½–2 *cups Tabbouleh (see p. 8) or store-bought tabbouleh*
> 3 *cups (25 fl. oz., 780 ml) vegetable broth (see pp. 37–8)*
> 1 *medium to large egg, lightly beaten*
> ⅓ *cup (3 fl. oz., 90 ml) lemon juice, or more to taste*
> *salt and freshly ground black pepper, to taste*

Lightly sauté the garlic in the oil until the garlic has softened and turned lightly golden brown.

Add the Tabbouleh and broth, bring to the boil, then remove the pan from the heat.

Combine the egg and lemon juice, then ladle in a little of the hot tabbouleh and broth mixture. Stir well and add the egg, lemon, and broth mixture to the rest of the hot broth and tabbouleh. The mixture should form a creamy emulsion, not scrambled egg.

Stir well, then return the pan to the heat for a moment or two, stirring well to be sure the egg is cooked through. The mixture will thicken slightly.

Serve immediately, with extra lemon juice, and salt and pepper to taste.

OPPOSITE: Green Bean, Potato, and Olive Soup from the Basque Shepherds of California's Central Valley

GREEN BEAN, POTATO, AND OLIVE SOUP FROM THE BASQUE SHEPHERDS OF CALIFORNIA'S CENTRAL VALLEY

Serves 4

California's great Central Valley stretches from the north of the state to the south, from the gentle coastal mountain range to the rugged and intimidating Sierra Nevada. Throughout the hilly areas that border the valley are huge flocks of sheep, still tended to by the Basque shepherds who migrated and settled the region. They still come, bringing their traditional skills to the melting pot of cultures, ethnic groups, hi-tech industry, and so on that is modern California.

The following soup is marvelous. Inspired by the cooking of the Californian Basques, it consists of green beans and potato in a garlicky broth, ladled over bits of cheese and olives. As the cheese melts, it enriches the simple broth, while the olives add a salty accent. Serve with crusty bread, preferably one made from a sourdough starter.

> 1 *medium new potato, diced*
> 2 *tablespoons olive oil*
> 4–6 *garlic cloves, coarsely chopped*
> 4 *cups (1¾ imp. pints, 1 litre) vegetable broth (see pp. 37–8)*
> 3½–4 *oz. (100–125 g) green or string beans (fresh or frozen), cut into 1–2-in. (2.5–5-cm) lengths*
> 2 *tablespoons tomato paste (purée)*
> 6–8 *oz. (185–250 g) mild cheddar or Monterey Jack cheese, diced*
> 10–15 *black olives (kalamata, oil-cured), pitted and halved, or diced*
> *several sprigs of fresh basil (optional)*
> ¼ *teaspoon dried oregano leaves, crumbled*

Sauté the potato in the olive oil and, when it has lightly browned, add the garlic and continue cooking for a few moments, or until the garlic is very fragrant and lightly golden.

Add the broth, bring to the boil, then reduce the heat and simmer for about 5 minutes, or until the potato has cooked through. Add the beans and tomato paste, and continue to cook for a few minutes until the beans are just tender.

Meanwhile, prepare each bowl by placing a little of the diced cheese, olives, basil (if using), and oregano in the bottom. Ladle the hot soup over the cheese, olives, and herbs. Serve immediately.

MISSION VIEJO SPICY POTAGE OF BARLEY AND VEGETABLES SEASONED WITH REFRIED BEANS AND PEANUT BUTTER

Serves 4

The name *mission viejo* simply means the 'old mission', a name I've given to this soup because the rustic chili, tomato, and bean seasonings reflect the cookery style of the Native Americans and Spaniards that characterized the early days of the California (then known as Nueva España or 'New Spain') missions that formed a trail winding up the coast of California as far north as San Francisco.

Thickening a soup with *frijoles refritos*, or refried beans, gives a deep, substantial quality to the soup. Though it is a technique I came about by accident, no doubt frugal cooks throughout the Southwest of America and further afield have been doing the same for generations.

Serve this soup as a first course, accompanied by either flour tortillas or chapatis, and follow with a salad such as Sonoma Salad of Grilled Goat Cheese, Caramelized Pecans, and Spinach (see p. 2).

4 oz. (125 g) pearl barley
2 garlic cloves, chopped
1 tablespoon vegetable or olive oil
½–1 fresh green chili pepper, deseeded and chopped, or to taste
¼ green sweet pepper (capsicum), chopped
½ teaspoon ground cumin
½ teaspoon mild red chili powder or paprika if your fresh chili is very hot
6 oz. (185 g) chopped fresh or canned tomatoes, with juice
2 cups (16 fl. oz., 500 ml) vegetable broth (see pp. 37–8)
4 oz. (125 g) fresh or half a pack frozen, thawed, and squeezed dry spinach, thinly sliced
8 oz (250 g) home-made or canned refried beans
3 tablespoons chopped fresh coriander
8 oz. (250 g) diced mixed vegetables of choice (corn, peas, green or string beans, carrots, etc.)
pinch of dried oregano, crumbled
1–2 tablespoons peanut butter
salt and freshly ground black pepper, to taste

Put the barley into a pan, cover with water, bring to the boil, and simmer until tender. Drain, reserving the water for other use.

Lightly sauté the garlic in the oil until it has softened, then add the chili and sweet pepper, and sprinkle in the cumin and chili powder or paprika.

Cook for a few moments longer, then add the tomatoes, broth, and spinach. Cook for another 10 minutes or until the spinach is cooked through and the flavors have melded together.

Stir the refried beans into the soup, letting them dissolve and thicken the mixture, then add the coriander, mixed vegetables, oregano, and peanut butter. Cook the soup for a few minutes longer, then season to taste with salt and pepper. Serve.

SOPA DE TORTILLA — MEXICAN COUNTRYSIDE SOUP, LOS ANGELES-STYLE

Serves 4

Vegetable soup spiked with chilies, dressed with lime or lemon, ladled over creamy cheese, and topped with crunchy tortilla chips makes for an invigorating bowlful of complex flavors. Yet it is straightforward to prepare. The only special ingredients you will need are good-quality, not-too-salty tortilla chips. If you can only come by supermarket ones, use these anyway and adjust the saltiness of the soup accordingly.

This is a traditional Mexican soup enjoyed particularly in southern California, where the cuisine is decidedly 'south of the border' in accent. The vegetables in the recipe are merely suggestions — use whatever is best in the market.

3 garlic cloves, chopped
2 tablespoons oil (preferably olive oil)
1 carrot, diced
1 zucchini (courgette), diced
½ red sweet pepper (capsicum), diced
handful of green or string beans, cleaned and cut into bite-sized pieces
1 small to medium waxy potato, peeled and diced
2 ripe tomatoes, skinned and diced
¼ cabbage, chopped
4 cups (1¾ imp. pints, 1 litre) vegetable broth (see pp. 37–8)
¼ teaspoon ground cumin
pinch of dried oregano
salt and freshly ground black pepper, to taste
6 oz. (185 g) cheese (Lancashire, Cheshire, mild cheddar), cut into slices
2 fresh green chili peppers, chopped
2–3 tablespoons chopped fresh coriander
1 lime, cut into wedges
several handfuls of tortilla chips (see above)

Lightly sauté the garlic in the oil, then, when it has softened but not browned, add the carrot, zucchini, red sweet pepper, beans, potato, tomatoes, and cabbage. Cook them for a few moments in the garlicky oil, then add the broth and bring to the boil. Reduce the heat and simmer, uncovered, for about 10 minutes or until the vegetables are tender.

Season with the cumin, oregano, salt, and pepper. Sprinkle some cheese, chili, and coriander in the bottom of each bowl, ladle the soup over, bob wedges of lime in it, and top with slightly crumbled tortilla chips. Enjoy immediately.

NAPA VALLEY SUMMER GARDEN SOUP OF ZUCCHINI, TOMATO, YELLOW SWEET PEPPER, GARLIC, AND ROSEMARY

Serves 4

Sunny flavors make this a light, late-summer soup — perfect for supper in the garden, accompanied by a hearty but cooling salad and the sounds of a late summer's evening.

3 *garlic cloves, coarsely chopped*
2 *tablespoons butter*
2 *zucchini (courgettes), diced*
2 *yellow sweet peppers (capsicums), deseeded and diced*
¼ *cup (2 oz., 60 g) arborio rice*
6 *ripe Roma or plum tomatoes, diced (peeled if desired)*
½ *teaspoon fresh rosemary leaves, coarsely chopped*
4 *cups (1¾ imp. pints, 1 litre) richly flavored vegetable broth (see pp. 37–8)*

Sauté the garlic in the butter, not letting it brown. Stir in the zucchini, yellow sweet peppers, rice, tomatoes, and rosemary, stirring them all into the garlic butter until they are evenly cloaked in it.

Pour in the broth, bring to the boil, then reduce the heat and simmer, covered, until the rice is tender (about 20 minutes), adding more liquid if needed.

Serve immediately.

BELOW: Sopa de Tortilla *(top) and Napa Valley Summer Garden Soup of Zucchini, Tomato, Yellow Sweet Pepper, Garlic, and Rosemary (bottom)*

GILROY DOUBLE GARLIC SOUP

Serves 4

While it is the tiny one-road town of Gilroy that is known as the 'Garlic Capital of the USA', its neighbor, King City, quietly shares its ranking with garlic lovers. During the harvest, in fact, the air between the two towns is permeated with the scent of garlic, for the area grows 80 percent of the nation's consumption of the 'stinking rose'.

In honor of the harvest, each year Gilroy hosts a garlic festival, serving up great lashings of the deliciously pungent herb. Up and down the coast, garlic festivals abound during the harvest time. The passionate garlic lover can even join a Berkeley-based organization (called appropriately Lovers of the Stinking Rose) that promotes the health-giving and food-enhancing properties of the odoriferous bulb.

> 8 *garlic cloves, coarsely chopped*
> 2 *tablespoons olive oil*
> 1–2 *slices French bread, broken up*
> 8 *garlic cloves, peeled and left whole*
> 4 *cups* (1 ¾ *imp. pints,* 1 *litre*) *vegetable broth*
>   (*see pp.* 37–8)
> 1 *tablespoon fresh or* 1 *teaspoon dried sage leaves, chopped*
> 1 *egg, lightly beaten*
> 1 ½ *oz.* (50 *g*) *freshly grated Parmesan cheese*
> *salt and freshly ground black or* cayenne *pepper, to taste*

Lightly sauté the chopped garlic in the olive oil until it is just fragrant and lightly golden brown. Add the bread and lightly sauté it. Remove the pan from the heat and set to one side.

Combine the whole garlic cloves with the broth and sage in a saucepan. Bring to the boil, then reduce the heat and simmer until the garlic is tender.

Mix the egg with the cheese in a bowl.

In a blender or food processor, combine the cooked garlic cloves with the sautéed garlic and bread, using just enough of the broth to make a soupy mixture (otherwise it will spill out of the machine when you turn it on). Whirl until a smooth mixture results, adding more of the broth for a smooth consistency. Mix ½ cup (4 fl. oz., 125 ml) or so of the remaining broth with the egg and cheese mixture, then add this to the blender or food processor, and whirl until smooth.

Return this mixture to the hot broth in the pan, and, stirring to keep the egg from scrambling or forming threads, cook over a low to medium heat until the mixture has thickened slightly. Serve immediately, seasoned with pepper and salt, and more sage, to taste.

TORTELLONI IN BROTH WITH BROCCOLI AND HERBS

Serves 4

Stuffed pastas are available in a wide variety of shapes, fillings, and colors. They are a veritable treasure trove for vegetarians, with the most delicious fillings being the vegetal ones. In California, pasta emporia sell fresh pastas in overwhelming variety, prepared with vegetable and/or herb-seasoned doughs, as well as fillings — they are filled with spinach, herbs, cheese, artichokes, and cèpes (*porcini* mushrooms).

This soup floats a handful of large, stuffed ring-shaped pasta, tortelloni (the larger sibling of the tiny tortellini), in a gentle broth, along with fresh, crisp–tender broccoli and a sprinkling of fresh herbs, with a drizzle of extra virgin olive oil on top. Serve for a cozy supper, accompanied by bread, tomato wedges, and fresh chive-seasoned ewe or goat cheese, followed by a dessert of nectarines and blueberries (bilberries), with *biscotti* and a glass of red wine for dipping.

> 4 *cups* (1 ¾ *imp. pints,* 1 *litre*) *vegetable broth*
>   (*see pp.* 37–8)
> 12 *oz.* (375 *g*) *fresh tortelloni or other stuffed pasta, as desired*
> 1 *medium crown broccoli, cut into florets (stems peeled and cut into bite-sized pieces)*
> 2 *tablespoons or more extra virgin olive oil*
> 1 ½ *tablespoons chopped fresh chives*
> 1 *tablespoon chopped mixed fresh herbs (marjoram, sage, oregano, etc.)*

Pour the broth into a saucepan and bring to the boil. Add the tortelloni or other pasta, cook for a minute or two, then add the broccoli and cook over a high heat for about 5 minutes. (You want the broccoli to be crisp–tender at the same time as the pasta is just tender, so time it accordingly — different pastas take different cooking times, and the size of the broccoli pieces dictates the cooking time of the broccoli.)

Mix the oil, chives, and herbs together well.

Serve the soup in bowls, topping each serving with a drizzle of the rich, flavorful oil.

OPPOSITE: *Tortelloni in Broth with Broccoli and Herbs*

BISQUES

CASTROVILLE ARTICHOKE BISQUE
Serves 4

This bisque was inspired by the fields of gray-green artichokes that cover the oceanside cliffs along the Central Pacific Coast area in the region of Castroville, the self-proclaimed 'Artichoke Capital of the World'. Some say the Italian immigrant farmers originally introduced the artichoke to this region; others say it was the Spanish padres. Regardless, it has thrived. Here the 'thistles' grow luxuriously large and are particularly succulent as the fields are shrouded in soft sea mists until about midday, the artichokes gaining flavor from the salty air.

Artichokes are eaten here with gusto: whole, steamed to tenderness, then dipped into savory mayonnaise-based sauces, or the leaves are removed and coated in batter and deep-fried for the popular street snack.

My favorite is marinated artichoke hearts, the cooked hearts are preserved in a particularly tangy vinaigrette, put up in bottles, and are available in nearly any market, even the tiniest corner store. These little nuggets of flavor are good eaten as they are, straight from the jar, or mixed into salads of pasta, rice, tucked into sandwiches, diced and added to dressings or relishes, tossed into savory tomato rice dishes, and so on.

This bisque is another favorite: a silken essence of artichoke. With Gilroy and King City just a few miles down the road, another local ingredient, garlic, makes its ardent presence known. The soup is one of simplicity, thickened only by a little potato, enhancing its artichoke character rather than disguising it with heavy flour and cream.

> 4 large or 6 medium artichokes
> 2–3 garlic cloves, chopped
> 3 tablespoons unsalted butter
> 1 medium baking potato, peeled and diced
> 3¾ cups (1½ imp. pints, 935 ml) vegetable broth
>   (see pp. 37–8)
> salt and freshly ground black pepper, to taste

To prepare fresh artichokes, pull back the leaves of each artichoke individually. Each leaf will give a little snap, which shows that the flesh of the artichoke remains on the vegetable and that the leaf you discard is only waste. Peel the stem and pare away the bits of thistle around the base.

When you reach the tender leaves near the heart, stop removing them. Quarter the artichoke and, with a small paring knife, remove the sharp leaves inside and the furry choke.

Prevent the artichokes discoloring by placing them in a bowl of water to which you have added, and stirred in, a squeeze of lemon or a spoonful or two of all-purpose (plain) flour.

Lightly sauté the prepared artichokes and garlic in 1½ tablespoons of the butter.

Add the potato and broth, bring to the boil, then reduce the heat, cover, and simmer until the artichokes and potato are tender (about 10 minutes).

Purée the bisque in a blender or processor until it is smooth. Add salt and pepper, spoon into bowls and top each bowlful with a tiny pat of the remaining butter to stir in and enrich the soup. Serve immediately.

Variation

PUREE OF ASPARAGUS BISQUE: This simple purée takes only minutes to prepare and tastes as indisputably of asparagus as the recipe above does of artichoke.

In place of the artichokes, use about 1 lb. (500 g) of tender asparagus, cut into 1–1½-in. (2.5–4-cm) lengths. Add the asparagus to the pot after you add the potatoes, when the potatoes are tender. You only want to cook the asparagus until it is bright green and just tender enough to purée (undercooked, the asparagus will retain its bright color and fresh flavor; overcooked it will become a gray-green and taste a bit stale). Enrich the asparagus soup by reheating with 6–8 fl. oz. (185–250 ml) of milk, and serve with a pat of butter as before, plus a generous sprinkling of freshly grated Parmesan cheese and a few thin shreds of fresh basil.

PUMPKIN AND CHARD PUREE WITH NORTH AFRICAN FLAVORS
Serves 4

Robust in flavor, yet surprisingly light, this simple purée of pumpkin and chard (silver beet) makes a delightful fall (autumn) supper.

Sprinkling the soup with curry powder at the end rather than during the cooking gives a strong, undiluted aroma of the savory spice mixture and balances the earthy flavor of the cumin-scented, simmered pumpkin. Combined with olive oil and garlic, the flavor and aroma is redolent of North Africa, while the non-conformist collection of flavors, techniques, and ingredients makes the soup quintessentially Californian. In fact, North African spicing, close in spirit and taste to Mexican spicing, has become a part of Californian cuisine over the past 20 years. A number of restaurants offer credible couscous platters and tagines, and the excellent books of both Paula Wolfert and Claudia Roden on the subject continue to inspire.

4 garlic cloves, chopped
2 tablespoons olive oil
1 lb. (500 g) peeled, diced pumpkin or other orange winter
    squash
1½ teaspoons cumin seeds
4 oz. (125 g) raw chard (silver beet) or spinach, cut into
    thin ribbons
1½ quarts (2½ imp. pints, 1.5 litres) vegetable stock
    (see pp. 37–8)
½ cup (4 fl. oz., 125 ml) sour cream
1 teaspoon curry powder

Lightly sauté the garlic in the olive oil, then add the pumpkin or squash, and cumin seeds. Cook over a medium heat until the pumpkin or squash begins to cook through and the cumin seeds are releasing their fragrance.

Add the chard or spinach, and stock, then continue cooking for about 15 minutes, or until the vegetables are tender.

Purée the vegetables with enough of the stock to make a smooth purée in a blender or food processor, then add the sour cream and mix well.

Return the purée to the stock, stir well, and heat through. Serve immediately, each bowlful sprinkled with a little of the curry powder.

ALAN'S CALIFORNIAN CARROT PUREE WITH MEDITERRANEAN FLAVORS
Serves 4

While this carrot soup is flamboyantly flavored with the fragrant ingredients of the Mediterranean, it is not traditional — rather, it is from my own Californian kitchen, and the favorite food of my fiancé, Alan.

Full of red and green sweet peppers (capsicums), tomatoes, and garlic, this lively and robust bowlful is served topped with a shredding of raw carrots, a spoonful of sour cream or Greek yogurt, and a sprinkling of fresh herbs. The smooth, rich purée is enhanced by the freshness and textural contrast of the toppings. It makes a delicious beginning to a festive meal or, in larger portions and accompanied by a salad and crusty bread, a lovely supper.

1 medium or 2 small onion(s), coarsely chopped
3 garlic cloves, chopped
½ medium green sweet pepper (capsicum), diced
½ medium red sweet pepper (capsicum), diced
1 teaspoon fresh or ½ teaspoon dried thyme
2 tablespoons butter
3 medium carrots, thinly sliced
1 medium baking potato, peeled and diced
2 cups (16 fl. oz., 500 ml) vegetable broth (see pp. 37–8)
4 oz. (125 g) chopped fresh or canned tomatoes with juice
1 cup (8 fl. oz., 250 ml) milk
salt and freshly ground black pepper, to taste
fresh or dried thyme, to taste

GARNISH
2 tablespoons chopped fresh parsley
1 medium carrot, grated
3 tablespoons sour cream or Greek yogurt

Sauté the onion, garlic, green and red sweet peppers, and thyme in the butter until they are limp and fragrant (3–5 minutes). Add the carrot and potato, and continue cooking for a few minutes longer.

Stir in the broth and tomato, bring to the boil, then reduce the heat and simmer, covered, until the vegetables are tender (about 20 minutes).

Purée the mixture until it is smooth in a blender or food processor. Add the milk, season with salt and pepper, and more thyme, if necessary, then heat until the bisque is very hot, but not boiling.

Garnish with a sprinkling of parsley, a pinch of grated carrot and a spoonful of sour cream or Greek yogurt. Serve immediately.

FRESH TOMATO BISQUE WITH EXUBERANT FRESH HERBS

Serves 4–6

Thick with puréed tomato and fragrant with garlic, this zesty soup is accented with a flurry of fresh herbs. I make this each year as soon as both ripe, sweet tomatoes and fresh herbs are in the market. While it is best this way, I have prepared this soup using a mixture of half canned tomatoes, half listless winter ones, and raided my windowsill herb garden for the herbs and the soup was still wonderful.

Serve accompanied by a wholegrain seeded bread — perhaps one that is crunchy with millet, poppy seeds, and cornmeal — and a salad of sliced avocados, roasted red sweet peppers (capsicums), and pimento-stuffed green olives dressed with wholegrain mustard vinaigrette.

1 medium to large or 2 small onion(s), coarsely chopped
3–4 garlic cloves, coarsely chopped
3 tablespoons butter
2¼ lbs. (1.125 kg) ripe tomatoes, coarsely chopped (skin if desired)
4 cups (1¾ imp. pints, 1 litre) vegetable broth (see pp. 37–8)
1¾ cups (14 fl. oz., 435 ml) milk

salt and freshly ground black pepper, to taste
2 tablespoons chopped fresh herbs (marjoram, thyme, oregano, etc.)
2 tablespoons chopped fresh parsley and/or fresh sweet basil

GARNISH
½ cup (4 fl. oz., 125 ml) sour cream or Greek yogurt

Sauté the onion and garlic lightly in the butter until they are golden brown, then add the tomatoes and continue to cook the mixture for a few minutes longer until the tomatoes start to become cooked and slightly saucy. Stir in the broth and simmer, uncovered, for 20–30 minutes.

Purée in a blender or food processor, then pass the mixture through a sieve to remove any stringy bits of tomato skin if desired. Return the mixture to the pan and add the milk, salt and pepper, half the herbs, and half the parsley and/or basil. Heat the bisque through, but do not let it boil.

Serve the bisque in individual bowls, each portion garnished with a spoonful of the sour cream or Greek yogurt, and a sprinkling of the remaining herbs and parsley and/or basil.

BELOW: *Fresh Tomato Bisque with Exuberant Fresh Herbs*

SPINACH BISQUE
Serves 4

This soup is very green and tastes of the essence of spinach. Serve as a first course, followed by a platter of pasta, a bowl of fresh lettuces and herbs, crusty bread, a chunk of ripe cheese, and then sweet, fresh pears to end the meal.

1 lb. (500 g) fresh or frozen spinach leaves, well washed
  and cleaned, or defrosted and squeezed dry
1–2 garlic cloves, chopped
2 tablespoons unsalted butter, plus a little extra for
  garnishing
2 tablespoons all-purpose (plain) flour
2½–3¾ cups (1–1½ imp. pints, 625–935 ml) vegetable
  broth (see pp. 37–8)
1 cup (8 fl. oz., 250 ml) milk
3 scallions (spring onions), thinly sliced
salt and freshly ground black pepper, to taste

Cook the spinach in a small amount of water until it is just tender. Remove it from the cooking liquid and put into a bowl on one side to cool. Reserve the cooking liquid for the soup.

When the spinach has cooled, squeeze it well, reserving the juices as well. Coarsely chop or cut up the squeeze-dried spinach and set aside.

Heat the garlic in the butter and, when the butter melts, sprinkle in the flour and cook them together until the garlic has softened a little and the flour is lightly golden brown. Off the heat, stir in a little bit of the broth to make a paste, then gradually add more broth and stir it in well until you have added all the broth and have a smooth bisque.

Cook the bisque over a medium heat until it has thickened slightly, then add the spinach and the reserved juices, and heat through.

Purée the mixture (if using a blender, do this in small batches so that the hot soup doesn't come sputtering out of the top of the machine).

Return the purée to the pan, add the milk and scallions, and heat together. Season with salt and pepper, and serve immediately, each portion topped with a nugget of the butter to melt in.

COLD SOUP

See also 'Grilled foods' (p. 80) for a wonderful chilled, puréed gazpacho of grilled vegetables.

ICED CUCUMBER YOGURT SOUP WITH GINGER
Serves 4

The day had been blazingly hot, just as an August day should be, and I thought a cooling, light soup would be the perfect summer supper. While the soup was chilling, however, and I was assembling the rest of the meal, the foghorns began their mournful wail and soft billows of white fog came creeping in. Suddenly a chilled soup seemed out of place and I yearned for a hearty potage instead! The soup was lovely, though. A light and refreshing start to the meal. Enjoy as a first course to a hearty, spicy main dish: couscous, pasta, or rice with savory vegetables.

1 medium cucumber, diced
2 garlic cloves, finely chopped
2 cups (16 fl. oz., 500 ml) plain yogurt
2⅔ cups (21 fl. oz., 655 ml) vegetable broth, at room
  temperature (see pp. 37–8)
salt and cayenne or freshly ground black pepper, to taste
⅛–¼ teaspoon ground ginger

Whirl the cucumber and garlic in a blender or food processor, adding enough yogurt to facilitate the puréeing. When the texture is smoothish, add the remaining yogurt and broth, and whirl until smooth.

Season with salt and cayenne or black pepper, and chill for at least 2 hours.

Serve each portion sprinkled with a small amount of the ground ginger.

Pastas & Grains

Pasta, this most ancient of foods that was known not that long ago in most homes as either spaghetti or macaroni, has now become a mainstay of Californian cuisine. The variety available is nearly endless, with the myriad of Italian dried pastas; wholefood pastas prepared from corn, buckwheat, whole-wheat (wholemeal) flour, rye, and so on; Eastern pastas from rice, yam, translucent mung bean flour and others; plus the wide array of fresh pastas, prepared not only with doughs such as red chili, cèpe (porcini mushroom), fresh herb, spinach, and saffron, but also with a wide variety of savory fillings. Artichokes, eggplants (aubergines), sweet peppers (capsicums), mild green chili peppers, pesto, spinach and ricotta, cèpes, potatoes, pumpkin, turnips, leeks, asparagus, even beets (beetroot) are among the vegetables puréed and stuffed into fresh pasta skins, or tossed with tender pasta ribbons. Cheeses such as mozzarella, feta, goat or ewe cheese, and ricotta — on their own or mixed with garlic, herbs, olives, and other seasonings — make for delicious and distinctively Californian pastas.

Grains are prepared with enthusiasm and strong spicing in California. A wider variety of grains are eaten in this state than in the rest of the USA. They are not usually blanketed in butter or cosseted in cream, as they traditionally may be in the rest of the country. Risotti and pilafs may be chockful of vegetables and herbs, based on a wide variety of rices and grains, polenta may be topped with spicy olive oil, and couscous may be rich with European or Mexican flavors as often as North African.

OPPOSITE: *Spaghetti with Asparagus and Mint (top), Whole-Wheat Spaghetti with Goat Cheese, Tomatoes, and Two Kinds of Olives (center left), and Angel Hair Pasta with Tomatoes, Field Mushrooms, and Roasted Garlic (bottom right)*

WHOLE-WHEAT SPAGHETTI WITH GOAT CHEESE, TOMATOES, AND TWO KINDS OF OLIVES

Serves 4

Nutty-tasting with a delightfully supple character, whole-wheat (wholemeal) pasta lends itself to robust seasoning. This dish is a perfect example, filled with gypsy-like colors and lusty flavors, and typical of Californian enthusiasm.

If serving as a main course, you might begin the meal with a sprightly, but not too spicy, soup such as Spinach Bisque (see p. 49) or perhaps an appetizer of Mexican-spiced Pepita Spread Served with Spinach and Crusty Bread (see p. 25).

1 lb. (500 g) whole-wheat (wholemeal) spaghetti (preferably Italian)
15 oil-cured black olives, pitted and halved
15 green Mediterranean-type olives, pitted and halved
3 garlic cloves, chopped
6–8 ripe tomatoes, deseeded and diced (skin if desired)
3 tablespoons extra virgin olive oil
3–4 oz. (90–125 g) creamy, tangy fresh goat cheese, crumbled
generous handful of fresh basil leaves, torn or coarsely cut or spoonful of good-quality pesto
freshly ground black pepper, to taste

Boil the spaghetti in salted, boiling water until *al dente*, then drain.

Meanwhile, combine the black and green olives, garlic, tomatoes, and olive oil.

Toss the hot, drained pasta with the olive, garlic, tomato, and oil mixture, then add the goat cheese, basil, and black pepper. Serve immediately.

ANGEL HAIR PASTA WITH TOMATOES, FIELD MUSHROOMS, AND ROASTED GARLIC

Serves 4

California, as noted earlier, is garlic-mad. We eat it in everything except desserts, and even then such restaurants as Berkeley's Chez Panisse have been known to dish up such goodies as garlic sherbet and garlic and wine-poached figs at their annual Bastille Day garlic bash!

When garlic is roasted in whole, unpeeled cloves, it becomes sweet and tender, like fragrant light butter, ready to spread on bread or simply squeezed into the mouth. The tender purée can also be squeezed out of its cloves and used as the base for creamy sauces or soups. Adding whole nuggets of these tender garlic cloves to a pasta dish is typical of California's peculiar passion for the herb.

While the recipe is at its sophisticated best with a variety of exotic mushrooms, it is also perfectly delicious with ordinary, everyday supermarket ones.

4 whole heads of garlic
1/3 cup (3 fl. oz., 90 ml) extra virgin olive oil
4 oz. (125 g) fresh mushrooms (shiitake, chanterelle, oyster, a combination of these or others), thinly sliced
6–8 ripe tomatoes, peeled, deseeded, and diced
2–3 tablespoons tomato purée (passata)
12 oz. (375 g) dried angel hair pasta (cappelli d'angelo) or cappellini or vermicelli nests

GARNISH
salt and freshly ground black pepper, to taste
1 tablespoon fresh thyme or oregano, chopped
Parmesan cheese, freshly grated, to taste

Preheat the oven to 350°F (180°C).

Cut off just enough of the tops of the heads of the garlic to expose the cloves inside. Rub them all over with some of the olive oil, then place them cut side down in a shallow baking pan. Roast for 35–45 minutes or until the buds have softened, turning them occasionally if they begin to brown.

Remove the garlic from the oven and leave until the heads are cool enough to handle.

When cool, hold the uncut end and, with your fingers, squeeze out the soft flesh. Set it aside.

Heat 2 tablespoons of the olive oil in a skillet or frying pan, and lightly sauté the mushrooms until they have lightly browned in spots, but are still firm. Remove them from the pan and reserve. Add the tomatoes to the pan and lightly sauté them in the remaining olive oil, then pour in the purée and cook for several minutes over a high heat, stirring, until it reduces a little to a thickened sauce-like consistency. Set aside.

Cook the pasta in a large pot of boiling, salted water for just 3–4 minutes (it cooks very quickly), then drain.

Meanwhile, add the reserved mushrooms and roasted garlic to the tomatoes, and heat until piping hot. Add the hot, drained pasta and toss them together.

Serve immediately, sprinkled with salt and pepper, the thyme or oregano and the Parmesan cheese.

CAPPELLINI WITH RAINBOW TOMATOES VINAIGRETTE

Serves 4

Ripe, sweet tomatoes, glistening with olive oil and a dash of tangy balsamic vinegar, make a refreshing salady sauce for the delicate *cappellini*. If yellow, orange, green, and red tomatoes are available, choose as wide a variety of shades as you can. They give a depth and richness to what is a simple dish. If you find multicolored tomatoes are unavailable, choose Roma or plum tomatoes instead. Unlike most tomato-sauced pasta dishes, this one needs to be made with sweet, ripe, flavorful, in-season tomatoes.

Enjoy this as a first course, followed by Leah's Stirred Zucchini Frittata (see p. 116), that tender scramble of grated zucchini (courgettes) bound together with eggs and cheese. For dessert? A refreshingly fruity sorbet, such as kiwi fruit (p. 164), or a mixture of sorbet and vanilla ice cream.

12 oz. (375 g) cappellini or *angel hair pasta* (cappelli d'angelo) or *vermicelli nests*
5 garlic cloves, finely chopped
½ cup (4 fl. oz., 125 ml) extra virgin olive oil
salt and freshly ground black pepper, to taste
dash of sugar, if needed
15–18 ripe tomatoes (preferably assorted colors and shapes)
1 tablespoon balsamic vinegar
1 tablespoon or so fresh herbs (thyme, marjoram, oregano, basil, etc.)

Boil the pasta in plenty of salted water until just tender (about 3 minutes), then drain.

Toss the hot, drained pasta with 3 of the garlic cloves and the olive oil. Season with salt and pepper. Set aside and leave to cool to room temperature.

Meanwhile, cut the tomatoes into quarters and mix them with the remaining garlic, the balsamic vinegar, and some salt and pepper (plus a dash of sugar if the tomatoes are sharp). Leave to marinate for at least 15 minutes. (If you prepare this dish in advance, the tomatoes may be marinated for up to 2 days.)

Serve the cooled garlic and olive oil-dressed pasta topped with the marinated tomatoes, and sprinkle the herbs over the top.

BELOW: Cappellini *with Rainbow Tomatoes Vinaigrette*

FARFALLE WITH MUSHROOMS, PEAS, AND GOAT OR EWE CHEESE

Serves 4

Not that long ago in California, goat cheese would have elicited a wary expression of trepidation from the prospective diner, but now it produces a smile of eager anticipation and culinary pride.

Goat cheese has become nearly synonymous with Californian cuisine. This is due in large part to Sonoma County's Laura Chenel, whose passion for goats led her to found a thriving business, California Chèvre, which produces cheeses to rival many of those made in France. Ewe cheese is similarly delicious though less well known. Petaluma's Bell Weather Farms produce marvelous sheep cheese in a variety of French/Mediterranean styles.

The fresh, slightly tangy nature of these cheeses combines brilliantly with much of the food upon which Californians dote. Its creamy freshness is delicious with almost any other ingredient on offer in the market — pungent black olives, tart green ones, strips of roasted sweet peppers (capsicums), ratatouille-type vegetable mixtures, fennel-seasoned tomato sauce, fresh herbs, garlic, green or string beans, flakes of hot dried red chili pepper, strips of roasted and peeled, marinated green chili pepper, and others. These robust combinations can go anywhere: on a pizza, in a sandwich, on top of a salad or saucing a plate of pasta.

The Mediterranean flavors of olive oil, garlic, herbs, and so on marry so compatibly with chèvre. So, too, the more assertive Middle-Eastern flavors that have added their savor to our cuisine. Mexican food as well, with its chilies, spices, and hearty bean, corn and vegetable dishes, is delicious with goat cheese. Indeed, the lightness of the cheese is similar to many of the cheeses available 'south of the border' and, further, the faint fragrant goat scent gives these robust dishes a certain finesse they would otherwise lack.

Goat cheese makes the most wonderful sauce for pasta, melted tenderly into the hot, chewy strands. In the following dish, tender *farfalle* is combined with the goat cheese, along with the spring-like freshness of peas and mushrooms. Cèpes (*porcini* mushrooms) add a particular piquancy and amplify the forest flavor of the fresh mushrooms, but if they are unavailable or prohibitively expensive, simply omit them as the dish will still be delicious.

1–2 oz. (30–60 g) cèpes (porcini) or *other flavored dried mushrooms*
½ cup (4 fl. oz., 125 ml) hot (not boiling) water
4 oz. (125 g) fresh mushrooms, diced or coarsely chopped
2 tablespoons butter
2 garlic cloves, chopped
12 oz. (375 g) farfalle (butterfly pasta) or penne (pasta quills)
4 oz. (125 g) fresh or frozen green peas
2 tablespoons olive oil
4 oz. (125 g) soft, fresh goat or ewe cheese (preferably with chives, herbs, or garlic), broken into bite-sized pieces
freshly ground black pepper, to taste

Put the cèpes or dried mushrooms in a bowl and pour the hot water over them. Cover and leave for 15 minutes or until the mushrooms have rehydrated and have cooled enough to handle.

Remove the mushrooms from the water, reserving the liquid (you will need to strain it) for another use. Squeeze the mushrooms dry, reserving this liquid for later in the recipe. Put the mushrooms in a bowl of cool water, swish them around to rid them of any sand, then squeeze them dry again, discarding this water.

Coarsely chop the mushrooms and set aside.

Sauté the fresh mushrooms quickly in the butter over a high heat. When they have softened and parts have lightly browned, add the garlic and rehydrated mushrooms. Cook for a moment or two, then remove the pan from the heat.

Cook the pasta in boiling, salted water until it is almost *al dente*, then add the peas (if the peas are fresh, young, and tender, add them about 3 minutes before the pasta is ready; if frozen, add them just in time to heat through with the pasta).

When the pasta is *al dente* and the peas are cooked or heated through, drain and toss with the mushrooms, olive oil, and goat or ewe cheese. Serve immediately, offering black pepper to those who like it.

OPPOSITE: Farfalle *with Mushrooms, Peas, and Goat or Ewe Cheese*

WINE COUNTRY PASTA WITH FLAME-GRILLED VEGETABLES AND SUN-DRIED TOMATOES

Serves 4

Flame-grilled vegetables tossed with *al dente spaghettini* make up what is an almost essential Californian pasta dish: full of strong, robust flavor, but light. It is an excellent day-after-a-barbecue dish; simply grill extra vegetables on the day and save them for this dish.

½ x recipe Grilled Old and New World Vegetables (see p. 78), including the juices accumulated during grilling
12 oz. (375 g) spaghettini *or other thin pasta (such as* cappellini)
4 garlic cloves, chopped
2–3 tablespoons extra virgin olive oil
1–2 tablespoons tomato purée (passata)

10–15 sun-dried tomatoes, cut into julienne
dash of balsamic vinegar
salt and freshly ground black pepper, to taste

GARNISH
handful of fresh basil or other fresh herb, coarsely chopped or torn

Cut the grilled vegetables into julienne and set to one side.

Cook the *spaghettini* or other pasta in boiling, salted water until *al dente*, then drain.

Toss the hot pasta with the garlic, olive oil, tomato purée, sun-dried tomatoes, balsamic vinegar, salt and pepper, and the reserved vegetables. Serve immediately, sprinkled with the fresh herbs.

Variation
Simply serve the above tossed with 10 or so oil-cured black olives that have been pitted and halved.

Roast Garlic and Cumin-Dusted Eggplant with Spaghettini and Lemon

Serves 4

Roasted garlic, cumin-dusted eggplant (aubergine) and sharp, sour lemon make a pasta dish refreshingly removed from the traditional spaghetti with tomato sauce. The Middle-Eastern flavors put together with Californian irreverence make this dish delicious for a picnic supper or summer lunch, along with a selection of *meze*-type vegetables or appetizer dishes, such as Mexican-spiced Pepita Spread Served with Spinach and Crusty Bread (see p. 25), sliced tomatoes topped with herbs, olives awash in a garlicky Cumin and Citrus Vinaigrette (see p. 139), or cucumbers topped with mint, lightly marinated onion, and crumbled feta.

3 heads of garlic, broken into cloves and unpeeled

3–4 tablespoons extra virgin olive oil

salt, to taste

1 small to medium eggplant (aubergine), thinly sliced lengthwise

1–2 teaspoons ground cumin, or as needed

1 lb. (500 g) thin spaghettini or vermicelli

salt and cayenne pepper, to taste

2 garlic cloves, peeled and chopped

juice of ½ lemon

GARNISH
2 teaspoons chopped fresh coriander or parsley

Place the whole unpeeled garlic cloves in a single layer in a baking pan. Sprinkle 2 tablespoons of the olive oil and salt to taste over them. Roast in a 350°F (180°C) oven for 40 minutes, or until the cloves are tender (for a more roasted flavor, roast at 400°–425°F (200°–220°C) for the last 10–15 minutes of the baking time). Remove from the oven and, when cool enough to handle, remove the cloves from their skins, tossing the cooked garlic flesh with the oil they have cooked in, if any remains. Brush the eggplant slices with a little of the olive oil and sprinkle each with a little of the cumin. Grill until browned in spots and tender, then remove from the heat and cut into matchsticks. Set aside.

Cook the pasta in boiling, salted water until it is just tender (about 3–4 minutes). Drain and toss with the chopped raw garlic, remaining olive oil and cumin, roasted garlic, and eggplant. Season with salt and cayenne pepper, lemon juice, and extra olive oil and cumin if needed. Serve at room temperature, garnished with the coriander or parsley.

OPPOSITE: *Wine Country Pasta with Flame-grilled Vegetables and Sun-dried Tomatoes (top left) and Pasta Solatia with Garlicky Green Beans, Tomatoes, and Olives (bottom right)*

BELOW: *Roast Garlic and Cumin-dusted Eggplant with* Spaghettini *and Lemon*

Pasta Solatia with Garlicky Green Beans, Tomatoes, and Olives

Serves 4

A bright little dish of pasta dressed in a sauce of fresh green or string beans and tomatoes with black olives. It sings of summer flavors and has no need of rich ingredients: it is straightforward and lively.

3 garlic cloves, coarsely chopped
2 tablespoons or so extra virgin olive oil
4 oz. (125 g) green or string beans
10 fresh, ripe tomatoes, deseeded and diced
2 tablespoons tomato paste (purée)
pinch of sugar, if need
salt and freshly ground black pepper, to taste
12 oz. (375 g) pasta (spaghetti, farfalle (butterfly pasta)
   or penne (pasta quills))
5–8 black Mediterranean-type olives, pitted and coarsely
   chopped
handful of coarsely chopped fresh sweet basil

Lightly sauté the garlic in the olive oil, then add the green or string beans and stir through. When well coated with the garlic oil, add the tomatoes and cook over a medium-high heat until the mixture becomes thick and saucy (about 5–8 minutes). Add the tomato paste and taste. Add a pinch of sugar if it tastes too sharp, and salt and pepper.

Cook the pasta in boiling, salted water until *al dente*, then drain.

Toss the hot pasta with the bean and tomato mixture, then sprinkle the olives and basil over the top. Serve at once, hot, or enjoy at room temperature.

Pesto Orzo with Diced Tomatoes, Toasted Pine Nuts, and Feta Cheese

Serves 4

Pesto-sauced *orzo* — that tiny, rice-shaped pasta — makes a delectable salad-like dish served at cool room temperature, splashed with balsamic vinegar.

For more elaborate presentation, hollow out the insides of medium-sized tomatoes, sprinkle the insides with salt and balsamic vinegar, then fill with the pesto-dressed *orzo*. Top with the pine nuts and serve garnished with crumbled feta cheese and sprigs of fresh basil.

Enjoy this as a summer first course, followed by Braised Tofu, Sweetcorn, and Zucchini with Mexican Flavors (see p. 97) or a grilled vegetable dish.

8 oz. (250 g) orzo
3–4 heaped tablespoons pesto, or to taste
6 ripe tomatoes, diced
a few drops of balsamic vinegar
salt, to taste
1 oz. (30 g) pine nuts, lightly toasted in an ungreased pan
4 oz. (125 g) feta cheese (preferably Greek sheep's milk),
   diced

Garnish
sprigs of fresh basil

Cook the *orzo* in boiling, salted water until it is *al dente*, then drain and leave to cool slightly. Toss with the pesto and set to one side.

Toss the tomatoes with the balsamic vinegar and salt.

Arrange the pasta on four serving plates next to a portion of the tomatoes. Sprinkle the pine nuts over the pasta, and then sprinkle the whole dish with the feta cheese. Serve garnished with the basil sprigs.

OPPOSITE: *Pesto Orzo with Diced Tomatoes, Toasted Pine Nuts, and Feta Cheese*

CHINESE SPICY NOODLE BOWL
Serves 4

This noodle dish is typical of the Californian penchant for Eastern pasta. Though it was inspired originally by several classic dishes from China and Vietnam, the way the two cuisines are put together is purely Californian. Serve as a first course, buffet dish, or midnight feast. It may be eaten either hot or cold, with hot sauce and cold condiments. Either way, it is a delight of textural as well as flavor contrasts.

As regards the inclusion of tomato ketchup, a word to those who consider it inauthentic and may be tempted to leave it out. The word itself is of Malaysian origin and its sweet, unsubtle flavor, which may be unwelcome in most dishes, plays a supporting role to the equally unsubtle hoisin sauce.

12 oz. (375 g) *Chinese-style egg noodles or fettucine-style noodles*
soy sauce and sesame oil, sufficient to toss the cooked noodles in
3 garlic cloves, chopped
1 tablespoon vegetable oil
10 oz. (310 g) tofu, frozen, thawed, squeezed dry, and crumbled or rehydrated soy mince or textured vegetable protein (TVP), rehydrated and drained
1 cup (8 fl. oz., 250 ml) hoisin sauce
½ cup (4 fl. oz., 125 ml) vegetable stock (see pp. 37–8)
pinch of Chinese five-spice powder
3 tablespoons tomato ketchup
2 tablespoons sugar or honey
1 tablespoon vinegar, or to taste
handful of cooked fresh or thawed frozen green peas
5–6 oz. (155–185 g) roasted peanuts, coarsely chopped
soy sauce, to taste
sesame oil, to taste
1 carrot, coarsely grated
½ cucumber, cut into julienne
handful of mung bean sprouts
fresh coriander leaves
3 scallions (spring onions), thinly sliced
several leaves of lettuce, thinly sliced or shredded

Boil the noodles in water until they are just tender, then rinse them in cool water and drain. Dress with several spoonfuls each of soy sauce and sesame oil, then put to one side.

Sauté the garlic briefly in the vegetable oil, then add the tofu or soy mince. Remove from the pan to a warm plate, and heat together the hoisin sauce, stock, five-spice powder, tomato ketchup, sugar or honey, and vinegar. Simmer the mixture for 5 minutes, or until it has thickened slightly, then return the sautéed garlic and tofu or soy mince mixture to the pan together with the peas and peanuts. Season with soy sauce and sesame oil.

Serve the noodles in Oriental bowls, topping them with a portion of the sauce and a sprinkling of the carrot, cucumber, bean sprouts, coriander, scallions, and lettuce.

SPAGHETTI WITH ASPARAGUS AND MINT
Serves 6

The sharp tang of late winter is deliciously bright combined with the first asparagus of spring, a glistening of olive oil, fresh mint, and parsley. Parmesan adds a salty accent. For a Greek touch, add a handful of coarsely chopped olives and use crumbled feta in place of the Parmesan.

1 lb. (500 g) spaghetti
1 lb. (500 g) fresh asparagus, trimmed and cut into 2-in. (5-cm) lengths
½ cup (4 fl. oz., 125 ml) extra virgin olive oil, or as needed
juice of 1 large lemon
4 tablespoons coarsely chopped or thinly sliced fresh mint leaves
3 tablespoons coarsely chopped fresh parsley
2 oz. (60 g) Parmesan cheese, freshly grated, or to taste
freshly ground black pepper, to taste

Bring a large pot of salted water to the boil and cook the spaghetti until it is half done.

To the boiling water and pasta, add the asparagus and continue cooking until the spaghetti is *al dente* and the asparagus is crisp–tender.

Drain them and toss with the olive oil, then add the lemon juice, mint, parsley, and cheese. Season with black pepper and serve immediately.

Variation
LEMON AND HERB PASTA WITH THE FLAVORS OF GREECE: Use 6–7 oz. (185–225 g) crumbled feta or goat cheese in place of the Parmesan, and toss in 10 or so kalamata or oil-cured black olives, pitted and halved, and half a chopped onion.

OPPOSITE: *Chinese Spicy Noodle Bowl*

GOAT CHEESE RAVIOLI IN CREAM
Serves 4

Decadently rich, the tender pasta is stuffed with tangy goat cheese and awash in a sauce of cream and Parmesan cheese. This makes a very special first course (it is too rich, really, to serve as a main course).

Making ravioli and other Italian/European-style pastas using won-ton, egg roll, and other Chinese pastas is a quick trick that works extremely well. The Chinese pastas are not only delicate once cooked, they are very easy to work with. Purchase them from Chinese food stores and use immediately or keep in the freezer for up to 6 months. They are then always at hand to stuff for nearly instant, fresh ravioli.

Serve this dish for a celebratory supper, followed by something simple with strong clear flavors and several lively sauces. For instance, a selection of grilled vegetables with Coriander and Lemon Salsa and Red Chili Aïoli (see pp. 102 and 142).

4 oz. (125 g) fresh goat cheese
½–1 garlic clove, finely chopped
2 tablespoons freshly grated Parmesan cheese
1 small egg, lightly beaten
¼ teaspoon fresh or pinch dried thyme
freshly ground black pepper, to taste
6–10 egg roll wrappers or home-made pasta squares
1 tablespoon unsalted butter, softened
3–4 tablespoons light (single) cream
extra Parmesan cheese, for sprinkling

GARNISH
whole chives (optional)

Break up the goat cheese with a fork and add the garlic, Parmesan cheese, egg, thyme, and black pepper.

Place about 1 tablespoon of the filling in the center of an egg roll wrapper or pasta square. Brush the edges with water and fold it in half on the diagonal, encasing the filling and forming a triangular shape. Seal the edges by pressing them together tightly. Leave stuffed pasta to sit on a floured plate for about 15 minutes (this helps to keep the edges together, but make sure that the plate is well-floured so that the moisture from the filling does not seep out through the delicate pasta and encourage it to tear or fall apart).

Tip the ravioli into plenty of boiling water. They are delicate and have a tendency to stick together, so be gentle with them. Cook over a medium-high heat, in gently boiling water, for only 1–2 minutes until the pasta is tender (home-made pasta squares will take longer than egg roll wrappers).

Drain immediately, taking care not to break the fragile ravioli.

Place several ravioli in each bowl, top with a little of the softened butter, a little cream, a sprinkling of the extra Parmesan cheese, and garnish with several of the whole chives (if using).

TORTELLINI WITH MUSHROOMS, TOMATO, CREAM, AND HERBS
Serves 4 as a main course

Any sort of stuffed pasta is delicious splashed with this tomato-tinted garlic and cream sauce. Filled with cheese, spinach, eggplant (aubergine), asparagus, cèpes (*porcini* mushrooms), sweet pepper (capsicum), artichoke, or whatever you choose, it is wonderful. For parties, I often assemble an assortment of pastas of various fillings and shapes, then serve them with this sauce.

3 garlic cloves, finely chopped
3 tablespoons unsalted butter
3 fresh or canned tomatoes, peeled, deseeded, and diced or chopped
¾ cup (6 fl. oz., 185 ml) light (single) cream
1 tablespoon tomato paste (purée)
½–1 teaspoon chopped fresh rosemary
2–4 oz. (60–125 g) mushrooms, coarsely chopped
1½ lbs. (750 g) stuffed fresh pasta or about 12–16 oz. (375–500 g) dried pasta
3 tablespoons coarsely chopped fresh basil or 2 tablespoons chopped fresh parsley, plus 1–2 teaspoons fresh marjoram, oregano, etc.
Parmesan or other grating cheese, to taste

Heat the garlic in 2 tablespoons of the butter over a medium–high heat, then add the tomatoes and stir until the garlic starts to release its aroma. Pour in the cream, tomato paste, and rosemary, and cook over a medium–high heat until the sauce has thickened a little and is full of flavor (about 5–10 minutes).

Meanwhile, sauté the mushrooms quickly in the remaining butter. When the sauce is ready, add the mushrooms to it and keep the sauce warm while you cook the pasta.

Cook the pasta in boiling, salted water, taking care not to overcook it. Drain and serve with the sauce, sprinkling the herbs and cheese over the top.

OPPOSITE: *Goat Cheese Ravioli in Cream (top) and Tortellini with Mushrooms, Tomato, Cream, and Herbs*

WHOLE-WHEAT PASTA WITH DICED POTATOES, PESTO, AND SUN-DRIED TOMATOES

Serves 4

Whole-wheat (wholemeal) pasta — chewy and tasting nuttily of wheat — takes readily to such sparkling tastes as pesto and sun-dried tomatoes. Adding a diced potato amplifies the earthy quality of the whole-wheat. This is a Californian innovation based on the Genoese tradition of serving *pasta al pesto* combined with potatoes.

3 *waxy potatoes, peeled and diced*
12 oz. (375 g) *whole-wheat (wholemeal) spaghetti*
2 *tablespoons olive oil*
2 *garlic cloves, chopped*

GARNISH

3–4 *tablespoons pesto, either home-made or store-bought*
10–12 *sun-dried tomatoes, or as desired, diced or cut into julienne*

Add the potatoes to a pot of boiling, salted water and cook for about 5 minutes, then add the spaghetti and continue cooking until the potatoes are just tender and the spaghetti is *al dente*. Drain (reserving the liquid for soup or other use).

Toss the pasta and potatoes with the olive oil and garlic, then serve, garnishing each plateful with a spoonful of the pesto and a scattering of the sun-dried tomatoes on top.

Variation
As above, but garnish with a handful of crisp–tender green or string beans as well as the pesto and sun-dried tomatoes.

OPPOSITE: *Oriental Cool Rice Noodles with Hot Chili, Green Onion Oil, Lime, Peanuts, and Cucumber*

BELOW: *Whole-Wheat Pasta with Diced Potatoes, Pesto, and Sun-dried Tomatoes*

Oriental Cool Rice Noodles with Hot Chili, Green Onion Oil, Lime, Peanuts, and Cucumber

Serves 4

Eastern flavors and ingredients have enhanced our entire coastal cuisine and nowhere is this effect more pronounced than in our pasta dishes. Here, green onion oil, a Vietnamese condiment, is used to season the stock-cooked pasta (a technique I first discovered in Venice), and the whole thing is garnished with a Thai flair — mint, peanuts, cucumbers, chili — a truly cross-cultural meal that is distinctively Californian.

Cooking the pasta in broth means that the brothy flavor permeates the pasta, adding extra flavor to this simply dressed dish. Be sure to reserve the cooking liquid rather than throw it away as it is wonderful for soups and other recipes.

> 12 oz. (375 g) wide rice noodles (also called vermicelli and usually Vietnamese)
> 4½ cups (1¾ imp. pints, 1 litre) broth of your choice, heated (see pp. 37–8)
> 4–6 scallions (spring onions), thinly sliced
> 3 tablespoons mild-flavored vegetable oil
> green onion oil, to taste
> 1–3 fresh green chili peppers, deseeded and thinly sliced
> 1 oz. (30 g) fresh mint leaves, torn or coarsely chopped
> ¼–½ cucumber, chopped or finely diced
> 1 oz. (30 g) roasted peanuts, coarsely chopped

Garnish
> 1 lime, cut into wedges

Cook the rice noodles in the broth once it is boiling, for half the required cooking time for the noodles. Let the noodles cool in the broth, testing them periodically to make sure that they do not overcook (if they do, drain immediately, reserving the cooking broth for another use).

Meanwhile, gently heat the scallions in the vegetable oil until tiny bubbles appear around the edge of the pan. Remove from the heat immediately and leave to cool.

Serve the drained noodles in Oriental bowls, each portion dressed with a teaspoon or so of the green onion oil, a scattering of the chili peppers, mint leaves, cucumber, and peanuts. Garnish each portion with a wedge of lime.

RICE

Drive along the raised freeways in the Great Central Valley at certain times of the year and it appears as if you are driving through the sea — all around the freeway is water, an endless expanse of water. It is not the sea, however, but the paddies being flooded to grow rice, which, since 1910, has been California's most important grain crop.

An interesting thing to note is that rice was originally grown as a crop to export, primarily to the Far East. In recent years, however, due to both gourmet trends and the increase in health-consciousness, interest in grains has increased enormously, giving rise to a thriving industry of specialty rices. In addition to the basic short-grain, long-grain and brown wholegrain rices, there are black, glutinous rices; Californian versions of both basmati and arborio rice, in both white and brown; *wehani*, a red, wholegrain rice; a rice with a slight pecan nut flavor — in fact, a nearly endless variety of them. This is true of rice products, too; there are crunchy puffed rice cakes, soft shimmery rice noodles, crispy rice breakfast cereals and rice bran syrup (said to have more cholesterol-inhibiting factors than oat bran), among others. The Central Valley is also home to the pricey, nutty grains called wild rice, which is, in fact, technically the seeds of an aquatic grass rather than a true rice. Wild rice is usually combined with other, blander and less expensive rice and an assortment of more exotic rice. Look for them in wholefood stores and supermarkets. Their robust flavor is particularly good with earthy accompaniments, such as sautéed mushrooms with sour cream, vinaigrette-dressed field salads, and grilled pumpkin slices spread with Red Chili Butter (see p. 145).

Rice dishes, though not eaten as frequently as pasta, are favored throughout the Golden State. You will find rice dishes for nearly all courses — piquant salads, savory soups, hearty stir-fries, stuffings for fresh, leafy vegetables, or simple accompaniments for saucy braises. Subtle pilafs can be made with brown rice, flavored with herbs or served with simple, savory salsa-like relishes. The Italian risotto is very popular. The potful of slowly cooked rice makes a perfect base for vegetarian dishes and gives itself readily and eagerly to the pan-cultural flavors that are the hallmark of Californian cuisine — Eastern ginger root, Hispanic chilies, fresh coriander, all are equally at home in a comforting risotto as they are in their more usual rice dishes.

Brown Rice Pilaf from Another Lifetime
Serves 4

This lovely pilaf entered my kitchen so long ago it seems like another lifetime, hence the name. It began with a recipe from Fresno for an Armenian pilaf, and over the years it has just evolved each time I have cooked it. Crunchy nuts, sautéed onions, sweet raisins, broken strands of browned vermicelli, and the fragrance of cinnamon all add distinctive savor to the nutty-tasting wholegrain rice.

This pilaf is good as a side dish, alongside eggplant (aubergine) or as a main course, surrounded by slices of grilled or pan-browned eggplant, Cumin-Roast Potatoes with Coriander and Lemon Salsa (see p. 102), tomato-sauced chickpeas (garbanzos), paprika- and thyme-seasoned sautéed pumpkin, and other such dishes. It is particularly good with yogurt and a hot sauce, each mouthful of rice mixture dabbed with a bit of the cooling yogurt and a tiny jolt of the hot stuff. A fresh platter of lettuces and herbs makes a perfect counterpoint. Rich rice, cooling, soft yogurt, a jazzy note of heat and the crispness of tartly-dressed greens — perfection.

⅓ cup (2 oz., 60 g) almonds, whole, shelled, and
   with skins
3 tablespoons butter or vegetable spread or oil
1 oz. (30 g) broken vermicelli or spaghetti
1½ cups (8 oz., 250 g) uncooked long-grain brown rice
⅓–½ cup (2–3 oz., 60–90 g) raisins or golden raisins
   (sultanas)
2 cups (16 fl. oz., 500 ml) vegetable stock (see pp. 37–8)
   or salted water
2 medium to large onions, thinly sliced
2 garlic cloves, chopped
¼–½ teaspoon ground cinnamon

ACCOMPANIMENTS
plain yogurt
hot sauce, either home-made salsa or hot store-bought one

Sauté the almonds in a teaspoon or two of the butter or spread or oil, until they have lightly browned, then put to one side.

Sauté the vermicelli or spaghetti in a teaspoon or two of the butter or spread or oil, until the pasta has browned slightly, then put to one side.

In 1 tablespoon of the butter or spread or oil, lightly sauté the rice until the grains are golden brown, then add the raisins or sultanas, stock or salted water, and the reserved pasta. Cover, bring to the boil, then reduce the heat and simmer over a low heat until the rice is *al dente* (about 30–40 minutes).

Meanwhile, sauté the onions and garlic in the remaining butter or spread or oil, until they are very limp and lightly browned in places. Season with the cinnamon, then fork this mixture into the pilaf with the reserved almonds. Serve accompanied by spoonfuls of yogurt and hot sauce at the edge of the plate.

Tarragon and Tomato Brown Rice Pilaf with Zucchini
Serves 4

Nutty brown rice is sautéed first in the savory flavors of olive oil and garlic, then combined with chunks of zesty zucchini (courgettes) and the piquant surprise of tarragon and tomatoes.

This makes a zesty, yet comforting main course, served on the same plate with a green salad dressed with a mustardy vinaigrette to which a splash of red wine has been added. Begin the meal with a starter portion of Smoked Tofu and Sun-dried Tomatoes in Olive Oil (see p. 17). For dessert, try lightly sweetened blackberries folded into rich Greek yogurt or soft frozen yogurt.

2 tablespoons olive oil
3–5 scallions (spring onions), thinly sliced
3 garlic cloves, chopped
1½ cups (8 oz., 50 g) long-grain brown rice
2 zucchini (courgettes), cut into large dice or small chunks
12 oz. (375 g) fresh or canned tomatoes, diced
1½ cups (12 fl. oz., 375 ml) vegetable stock, or as
   needed (see pp. 37–8)
1 teaspoon chopped fresh tarragon, or to taste
salt and freshly ground black pepper, to taste

In the olive oil, lightly sauté the scallions, half the garlic, and the rice until all are lightly golden brown. Add the zucchini and continue to sauté for a moment.

Add half the tomatoes, the stock, and the tarragon. Bring to the boil, cover, and reduce the heat. Cook the pilaf over a medium to low heat for 30 minutes, or until the rice is almost tender, then add the remaining garlic and tomatoes. Season with salt and pepper, and add more stock if needed. Simmer the pilaf for another 10–15 minutes or until the rice is *al dente.*

Serve as desired.

CUMIN-SCENTED MILLET AND CHEESE PILAF

Serves 4

This dish is Swiss-inspired, a delicious relic of the European pre-industrial age when wheat bread was not available to the average person, but other whole and unground grains were. Millet was one of them. It is a delicious grain and has relatively recently been rediscovered and embraced by contemporary Californian cooks. The thing to remember, however, is that millet seeds need not be toasted, otherwise they tend to be a bit gummy and lose their delightful crunch and round shape.

Millet is good in breads, muffins, Mexican dishes, soups, and in the following pilaf. Adding a jolt of cumin seeds is my own addition. The warm, dusky sauciness lifts this otherwise heavy dish. This is perfect winter food, to be eaten in a rustic bowl, perhaps next to a warming fire with the cat snoozing on your lap. Accompany the pilaf with a salad of slightly bitter greens such as *frisée* (curly endive).

1 medium onion, coarsely chopped
2 tablespoons unsalted butter or vegetable oil
4 oz. (125 g) millet
2 teaspoons cumin seeds
3 cups (24 fl. oz., 750 ml) vegetable stock (see pp. 37–8)
4 oz. (125 g) Gruyère-type cheese, coarsely grated
freshly ground black pepper, to taste

Sauté the onion in the butter or oil until it has softened, then add the millet and cumin seeds.

Raise the heat and let the millet and cumin lightly brown, stirring from time to time.

Add the stock, reduce the heat to medium, cover, and cook for 15–20 minutes.

Fork the cheese into the millet, then toss them together well, letting the cheese melt into a delicious, though rather messy, potful. Season with black pepper. Enjoy immediately.

TAMALE POLENTA PIE
Serves 4

Tamale pie originated somewhere in the West — some people say Texas, others California. It comes in a wide variety of guises, but the basic style is a combination of Mexican flavors and polenta or cornmeal. While it may be prepared in pie form, with the polenta or cornmeal formed into a crust, it is more often prepared casserole-style, with all the ingredients baked together. Not only is it easier this way, it actually tastes better.

It is a dish that was once doted on, but is now rather unfashionable, no doubt because any number of errant ingredients began to be added — leftovers of nearly any persuasion, too salty corn chips, canned soups and vegetables, and so on, turning the basic, honest dish into a confusing muddle of flavors.

Real tamale pie, however, is absolutely delicious — streamlined down to its basics of corn and chili in a tomato and polenta or cornmeal porridge-like mixture, blanketed in a rich layer of melting cheese, served with a spoonful of sour cream, a sprinkling of chopped scallions (spring onions), and a scattering of diced black olives. The crisp, pungent onion, rich tangy olives, and cool, creamy sour cream contrast well with the hearty, sizzling hot casserole.

2–3 onions, coarsely chopped
3 garlic cloves, chopped
1 green sweet pepper (capsicum), diced
1–2 fresh green chili peppers, deseeded and chopped, to taste
   but not too spicy
2 tablespoons olive oil
1 teaspoon mild chili powder
1 teaspoon paprika
1/2 teaspoon ground cumin, or to taste
1 lb. (500 g) fresh or frozen sweetcorn
8 oz. (250 g) polenta or cornmeal
2 cups (16 fl. oz., 500 ml) water or vegetable broth
   (see pp. 37–8), plus more if needed
1 1/2 lbs. (750 g) fresh or canned tomatoes, diced,
   with juice
12 oz. (375 g), approximately, sharp cheddar cheese,
   thinly sliced or grated

Preheat the oven to 400°F (200°C).

Lightly sauté the onions, garlic, green sweet pepper, and chili in the olive oil until they have softened.

Sprinkle in the chili powder, paprika, and cumin. Cook for 1–2 minutes, then add the sweetcorn, polenta or cornmeal, water or broth, and tomatoes. Cook, stirring, over a medium heat until the mixture thickens and the polenta or cornmeal is cooked through and no longer grainy (about 30 minutes — the exact time will vary depending upon the polenta or cornmeal you use). Add more water if needed to achieve a porridge-like consistency.

Pour the mixture into a baking dish and top with the cheese. Bake for 15–20 minutes, until the cheese topping has melted and lightly browned. Serve immediately, spooned onto plates in such a way that each serving has some of the crusty bottom and melted cheese topping.

OPPOSITE: *Tamale Polenta Pie*

RISOTTO VERDE WITH BASIL AND GREEN BEANS

Serves 4

Flecked with green and scented with garlic and basil, this risotto has more than a whiff of blue cheese stirred in, as well as the more expected Parmesan.

For part of the liquid, I often use the cooking liquid from spinach — its green hue amplifies the green of the basil and its vegetable flavor enriches the dish. It also appeals to my sense of healthful frugality — nothing is wasted; vitamins are gained.

If you have no fresh basil, just spoon in a generous amount of pesto towards the end of the cooking time.

Any sort of sharp blue cheese is good here, but if you have no blue cheese, crumbled feta, ewe, or goat cheese is nice, too, in a slightly different way.

3 garlic cloves, chopped
1 tablespoon butter
2 cups (12 oz., 375 g) arborio rice
4½ cups (1¾ imp. pints, 1 litre) vegetable broth, hot (see pp. 37–8)
1 cup (8 fl. oz., 250 ml) light (single) cream
4 oz. (125 g) fresh or frozen green or string beans, blanched or thawed and cut into bite-sized pieces
4 oz. (125 g) sharp blue cheese (Roquefort, Gorgonzola, Danablu (Danish blue), etc.)
4–6 tablespoons coarsely grated Parmesan cheese
½ oz. (15 g) fresh basil, coarsely chopped

GARNISH
handful of extra fresh basil, chopped

Heat the garlic in the butter and when it has turned lightly golden and is aromatic, stir in the rice and toss them together over the heat to coat the grains in the golden butter. Continue to stir, adding ½ cup (4 fl. oz., 125 ml) of the broth, stirring until it has been absorbed. Repeat with another ½ cup of the broth, and so on, until all the broth has been absorbed and the rice is nearly tender.

Add the cream and beans, and continue cooking until the rice is *al dente* tender, but no more than that. The cream will bubble and boil up, but that is fine.

When the rice is ready, stir in the blue cheese, Parmesan, and basil. Serve immediately, each portion topped with a sprinkling of the extra basil to garnish.

OPPOSITE: *Risotto Verde with Basil and Green Beans (top right) and Creamy Corn and Tomato Risotto with Fresh Coriander (bottom left)*

CREAMY CORN AND TOMATO RISOTTO WITH FRESH CORIANDER

Serves 4

Kernels of sweetcorn, the tart–savory taste of tomatoes, and the pungent shock of coriander all flavor creamy grains of arborio rice, along with a last-minute splash of cream. I have experimented with embellishing this delectable risotto, including a sprinkling of mild chili powder, a grating of ginger root, and a shake of Parmesan, but it really is best just the way it is with, perhaps, a little finely chopped scallion (spring onion).

1 medium to large or 2 small to medium onion(s), chopped
3 garlic cloves, chopped
1 green sweet pepper (capsicum), diced
½–1 fresh green chili pepper, chopped, or to taste
4 tablespoons olive or vegetable oil
2 cups (12 oz., 375 g) arborio rice
3–4 cups (24–36 fl. oz., 750 ml–1 litre) vegetable stock, heated (see pp. 37–8)
1 lb. (500 g) chopped fresh or canned tomatoes, with juices
1 lb. (500 g) fresh or frozen sweetcorn
3–4 tablespoons coarsely chopped fresh coriander
1–1¼ cups (8–10 fl. oz., 250–310 ml) light (single) cream
salt and freshly ground black pepper, to taste
2 scallions (spring onions), thinly sliced (optional)

Lightly sauté the onions, garlic, sweet pepper, and chili in the oil until they have softened and lightly browned in places. Add the rice and stir as you cook, letting the grains go lightly golden brown in the onion and pepper mixture.

Slowly add the hot stock, beginning with about ½ cup (4 fl. oz., 125 ml), stirring until it has been absorbed, then another ½ cup, and so on, until all the broth has been absorbed, alternating with adding in the tomatoes. When the rice is nearly done, stir in the sweetcorn and coriander, and continue stirring until the rice grains are almost *al dente*.

Add the cream, stirring and cooking until the mixture is a delicious mass of *al dente* rice grains coated in the creamy, savory sauce. Season with salt and pepper, and serve immediately, sprinkled with the scallions (if using).

Variation

SWEETCORN AND ARBORIO RICE HORS D'OEUVRES: I discovered by accident that leftover sweetcorn risotto, left to cool to room temperature and spread onto very crisp water crackers, makes an unexpectedly delicious canapé or appetizer.

Soft Creamy Polenta with Sage and Garlic Oil

Serves 4

Corn, indigenous to the Americas, has long featured in the diets of its people. The Native Americans grew it and ate it in a wide variety of guises, depending upon the region in which they lived. The explorers brought corn home to Europe where it flourished, both as it came or dried as fodder for their animals and ground for their owners, becoming *polenta* in Italy and *mamaliga* in Romania.

It was in this form that it first returned to the USA during the waves of Eastern European and Italian immigration. More recently, polenta has become chic on the West Coast, due in part to a passion for all things Italian, and also because the creamy cornmeal mixture pairs so well with the Mediterranean-inspired cuisine of the coast. This recipe is a simple but rich little polenta. Embellish it if you wish: crumbled Gorgonzola, chopped fresh rosemary, diced lightly stewed ripe fresh or canned tomatoes, or sun-dried tomatoes. Coarsely grated Parmesan cheese always makes a delicious addition.

> 3 tablespoons olive oil
> 1 teaspoon dried or 2 teaspoons fresh sage leaves, coarsely chopped
> 2–3 garlic cloves, chopped
> 4 oz. (125 g) polenta or coarse cornmeal
> 2¼–3¾ cups (18–21 fl. oz., 560–655 ml) water
> ½ cup (4 fl. oz., 125 ml) milk
> salt and freshly ground black pepper, to taste

Prepare the sage and garlic oil first. Gently heat the olive oil in a pan with the sage until it is just hot (tiny bubbles will form around the edge). Do not let the sage brown as it can then develop an unpleasantly strong, bitter flavor. Add the garlic to the oil and let it cook for a few more moments. Remove from the heat.

Pour the sage and garlic oil into a bowl and leave to cool. Do not wash the cooking pan — use it to cook the polenta. First, mix the polenta or cornmeal with ½ cup (4 fl. oz., 125 ml) of the water, and stir to combine well. Leave the mixture for a few minutes to swell, then add half the remaining water and cook over a medium-high heat, stirring until the cornmeal cooks through and is smooth. Add more water as needed until the polenta is smooth, thick, and not grainy.

Stir in the milk and continue to cook for a few minutes (the mixture should be soft and smooth). Leave to sit for several minutes to develop its flavor.

Serve the polenta spooned into bowls, each garnished with a spoonful of the sage and garlic oil, and salt and pepper.

Couscous with Green Beans and Cumin Butter

Serves 4

Couscous, that pasta-like dish of tiny nuggets of semolina dough, is the basis of dishes throughout the Middle East. In Egypt, it is served with milk, sugar, and cinnamon for breakfast or as a comforting snack; in Morocco and Tunisia, it is covered with robust rustic stews and served with a peppery seasoning to enliven it all; in Italy, it is ladled with ginger-scented stews, often based on fish or seafood. Occasionally, couscous is layered into cakes and drenched with sweet syrup to make Middle Eastern sweets. I find that couscous makes a refreshing grain salad when tossed with diced tomatoes, seasoned with grated ginger root, and dressed with olive oil and lemon juice.

Since the late sixties, couscous has been a favorite in California — either as a main course or a side dish.

Here it is cooked with broth and beans, then seasoned with butter and cumin. Serve it alongside a Mediterranean vegetable ragoût or with any curried vegetable mélange.

> 8 oz. (250 g) couscous
> 1 cup (8 fl. oz., 250 ml) hot broth of choice, more if needed (see pp. 37–8)
> 6 oz. (185 g) fresh, young or thawed frozen whole green or string beans, cut into bite-sized lengths
> ½ teaspoon ground cumin
> 2 tablespoons unsalted butter, or to taste
> salt and cayenne pepper, to taste

Pour the couscous into a pan and add the hot broth and beans. Leave the mixture to sit for a minute or two, then bring it to the boil. Simmer for a few minutes until the couscous is tender, then fluff with a fork.

Season with the cumin, butter, salt, and cayenne pepper. Serve immediately.

Variation

In place of the beans, use a generous amount of butter-sautéed mushrooms: choose either shiitake or a selection of exotic fungi.

OPPOSITE: *Couscous with Green Beans and Cumin Butter*

Grilled Foods

*T*he scent of savory foods grilling over an open fire characterizes the cookery of California, and has done since the earliest coastal dwellers, the Native American tribes, lived there.

Californians love the clean, smoky flavors of food from the grill and the fact that such food suits the strong flavors of garlic, chilies, and savory oils that West Coast cuisine is all about, rather than the heavy creams and butter sauces favored in other regions and in traditional Northern European cuisine. Barbecuing is a relaxing way of entertaining, too: informal, friendly, creative, and convivial, fitting the Californian's laid-back lifestyle perfectly. In the land of patios and decks, swimming pools and hot tubs, sliding glass doors opening onto year-round gardens, few homes are without a barbecue or grill — even tiny city-bound flats.

The delicious flavors that open-fire cooking bring to vegetables have become popular elsewhere in recent years — both in chic restaurants and at home. You will find such robust dishes as smoky eggplants (aubergines), sliced grilled garden vegetables, nuggets of sweet and charred corn slathered with chili butter, yams roasted to a caramel sweetness over an open flame, potatoes marinated then grilled to a hearty, herbal intensity, as well as sauces and soups prepared from grilled vegetables. Even the simplest grilled vegetable makes the basis of endless meatless meals when served California-style, with a spicy salsa or savory herbed sauce.

CEBOLLAS Y AJO ASADO —
GRILLED SCALLIONS

Serves 4

This is a traditional Mexican dish that has its roots in
Spain. Recently it has drifted north of the Mexican
border and is especially popular in Los Angeles,
where in stylish restaurants they come piled alongside
the main course, accompanied by lots of black beans
and warm, tenderly soft corn tortillas. Grilled
scallions (spring onions) are equally at home in back
garden barbecues, and Angelenos, passionate about
fitness, are devotees of grilled dishes based on
vegetables.

Marinating the scallions gives more of a flavor
dimension to the dish. Although you can grill them
without marinating, they do not taste as special.
While scallions are easily available, when baby leeks
and green garlic shoots are in season, by all means
cook them in this way, too. The onion flavor is
softened, contrasted with the smoky flavor imbued by
the coals.

I have made these without grilling them as well, by
quickly browning them on a very hot, ungreased
skillet or frying pan. They are very good prepared
this way.

12 or so scallions (spring onions) or green garlic shoots and
*   baby leeks, cleaned and cut into halves lengthwise*
4 tablespoons extra virgin olive oil
1 teaspoon Dijon-type mustard
1 teaspoon lemon juice or balsamic vinegar
2 teaspoons fresh thyme, chopped
¼ teaspoon salt
½ teaspoon black pepper

Combine the scallions or garlic shoots and leeks with
the remaining ingredients. Leave them to marinate for
at least an hour.

Remove the scallions from the marinade after this
time, reserving any marinade.

Grill the scallions quickly, about 5–8 minutes on
each side, or 2–3 minutes in a hot pan, depending on
how big and mature the vegetables are.

Serve the grilled scallions cut into bite-sized
lengths, tossed in any reserved marinade.

GRILLED POTATO SLICES AND
MIXED SWEET PEPPERS WITH
SAUCES AND RELISHES

Serves 4

Cooking the potatoes until they are almost tender,
marinating them in olive oil, garlic, and herbs, then
grilling them over a barbecue results in potatoes like no
others as they are suffused with the fragrance of the
marinade and the smoky flavors of the barbecue. The
potatoes are unpeeled as the peel's flavor contributes to
the rustic, substantial quality of the dish. Potato slices
are served with grilled sweet peppers (capsicums), a
creamy aïoli (see pp. 142–3), and the tangy, herby
Olivada and Sweet Basil Pesto (see p. 142).

Nearly any sauce is good with these grilled potatoes
and peppers. Experiment with Gazpacho Vinaigrette,
Chunky Avocado Salsa, or Red Chili Aïoli (see
pp. 140, 138, and 142), for example.

3 lbs. (1.5 kg) large floury potatoes, scrubbed but unpeeled
½ cup (4 fl. oz., 125 ml) extra virgin olive oil
4 garlic cloves, finely chopped
1 tablespoon vinegar or lemon juice
1 teaspoon dried oregano
salt and freshly ground black pepper, to taste
1 red sweet pepper (capsicum), deseeded and cut into quarters
1 yellow sweet pepper (capsicum), deseeded and cut into
*   quarters*

TO SERVE
sauces and relishes of choice (see above)

Cook the potatoes for about 20 minutes in boiling
water, until they have almost cooked through (they
should be slightly less cooked than *al dente*).

Drain and leave them to cool.

When the potatoes are cool enough to handle, cut
them lengthwise into slices about ½ in. (1.5 cm)
thick. Toss the potato slices in the olive oil, garlic,
vinegar or lemon juice, oregano, and salt and pepper.
Leave them to marinate for at least an hour.

Prepare the barbecue. When the coals turn from red
hot to white, they are ready to cook over. Remove the
potato slices from the marinade and grill them for
about 3 minutes on each side. Place the sweet peppers
on the grill, too, brushing them with any leftover
marinade, and cooking until they have lightly browned
in places.

Serve the grilled potato and peppers immediately,
garnished with a dab each of the sauces and relishes
of your choice.

Variations

GRILLED BABY ARTICHOKES OR ARTICHOKE HEARTS: Use the same method as in the above recipe, but with nearly tender artichokes instead of potatoes (see p. 7 for details of how to prepare artichokes).

A DELICIOUS SANDWICH: Grilled artichoke heart slices make a tasty sandwich, nestled into a crusty roll that has been generously spread with blue cheese mixed with butter, a handful of alfalfa sprouts, and a sprinkling of toasted hazelnuts.

GRILLED EGGPLANT SLICES WITH CUMIN, MELTED CHEESE, AND SALSA

Serves 4

'Steaks' of eggplant (aubergine) are brushed with oil and browned on an open fire, topped with cumin and melted cheese, then served with the salsa of your choice. They make a delicious main dish for any barbecue, and any leftovers make succulent next-day sandwiches, especially tucked into crusty rolls that have been stuffed with hot refried beans and, perhaps, some roasted or pickled mild chili peppers.

1 large or *2 medium eggplant(s) (aubergine(s)), cut into*
* thick slices*
olive oil, for brushing
2 teaspoons or so ground cumin, for sprinkling
salt and freshly ground black pepper, to taste
about 12 oz. (375 g) white cheese for melting (sharp cheddar,
* Monterey Jack, etc.)*

ACCOMPANIMENT
salsa of choice (see p. 138)

Brush the eggplant slices on each side with the olive oil, then sprinkle the cumin, salt, and pepper over them.

Grill the slices over a barbecue, laying them on a piece of foil on the rack to keep them from falling through and also keeping the juices. Alternatively, prepare the slices under a hot broiler (grill).

When the eggplant is just tender and has lightly browned, top each with a slice of cheese and return to the heat to melt the cheese.

Serve immediately, with the cheese hot and sizzling, accompanied by your choice of salsa.

PAGE 74: Cebollas y Ajo Asado — *Grilled Scallions*
BELOW: *Grilled Eggplant Slices with Cumin, Melted Cheese, and Salsa*

GRILLED OLD AND NEW WORLD VEGETABLES

Serves 6

An assortment of fresh vegetables, marinated in garlic and olive oil, grilled over coals, is one of the definitions of the Californian cuisine of today.

Serve the assortment of vegetables with a spoonful of your favorite aïoli, and a croûte of country bread spread with olive paste. Prepare a double batch as any leftovers are fantastic tossed in pasta, simmered in soup, diced and dressed with tahini or vinaigrette, eaten as a salad . . .

> 6 heads of garlic, left whole and unpeeled
> 3 red onions, cut lengthwise into halves or *a handful of baby garlic cloves or baby leeks*
> olive oil, as desired
> salt and freshly ground black pepper, to taste
> *herbes de Provence*, to taste
> 1 Florence fennel (finocchio), thickly sliced lengthwise
> 1 red sweet pepper (capsicum), deseeded and cut into quarters
> 1 yellow sweet pepper (capsicum), deseeded and cut into quarters
> 2 medium zucchini (courgettes), cut into halves lengthwise or thick slices lengthwise
> 2 small yellow squash (marrow), cut into thick slices lengthwise (optional)
> dash of balsamic vinegar
> 3–5 garlic cloves, chopped
> 1 small eggplant (aubergine), cut into thick slices lengthwise
> 8 oz. (250 g), approximately, pumpkin, peeled and sliced thickly or sweet potato (kumara), blanched then cut into halves
> 4–6 tomatoes, cut into halves
> 1 loaf baguette or crusty country bread
> garlic cloves, as required
> olive paste (olivada), for spreading, or *Olivada and Sweet Basil Pesto (see p. 142)*
> aïoli (see pp. 142–3), as desired

Put the garlic and onions or baby garlic or baby leeks into a bowl and toss with several tablespoons of the olive oil. Season with the salt and pepper, and *herbes de Provence*. Leave to marinate for at least an hour.

Dress the fennel, sweet peppers, zucchini, and squash with several spoonfuls of olive oil, the balsamic vinegar, half the chopped garlic, and salt and pepper to taste. Leave to marinate for at least an hour.

Brush the eggplant and pumpkin slices, and tomatoes, with olive oil and the rest of the chopped garlic.

Sprinkle salt and pepper over them and leave to marinate also.

When ready, grill the vegetables over a barbecue. When grilling the vegetables, use a piece of foil over the grilling grid to prevent the vegetables falling in when they soften. This has the added advantage of preserving the delicious vegetable juices.

Cut the vegetables into bite-sized pieces or leave them whole and rustic-looking as you prefer.

Toast the bread slices on the grill, then brush them with olive oil and rub cut garlic cloves over them. Spread the toasted bread with the olive paste or Olivada and Sweet Basil Pesto.

Serve the vegetables piled onto a plate, accompanied by spoonfuls of the aïoli and prepared bread.

Leftovers

Olive oil and aromatic basted grilled vegetables make a good base for a variety of delicious dishes. Prepare a double amount of grilled vegetables as given above and use the leftovers for Wine Country Pasta with Flame-grilled Vegetables and Sun-dried Tomatoes (see p. 56) or the following two simple soups and sandwiches. Do not be fooled by the ease of preparation into thinking that they are nothing special — they are robust and lusty little dishes.

Variation

For a Mexican flavor, serve a simple sauce of chopped coriander, seasoned with lime juice and chopped green chili peppers and Red Chili Aïoli (see p. 142) in place of the aïoli. Accompany the dish with Bowl o' Red (see pp. 94–5) and soft corn tortillas instead of the garlic- and olive spread-topped bread.

OPPOSITE: *Grilled Old and New World Vegetables*

GRILLED VEGETABLE SOUP WITH GARLIC AND CUMIN
Serves 4

Strikingly simple, with a depth of flavor provided by the smoke of the barbecue. The flavoring is adapted from the Yucatán Peninsula of Mexico where flame-roasted vegetables add their savor to a wide variety of foods. This soup is, however, typically Californian: vividly flavored, yet light; innovative, yet cozy.

3 ³/₄ cups (1 ¹/₂ imp. pints, 935 ml) stock (see pp. 37–8)
8 ripe, sweet fresh or canned tomatoes, diced
the following vegetables grilled as for Grilled Old and New
   World Vegetables (see p. 78):
      1 red sweet pepper (capsicum), deseeded and cut into
        quarters
      1 green sweet pepper (capsicum), deseeded and cut into
        quarters
      1 zucchini (courgette), sliced
      2 tomatoes, halved
      ¹/₄ eggplant (aubergine), sliced
      sweetcorn from 1 cob
      1 potato, sliced
      5 scallions (spring onions)
      cloves of ¹/₂ head of garlic, the tender roasted flesh
        squeezed out and the skin discarded
1–2 garlic cloves, finely chopped
salt and freshly ground black pepper, if needed
cumin seeds, toasted and lightly crushed (see p. 144)
dash of hot pepper sauce (such as Tabasco)

Combine the stock and tomatoes, and bring to the boil.

Dice all the cooked vegetables, except the corn, and add them to the stock and tomato mixture. Bring to the boil. Simmer for 5–10 minutes to meld the flavors.

Add the chopped garlic, taste, and add salt and pepper if necessary. Serve each portion sprinkled with a little toasted and crushed cumin seed, and a tiny dash of hot pepper sauce.

SMOOTH GAZPACHO OF GRILLED VEGETABLES
Serves 4

Much like the Spanish *salmorejo*, or smooth, thick gazpacho, this smooth chilled purée of grilled vegetables tastes at once hearty and refreshing. A rather nice way of serving it is with a few ice cubes made from tomato juice melting into the soup. The potato thickens the mixture, giving it an almost creamy consistency without heaviness, while the vegetables, savory seasonings, oil, and vinegar impart refreshing tang.

   choose from the following vegetables and grill as for Grilled
   Old and New World Vegetables (see p. 78):
      1 potato, sliced
      1 red sweet pepper (capsicum), roasted, peeled, and chopped
      1 green sweet pepper (capsicum), roasted, peeled, and
        chopped
      4 tomatoes, skins removed and flesh coarsely chopped
        (reserve juices)
      1 zucchini (courgette), sliced
      ¹/₂ eggplant (aubergine), coarsely chopped
      sweetcorn from 1–2 cobs
      3–5 scallions (spring onions), coarsely chopped
¹/₂ cup (4 fl. oz., 125 ml) tomato juice
1 ¹/₂ cups (12 fl. oz., 375 ml) vegetable stock (see pp. 37–8)
3 tablespoons olive oil
1 teaspoon sherry or red wine vinegar, or to taste
1 garlic clove, finely chopped
salt, cayenne, and freshly ground black pepper, to taste

GARNISH
ice cubes or ice cubes made from tomato juice

Dice the vegetables you have grilled, except the corn.

Combine the vegetables with the tomato juice, and purée them in a blender or food processor. Add the stock, olive oil, sherry or vinegar, and garlic. Whirl them together until a smooth mixture results. Season to taste with salt, cayenne, and black pepper.

Serve chilled with several ice cubes or the tomato ice cubes floating on top.

OPPOSITE: Roast Vegetable and Goat or Ewe Cheese Sandwich on Country Bread

ROAST VEGETABLE AND GOAT OR EWE CHEESE SANDWICH ON COUNTRY BREAD

Serves 1

Sliced country bread, spread with tangy, fresh cheese and topped with grilled vegetables and oil-cured black olives is a zesty sandwich.

2 thick slices country bread, such as ciabatta
several spoonfuls of soft goat or ewe cheese, preferably garlic and herb flavored
1 portion sliced grilled vegetables (sweet peppers (capsicums), eggplant (aubergine), onions)
olive oil and balsamic vinegar, to taste
2–3 oil-cured black olives, pitted and halved

Place the bread on a plate and spread the goat or ewe cheese on it.

Toss the vegetables with the olive oil and balsamic vinegar, then arrange them on top of the cheese-spread bread. Drizzle any leftover oil and vinegar onto the second piece of bread.

Put the olives on top of the vegetables and top with the second slice of bread.

Variation

GRILLED VEGETABLE AND GOAT CHEESE PIZZA: Spread the sliced grilled vegetables over the pizza dough, dot with olives, goat or ewe cheese, chopped garlic, and mozzarella cheese, and bake as directed for pizza recipe (see p. 134).

GRILLED EGGPLANT SLICES WITH RED CHILI AIOLI

Serves 4

I do not usually salt eggplant (aubergine). Perhaps I am lucky, but my eggplant is never bitter. If you have had a problem with bitter eggplant, by all means salt it, drain, rinse, and dry, then proceed with the grilling. (Salted eggplant does not soak up as much oil, however.) A good way to tell if the vegetable is bitter ahead of time is to taste a tiny bit raw.

> 2–3 small to medium or 1 medium to large eggplant(s)
>   (aubergine(s)), cut into 1/8–1/4 in. (3–6 mm) thick
>   slices lengthwise
> olive oil, as needed
> 1/2 teaspoon ground cumin, or to taste
> salt and freshly ground black pepper, to taste
>
> **GARNISH**
> *Red Chili Aïoli (see p. 142)*

Brush the eggplant slices with the olive oil, then sprinkle cumin, salt, and pepper over them.

Grill the slices on each side over or under a hot grill until they have lightly browned and are tender.

Serve garnished with spoonfuls of the Red Chili Aïoli.

Leftovers

CRUSTY GRILLED EGGPLANT SANDWICH WITH RED CHILI AIOLI: Spread Red Chili Aïoli thickly over the bottom half of a chunk of crusty French bread or baguette, top with the eggplant (aubergine) slices, then with a handful of arugula (rocket) or *mesclun*, a few strips of red sweet pepper (capsicum) (either fresh or roasted and peeled), then a little more Red Chili Aïoli. Close the sandwich and enjoy warm or at room temperature.

Variation

GRILLED EGGPLANT WITH GOLDEN SHALLOTS AND PARSLEY: Brush the eggplant (aubergine) slices with olive oil, salt, and pepper. Grill as above, then sprinkle the slices with a little lemon juice and a scattering of chopped golden shallots and parsley.

OPPOSITE: Queso Asado — *Mexican Grilled Cheese with Green Olive Salsa*

GRILLED EGGPLANT WITH PACIFIC RIM PESTO

Serves 4

Tender, smoky-flavored eggplant (aubergine) is delicious dressed with a pesto-like seasoning paste of garlic, chilies, mint, coriander, and peanuts. It is equally good with sliced, pan-browned eggplant or with Oriental-style stuffed pasta.

> 4 eggplants (aubergines), cut into halves lengthwise
> 2 tablespoons vegetable oil
> 1 tablespoon sesame oil
> 2 garlic cloves, chopped
> salt and freshly ground black pepper, to taste
>
> **ACCOMPANIMENT**
> *Pacific Rim Pesto (see p. 142)*

Brush the eggplant with a mixture of the vegetable oil, sesame oil, garlic, and salt and pepper. Leave the eggplant on one side while you prepare the barbecue and make the pesto.

Grill the eggplant over white-hot coals, lining the rack with foil, or pan-brown if not barbecuing. Serve immediately with a spoonful of Pacific Rim Pesto.

QUESO ASADO — MEXICAN GRILLED CHEESE WITH GREEN OLIVE SALSA

Serves 4

Queso asado is simply cheese grilled or melted over an open fire. It is somewhat like the French *raclette*, but, being Mexican, is served with assorted spicy and variously textured toppings.

It is a specialty of the northern region of Mexico, Sonora, from which many of California's Hispanic population originate. The cheese is placed on top of the hot grill, alongside whatever else is cooking over the coals, and left to melt and sizzle deliciously. Topped with a salsa or assortment of toppings and served as an appetizer, it is dipped into with soft flour tortillas. *Queso asado* has been adapted perfectly to West Coast summer barbecues or if the Pacific coast summer fog drives you indoors, the dish can easily be made using the kitchen broiler (grill).

Any sort of salsa or savory topping may be served as an accompaniment for *queso asado*, but your selection should be deliciously varied: diced, fresh hot chili peppers, cinnamon-scented tomato sauce (perhaps with raisins and/or green olives), lemony salsa verde (green tomatillo (husk tomato) and chili sauce), thinly sliced onions, chili peppers, roasted sweet peppers or mild chili peppers, a sprinkling of corn, diced radishes, coriander leaves, and so on. Sometimes the cheese itself is a mixture of cheeses, seasoned generously with lashings of garlic, chili peppers, and herbs.

In this version, a simple slab of cheese is melted to sizzling, then topped with a mixture of onions, tomatoes, coriander, chilies, green olives, and lime. Serve with crusty bread, soft naan, or flour tortillas; grilled baby leeks, garlic shoots, or scallions (spring onions); and, perhaps, a bowl of earthy refried beans.

12–16 oz. (375–500 g) white melting cheese (preferably Monterey or Sonoma Jack), cut into thick slices

GREEN OLIVE SALSA
2 garlic cloves, finely chopped
1 onion, finely chopped
3 ripe fresh tomatoes, diced
3 fresh green chili peppers, or to taste, thinly sliced or coarsely chopped

2 oz. (60 g) fresh coriander leaves, coarsely chopped or mixture of fresh parsley and coriander
10–15 pimento-stuffed green olives, coarsely chopped
salt and freshly ground black pepper, to taste
½ teaspoon ground cumin
juice of 1 lime

ACCOMPANIMENT
crusty bread or soft fresh naan or flour tortillas

Lay the cheese slices in individual casserole dishes or arrange them in a single layer in one large casserole, allowing enough space around each slice for the cheese to spread and melt into, and get all sizzly around the edges.

Cook the cheese over a hot barbecue or under a hot broiler (grill) until it has almost melted completely and is sizzling.

Meanwhile, make the salsa by combining the remaining ingredients.

Serve the hot cheese with the salsa, and accompany with the crusty bread or naan or tortillas to dip into the cheese and salsa.

FIRE-ROASTED YAMS TWO WAYS

Serves 4

Roasting yams or sweet potatoes in the ashes of an open fire is one of the best ways to cook these sweet and hearty tubers. This method seems to roast the sugars of the vegetable into a flavor that is at once caramelly yet earthily vegetal.

A sprinkle of salt and a puddle of melted butter are all one needs to enjoy the roasted yams. For variety, try a spicy red chili butter to melt into the gash-opened vegetable or, for a tasty topping that is also nearly fat-free, a drizzle of soy sauce and sprinkling of toasted sesame seeds.

4 small to medium yams or sweet potatoes (kumara), washed
either 1 x recipe Red Chili Butter (see p. 145) or 2 oz. (60 g)
toasted sesame seeds and soy sauce, to taste

Prick the yams or sweet potatoes with a fork (this stops them from exploding in the heat). Wrap in foil individually.

Place in the white-hot coals of an open fire or barbecue (alternatively, bake in a hot 425°F (220°C) oven) for about 30–50 minutes, depending on the size of the vegetables, until they are softly tender inside.

They may also be left unwrapped and grilled slowly over the hot coals. Remove the yams or sweet potatoes to a plate and cut them open down the center. Serve immediately, buttered with the spicy Red Chili Butter or sprinkled with the sesame seeds and soy sauce.

OPPOSITE: *Double Pesto* Spiedini
BELOW: *Fire-roasted Yams Two Ways (made here with sweet potato)*

DOUBLE PESTO SPIEDINI

Serves 4

Spiedini are skewers loaded alternately with cheese and chunks of bread, seasoned with garlicky olive oil, and then grilled. This Roman specialty has been made Californian by the addition of pesto and the totally inauthentic sun-dried tomato pesto, made from sun-dried tomatoes and basil. The bread grills to a crusty, garlicky deliciousness and the cheese melts creamily, all enlivened further by the delectably strong flavors and perfumes of sun-dried tomato, basil, and garlic. Vary this dish by preparing it with different pestos: each will add its own distinctive 'zing'.

Take care when grilling not to let the cheese melt so much that it slithers off the skewers. If you are worried that the heat of the barbecue will be too great, grill indoors under a medium hot broiler (grill) instead.

¼ cup (2 fl. oz., 60 ml) extra virgin olive oil

3 garlic cloves, finely chopped

¼ teaspoon salt

10 oz. (310 g) French loaf, cut into 1-in. (2.5-cm) cubes

12 oz. (375 g) melting white cheese (such as Jack or mozzarella), cut into ½-in. (1.5-cm) pieces

½ x each of 2 recipes for pesto (such as traditional basil Pesto, Sun-dried Tomato Pesto, Californian Coriander Pesto, or Olivada and Sweet Basil Pesto, see pp. 141 and 142. Good-quality bottled ones are also fine.)

Combine the olive oil with the garlic and salt, and toss the bread cubes in the mixture. Thread the bread and cheese alternately onto the skewers, dabbing each with alternating pestos, taking care that the cheese is tightly wedged in.

Grill the threaded skewers over the coals before they are too hot, about 4–6 in. (10–15 cm) from the fire. Turn the skewers often and remove from the grill when the cheese just starts to melt (5 minutes or so). Serve immediately, accompanied by extra pesto or olive paste.

Variations

Omit the pesto entirely and skewer the bread and cheese with basil leaves and sun-dried tomato halves. Alternatively, dab the bread and cheese with both pestos and serve with olive paste.

DOUBLE PESTO PIZZAS: Top either a pizza base or sliced baguette with a spoonful each of sun-dried tomato pesto and basil pesto, top with shredded Jack or mozzarella, and grill until the cheese is melting and sizzling. Serve immediately as an appetizer or snack.

DOUBLE PESTO GRILLED CHEESE SANDWICHES: Spread one slice of whole-wheat (wholemeal) bread with sun-dried tomato pesto, then top with sliced white cheese. Spread a second slice of bread with basil pesto, then close the sandwich and press together well. Cut into four pieces and heat in a hot, lightly oiled pan, until the bread is fried golden and the cheese has melted. Serve as an appetizer or for a midnight snack.

Sautés, Braises, & Casseroles

T*he vegetables of the season, sautéed crisply, braised deeply, or baked into savory casseroles, make a delightful focal point for any meal. Strong flavorings, spices, and seasoning pastes add character and allure to these hearty dishes.*

I usually wander through the farmers' market, searching for whatever is sparklingly fresh and most delicious. Whichever vegetable I choose goes into a sauté pan, or is tossed into a simmering sauce or layered with beans or tofu for a spicy casserole. Strewn with fresh herbs — and often enough garlic to eliminate any threat of vampires — seldom does a dish please me more. Feel free to substitute whatever is freshest for whatever the recipe calls for — enjoy the inspiration of the season. Artichokes are often delicious in place of asparagus, corn and sweet peppers (capsicums) in place of zucchini (courgettes), zucchini in place of eggplant (aubergine), and so on. Using your imagination will be worth it: not only is fresh best, but you also add your own imprint, often improving on the original.

Asparagus Simmered in Garlic-scented Chili-spiked Tomato Sauce
Serves 4

So simple, so deliciously seasonal, tender asparagus is simmered in garlicky tomato sauce, enlivened by a shot of hot pepper sauce and a sprinkling of parsley. It is a variation of a dish I enjoyed during a stay in Italy, evocative of midsummer, when the days are warm and very, very long and the last of the asparagus beckons from the market stall. Serve it hot, spooned over any sort of pasta, especially plump, mushroom-stuffed ravioli, or in a shallow soup bowl, each portion topped with a perfect poached egg. It is also lovely at room temperature, spooned over rustic country bread as an appetizer, *bruschetta*-style. Use as a sandwich filling with thinly sliced mozzarella cheese stuffed into a crusty roll along with the spicy asparagus, then heated until crisp, toasted, and the cheese just melting.

1½ lbs. (750 g) asparagus, preferably the tiny, thin shoots rather than thick, plump ones
6 garlic cloves, chopped
2 tablespoons or so olive oil
2 lbs. (1 kg) fresh or canned tomatoes, diced
pinch of sugar
salt and freshly ground black pepper, to taste
1 vegetable bouillon (stock) cube (optional), for a stronger flavor
1–3 teaspoons, or to taste, fresh thyme leaves, coarsely chopped
dash or two of hot pepper sauce (such as Tabasco), to taste
1–2 tablespoons coarsely chopped fresh flat-leaf (Italian) parsley

ACCOMPANIMENTS
either 4 portions cooked pasta or 4 poached eggs
handful of fresh parsley, chopped

Snap off the ends of the asparagus. Take the tender tips and cut them into bite-sized pieces (reserve the tougher ends to be peeled and diced for another purpose, such as soup), and put to one side.

Warm the garlic in the olive oil. When it starts to release its aroma, add the asparagus and cook it briefly in the garlicky oil. Add the tomatoes, sugar, salt, pepper, and bouillon cube (if using). Cook the mixture over a medium-high heat until it has thickened.

Season with the fresh thyme and hot pepper sauce, then serve hot poured over the pasta or in a bowl topped with a poached egg, and the parsley sprinkled over the top. Alternatively, serve at room temperature.

Variation
PIZZA D'ASPARAGI: For an absolutely delicious asparagus pizza, prepare the above recipe using plump asparagus and without the bouillon (stock) cube. When the sauce has cooled, spread it thickly over the basic pizza dough made with olive oil given on p. 134, which has been rolled out thinly and put on a lightly greased flat baking sheet. Top with thinly sliced mozzarella or fontina cheese, and sprinkle with a little grated Parmesan. Bake the pizza in a 400°F (200°C) oven for 20–30 minutes, or until the dough has puffed, turned golden brown at the edges, is cooked in the middle, and the cheese is bubbling and golden almost all over.

Sauteed Zucchini in a Pool of Saffron-scented Puree
Serves 4

The presentation of this dish is elegant: slices of sautéed zucchini (courgette) lie in a pool of shamelessly extravagant saffroned zucchini purée. The sauce is more like a thick soup, thickened and enriched not by the addition of flour, butter or cream, but merely by means of the puréed vegetable itself.

1 medium to large onion, chopped
¼ cup (2 fl. oz., 60 ml) olive oil
8 oz. (250 g) zucchini (courgettes) or yellow squash (marrow), diced, for the sauce
3 oz. (90 g) fresh flat-leaf (Italian) parsley, coarsely chopped
1 teaspoon saffron
1½ cups (12 fl. oz., 375 ml) vegetable stock (see pp. 37–8)
freshly ground black pepper, to taste
4 medium zucchini (courgettes) or golden zucchini, for slicing and sautéing
olive oil, for sautéing

Lightly sauté the onions in the olive oil until they have just softened, then add the zucchini or squash for the sauce and two-thirds of the parsley. Cook over a low heat until the zucchini or squash is almost tender (about 5 minutes).

Meanwhile, dissolve the saffron in 2 tablespoons or so of warm water. Stir, then add it to the sautéed onion and zucchini mixture, together with ⅓ cup (3 fl. oz., 90 ml) or so of the stock. Simmer until the zucchini has cooked through and the liquid has mostly been absorbed. Season with black pepper. Purée in a blender or food processor, adding remaining stock to form a thick, smoothish sauce. Set aside.

Slice the remaining zucchini and taste a little of each to see if they seem bitter or astringent. If so, sprinkle them with salt and leave until the bitter juices come to the surface in little droplets, then rinse and pat them dry. Sauté the sliced zucchini quickly in sufficient olive oil, taking care not to break them up as they will then look like some sort of squash stew.

Spoon the purée onto individual plates, then top each with an arrangement of the sautéed zucchini. Garnish by sprinkling the rest of the parsley over the border of purée around the edge of the plate. Serve immediately, perhaps with some crusty bread to scoop up all the delicious sauce.

Variation

PUREE OF ZUCCHINI SOUP WITH SAFFRON: Follow the above recipe, but omit the sautéed zucchini (courgettes) and increase the amount of stock you add to $3\frac{3}{4}$ cups ($1\frac{1}{2}$ imp. pints, 935 ml). Serve either hot or at room temperature.

XIN-XIM — BAHIAN TOMATO AND COCONUT STEW WITH RED BEANS, BROCCOLI, AND RICE
Serves 4

This dish is a result of Brazilian and Afro-Caribbean influences on Californian cooking. The flavors are Amerindian, African and Portuguese, combined with the essentially Californian ingredients of broccoli, beans, rice, and fresh herbs.

XIN-XIM SAUCE
3 medium onions, chopped
3–4 garlic cloves, chopped
2–3 fresh green chili peppers, deseeded and chopped
2 tablespoons olive oil
1 tablespoon paprika
$\frac{1}{4}$ teaspoon ground ginger
$\frac{1}{4}$ teaspoon ground cinnamon
pinch of ground nutmeg
1 lb. (500 g) fresh or canned tomatoes, chopped
1 cup (8 fl. oz., 250 ml) vegetable broth (see pp. 37–8)
$\frac{1}{2}$ cup ($\frac{1}{2}$ oz., 15 g) fresh coriander, or more, to taste, coarsely chopped
$\frac{1}{2}$ cup ($\frac{1}{2}$ oz., 15 g) fresh mint leaves, coarsely chopped
1 cup (8 fl. oz., 250 ml) coconut milk
$\frac{1}{2}$ cup (4 oz., 125 g) smooth peanut butter
juice of $\frac{1}{2}$–1 lemon, or to taste
1 oz. (30 g) dry-roasted peanuts, coarsely chopped

RED BEANS AND BROCCOLI
1 small to medium green sweet pepper (capsicum), coarsely chopped
2 elephant garlic cloves, diced, or 2 garlic cloves, plus $\frac{1}{2}$ onion, chopped
2 tablespoons olive oil
1 tablespoon all-purpose (plain) flour
$\frac{1}{2}$ cup (4 fl. oz., 125 ml) vegetable broth (see pp. 37–8)
salt and coarsely ground black pepper, to taste
1 large bunch or 2 small bunches of broccoli, cut into bite-sized pieces and any tough stems peeled and cut into bite-sized pieces
1 lb. (500 g) cooked kidney beans (8 oz. (250 g) uncooked), drained
4 portions plain cooked brown or white rice

ACCOMPANIMENT
salsa or pickled chili peppers, to taste

Make the Xin-Xim Sauce. Sauté the onions, garlic, and chili peppers in the olive oil until they have softened. Add the paprika, ginger, cinnamon, and nutmeg. Cook for a moment, then stir in the tomatoes and broth. Cook, uncovered, over high heat for 10–15 minutes, or until the mixture has reduced to the consistency of a sauce. Stir in the coriander, mint, coconut milk, peanut butter, and lemon juice. Cook over a medium heat until the sauce has thickened a little more (only a few minutes). It will be soupy. Set the pan to one side while you prepare the red beans and broccoli.

Sauté the sweet pepper and garlic or garlic and onions in the olive oil until they have softened. Sprinkle in the flour and cook, stirring, until it is golden brown (about 3 minutes). Remove from the heat, add the broth gradually, stirring it to combine, then return the pan to the heat and cook, stirring, over a medium heat until the mixture is smooth and has thickened (about 5 minutes). Season with salt and pepper. Add the broccoli and beans, and cook for about 5 minutes longer until the broccoli is tender.

Sprinkle the peanuts over the Xin-Xim Sauce and serve the red bean and broccoli mixture ladled over the rice, garnished with a generous portion of Xin-Xim Sauce. Offer salsa or pickled chilies on the side for each person to sample as they please.

PAGE 86: *Sautéed Zucchini in a Pool of Saffron-scented Purée (left) and Asparagus Simmered in Garlic-scented Chili-spiked Tomato Sauce (right)*

MANY TREASURE VEGETABLES WITH PITA BREAD AND HOISIN SAUCE

Serves 4

Shiitake mushrooms are richly brown with a woodsy flavor. Another of my favorite fungi is tree fungus. Its consistency is chewy, rubbery, and crunchy all at the same time. Strange though it sounds, it is almost addictively good. Tree fungus is available in Asian food stores. This dish is inspired by Israeli immigrant friends who often ate take-out vegetable stir-fries tucked into their native pita breads. The bland bread is a delicious foil to the zesty vegetables and sweet–spicy hoisin sauce.

4–5 shiitake mushrooms

10 or so small tree fungus or cloud ears (optional)

1 garlic clove, chopped

1-in. (2.5-cm) piece of fresh ginger root, peeled and chopped

2 tablespoons vegetable oil

1 carrot, cut into julienne

½ white or Napa cabbage or Chinese leaf, thinly sliced

1 celery stick, cut on a diagonal

several pieces of firm tofu, fried (either buy it fried or fry it at home, see p. 23)

2 tablespoons vegetable broth (see pp. 37–8)

2 teaspoons soy sauce

2 teaspoons cornstarch (cornflour)

1 tablespoon sesame oil

ACCOMPANIMENTS

4 pita breads or other soft, flat bread (naan, chapati, etc.)

hoisin sauce, to taste

8 or so scallions (spring onions), cleaned, trimmed, and left whole

1 oz. (30 g) fresh coriander leaves

Put the shiitake mushrooms and tree fungus (if using) in separate bowls, and pour enough hot water over to cover them. Cover the bowls and leave the mushrooms to soak and soften for 20 minutes or so. Now remove them from the soaking liquid, rinse with clean water, and squeeze dry. Trim the shiitake mushrooms of their tough stems and cut the caps into strips. Thinly slice the tree fungus.

Stir-fry the garlic and ginger in the oil for 1 minute, then add the carrot, stir well, and spoon the mixture onto a warmed plate. Next, adding a tiny bit more oil to the wok if needed, stir-fry the cabbage or Chinese leaf and celery for just a minute. Remove these from the wok to the warmed plate with the garlic, ginger, and carrot. Quickly stir-fry the tofu in the wok, adding more oil if needed, then place the tofu with the rest of the reserved vegetables. Finally, stir-fry the mushrooms.

Mix the broth with the soy sauce and cornstarch in a pitcher (jug). Return all the vegetables to the wok and heat through over a medium-high heat. Add the broth mixture and cook for only a minute or two — just long enough for the liquid to thicken a little into a sauce.

Drizzle the sauced vegetables with the sesame oil and serve immediately, accompanied by the pita bread, hoisin sauce, scallions, and coriander. Have each diner make sandwiches using the scallions as paint brushes with which to spread the hoisin sauce inside each pita bread, then pile in the vegetables, garnishing with the onions and coriander.

BRAISED EGGPLANT WITH TOMATOES AND BORLOTTI BEANS

Serves 4

This rich braise mingles chunks of tender eggplant (aubergine) with meaty brown beans in an intensely tomato-flavored sauce. Serve it with a bowl of plain yogurt and cucumber salad, such as tzatziki, a bowl of brown rice and, perhaps, an omelet.

1 large or 2 medium eggplant(s) (aubergine(s)), cut into bite-sized chunks

salt, for sprinkling

several tablespoons olive oil, for frying

3–5 garlic cloves, chopped

½ onion, thinly sliced

2 lbs. (1 kg) diced tomatoes, fresh or canned

salt, sugar and freshly ground black pepper, to taste

6 oz. (185 g), approximately, canned borlotti or mottled shell beans, drained

2–3 tablespoons coarsely chopped fresh flat-leaf (Italian) parsley

Put the eggplant chunks in a colander and sprinkle salt very liberally over them. Leave for 30 minutes, then rinse them in water and pat dry with paper towels or absorbent kitchen paper.

Heat 2 tablespoons or so of olive oil in a skillet or frying pan, then add about half the garlic. When it is golden brown, add the eggplant chunks and let them brown lightly, turning from time to time until they are evenly colored (you may need to do this in several batches; the eggplant does not need to be cooked completely through as it will also be simmered).

Put the sautéed eggplant into a saucepan or other heavy-bottomed pan ready for simmering. In the skillet or frying pan, heat another tablespoon of the olive oil, then a little more of the garlic, the onion, and the tomatoes. Cook over a high heat until the mixture has reduced in volume by about half. Season with salt, sugar, and pepper.

Add the tomato sauce to the eggplant, together with the beans, parsley, and remaining garlic. Cover the pan and simmer over a low heat for about 20 minutes, or until the eggplant has finished cooking and the flavors have melded together.

Serve the braise hot or at room temperature.

OPPOSITE: *Many Treasure Vegetables with Pita Bread and Hoisin Sauce*

BELOW: *Braised Eggplant with Tomatoes and Borlotti Beans*

CALIFORNIAN CASSOULET

Serves 4

This savory casserole of creamy white beans baked with wine, broth, vegetables, and masses of garlic, enriched with a breadcrumb, olive oil, garlic, and parsley crust, is heartily delicious. It has an added bonus: it will not put your diners into a post-meal stupor, which traditional (meaty) cassoulets are legendary for doing.

I have combined the traditional white beans with lima (butter) beans. As the lima beans cook, they fall apart and impart a richness to the sauce, giving the cassoulet plenty of body.

Serve this cassoulet accompanied by a salad of *frisée* (curly endive) and other Continental leaves, mixed with fresh tarragon and chives, and cloaked with tangy vinaigrette.

1 lb. (500 g) dried white haricot or cannellini beans, soaked overnight or 5 cans cooked cannellini beans (approx. 8 oz. (250 g) each), drained

8 oz. (250 g) dried lima (butter) beans or 3 cans cooked lima beans, drained

1 medium potato, peeled and diced

1 medium red sweet pepper (capsicum), diced

1 medium carrot, diced

1–2 heads of garlic, cloves separated, peeled, and left whole

1 teaspoon herbes de Provence

1 teaspoon dried thyme

2½ cups (1 imp. pint, 625 ml) dry red wine (vin de Cahors)

1 lb. (500 g) fresh or canned tomatoes, chopped and with the juice

2½ cups (1 imp. pint, 625 ml) vegetable broth, or more if necessary (see pp. 37–8)

1–2 fresh chili peppers or Turkish-style pickled chili peppers, deseeded and chopped, or chopped

salt and freshly ground black pepper, to taste

3–4¼ cups (6–8 oz., 185–250 g), approximately, fresh breadcrumbs

3½ fl. oz. (100 ml) extra virgin olive oil

3 garlic cloves, chopped

3 tablespoons chopped fresh parsley

Drain the haricot or cannellini beans, pour them into a saucepan, cover with fresh water, then bring to the boil. Reduce the heat to a low simmer, cook for 1½–2 hours or until they are just tender, adding extra water if they seem too dry, then drain the beans. If using canned beans, omit this step.

Mix the cooked beans with the raw lima beans, potato, red sweet pepper, carrot, garlic, *herbes de Provence*, thyme, wine, tomatoes, broth, and chili peppers. Bring to the boil, then reduce the heat to very low and simmer, adding more broth as needed, until the beans are tender (about an hour). Stir the mixture from time to time during cooking, and take care that the beans at the bottom of the pot do not stick and burn. Season generously with salt and pepper.

Pour the mixture into a baking pan. The beans should be tender and the sauce should be thick, though somewhat soupy.

Mix the breadcrumbs with the olive oil, chopped garlic, and parsley. Spread a third of this mixture over the top of the beans and bake in a 350°F (180°C) oven for about 30 minutes, or until the top is golden brown and lightly crusty. Remove the pan from the oven and break up the crumb crust, stirring it into the beans, and add a little extra broth or wine at this point if the mixture seems too stodgy. Spread half the remaining breadcrumb mixture over the bean mixture as before and bake as before.

Remove the pan from the oven, stir the crust in, spread the rest of the breadcrumb mixture on top of the casserole and return it to the oven. Raise the oven temperature to about 400°F (200°C) and bake for another 15 minutes or until the top is crusty and golden brown. Serve immediately.

WHITE BEAN AND TOMATO STEW WITH OLIVADA TOPPING
Serves 6–8

Bean and tomato stew, topped with garlic and herb olive sauce, makes a hearty main course offering. In winter, it is delicious served piping hot, while in summer, it is refreshing served at cool to room temperature.

If olive paste is unavailable, make your own by puréeing pitted Mediterranean-style black olives with enough olive oil to make a rich, smooth paste.

OLIVADA SAUCE
1 large garlic clove, chopped
1 teaspoon fresh rosemary, finely chopped
2 teaspoons olivada or other black olive paste (see above)
3 tablespoons olive oil

WHITE BEAN STEW
12 oz. (375 g) dried white beans, rinsed and picked over, or 2 cans (about 8 oz. (250 g) each) cannellini beans, drained
1 medium carrot, diced
2 small to medium onions, thinly sliced
15 small to medium fresh or canned tomatoes, peeled and quartered, or chopped
2 medium to large potatoes, peeled and cut into large dice
2 tablespoons finely chopped fresh parsley
2 cups (16 fl. oz., 500 ml) vegetable broth (see pp. 37–8)
salt and freshly ground black pepper, to taste

Prepare the Olivada Sauce first. Combine the ingredients and chill while you prepare the stew.

For the stew, put the white beans in cold water, covering them by 3 in. (7.5 cm), soak overnight and then drain. Alternatively, put the beans into a large saucepan, cover them with cold water, bring to the boil, cover the pan, and then remove from the heat. Leave the beans to soak for an hour, then drain.

Mix the soaked beans with the carrot, onion, tomato, potato, parsley, and broth in a saucepan. Bring to the boil, cover the pan partially, and simmer until the beans are tender (1–1½ hours). Season to taste with salt and pepper. If using canned beans, first cook the carrot, onion, tomatoes, potatoes, parsley, and broth until the vegetables are tender (about 10 minutes), then add beans and simmer to meld the flavors (about 15 minutes).

Serve either hot or at room temperature with about a teaspoonful of the Olivada Sauce poured on top of each portion.

Leftovers
This makes a perfect base for a good minestrone soup. Simply thin with 2½ cups (1 imp. pint, 625 ml) broth, an assortment of chopped vegetables (such as chard (silver beet) or spinach, zucchini (courgette), potato), a handful of broken pasta, and serve hot, topped with some chopped fresh basil and a spoonful of pesto.

OPPOSITE: *Californian Cassoulet*

Black Bean Chili with Lime Cream

Serves 4

Inky black beans, tasting of chili and spices, are spiked with a shot of tart lime for a hearty, distinctive bowlful.

Black bean chili has become a recent quintessentially Californian dish, though the addition of lime-scented sour cream is my own. It adds a wonderful contrast. For a more classic dish, finish each bowlful with a handful of more elaborate toppings, such as grated cheddar cheese, sour cream, chopped scallions (spring onions), thin shreds of lettuce, or strips of roasted, mild, green chili peppers.

8 oz. (250 g) black beans, picked over
3 cups (24 fl. oz., 750 ml) vegetable broth (see pp. 37–8)
2 cups (16 fl. oz., 500 ml) tomato purée (passata) or fresh
*   tomatoes, diced*
2 tablespoons olive oil
2 onions, chopped
5 garlic cloves, chopped
1 fresh green chili pepper, deseeded and chopped
1 tablespoon ground cumin
1 teaspoon mild chili powder
1 teaspoon paprika
1 teaspoon oregano
hot pepper sauce (such as Tabasco), to taste
1/2 cup (4 fl. oz., 125 ml) sour cream
juice from 1/2 lime and grated zest from 1/4 lime
1 oz (30 g) fresh coriander

ACCOMPANIMENTS
2 fresh green chili peppers, deseeded and chopped
hot pepper sauce (such as Tabasco)

Pour the beans into a large saucepan and add enough water to cover them. Soak overnight or bring to the boil, remove the pan from the heat, and leave them to soak, covered, for an hour.

Drain, pour enough fresh water into the pan to cover the beans, and bring to the boil. Reduce the heat and simmer for about 1 1/2 hours or until the beans are tender.

Then add the broth, tomato purée or fresh tomatoes, and raise the heat to medium-high. Cook until the liquid reduces and thickens somewhat, and the beans are just beginning to fall apart.

Heat the olive oil in a skillet or frying pan. Sauté the onion and garlic until they have softened, then sprinkle in the chili pepper, spices and herbs,

including the hot pepper sauce, and cook through for a few moments to release their flavor. Add this mixture to the beans and simmer them together for another 20 minutes or so, stirring every so often so that the beans do not stick, and adjusting the liquid so that it is neither too soupy nor too thick.

Mix the sour cream with the lime juice and zest.

Serve each portion of the Black Bean Chili topped with a spoonful of the Lime Cream and a sprinkling of the coriander. Have extra chilies or hot sauce available for those who would like them.

Bowl o' Red

Serves 8

Authentic chili, also known as bowl o' red to aficionados, is based on mild, whole red chili peppers or chili powder. Beans have come to be a common ingredient, but this is not authentic and no chili purist would admit to including beans in their special recipe.

However, beans and red chili sauce are such perfect partners that only die-hards refuse their pairing — most of us simply spoon it up and enjoy. For vegetarians, especially, beans give the chili body and protein. You could also add texturized vegetable protein or soy mince to this end. Whatever you do, the thing about a bowl o' red is that, as long as you season it generously and it fairly singes with chili flavor, it will be good.

3 onions, chopped
4 garlic cloves, chopped
1 medium to large or 2 small green sweet pepper(s)
*   (capsicum(s)), deseeded and chopped or diced*
2–3 tablespoons vegetable oil
2 tablespoons mild red chili powder
2 tablespoons paprika
1 tablespoon ground cumin
1 bay leaf
2 teaspoons dried oregano
3 tablespoons masa harina (corn tortilla flour) or 2 corn
*   tortillas, lightly toasted and crumbled or cut into tiny*
*   pieces or a handful of tortilla chips, crumbled*
1 lb. (500 g) fresh or canned tomatoes, diced
3 cups (24 fl. oz., 750 ml) vegetable broth (see pp. 37–8) or
*   mixture of beer or lager and broth*
12 oz. (375 g) beans (borlotti or kidney), cooked and
*   drained, or 3 medium-sized cans, drained*
salt and freshly ground black pepper, to taste

GARNISHES
cheese, grated
lettuce, thinly sliced
onion, chopped
avocado, diced
hot pepper sauce (such as Tabasco)

Sauté the onions, garlic, and green sweet pepper in the oil until they have softened, then stir in the chili powder, paprika, and cumin. Cook for a minute or two. Add the bay leaf, oregano, *masa harina* or tortillas or tortilla chips, and stir everything together over the heat for a few minutes.

Add the tomatoes and broth or beer or lager and broth, bring to the boil, then reduce the heat and simmer until the chili has thickened and is flavorful (about 30 minutes).

Add the beans, heat them through and season to taste with salt and pepper. Serve, ladled into bowls, and let the diners choose the garnish or garnishes they prefer.

BELOW: *Black Bean Chili with Lime Cream (top left) and Bowl o' Red (bottom right)*

Spiced Potatoes, Green Beans, Eggplant, Chickpeas, and Tomatoes with Burmese Curry Sauce

Serves 4

California boasts numerous Burmese restaurants and the spicy cuisine rich with vegetables, noodles, crispy lentils, and aromatics is especially enticing for vegetarians. This dish, adopted from their repertoire, is delicious. The sauce is a variation of *panthe kaukswe*, the Burmese national dish of coconut-flavored curry sauce, eaten ladled over thin noodles with an assortment of variously flavored and textured toppings. I have further changed it. One day I had leftover sauce but no noodles, so I served the nutty, slightly spicy sauce with a curried stir-fry of vegetables and found it to be even better than the traditional Burmese dish. The mustard and cumin seeds in the vegetables add a pleasing texture, releasing their flavor and aroma as the little seeds burst as you chew.

Accompany my version with soft, chewy bread or naan or plain steamed rice, to balance the flavorful sauce and varied ingredients.

Burmese Curry Sauce

4 medium onions, chopped
6–8 garlic cloves, chopped
1½-in. (4-cm) piece of fresh ginger root, peeled and chopped
1 teaspoon ground turmeric
1 teaspoon curry powder
1 medium stalk of lemon grass, peeled and cut into 2-in. (5-cm) lengths, lightly crushed
2 tablespoons vegetable oil
1 tablespoon sesame oil
pinch of red chili flakes or cayenne pepper
2 tablespoons chickpea flour (besan)
2 cups (16 fl. oz., 500 ml) coconut milk or coconut cream from a block dissolved in hot water
1 cup (8 fl. oz., 250 ml) vegetable broth of choice (see pp. 37–8)
juice of 1 lime or lemon

Spiced Potatoes, Green Beans, Eggplant, Chickpeas, and Tomatoes

6 garlic cloves, coarsely chopped
3 tablespoons vegetable oil, or more if necessary
2 teaspoons mustard seeds
1 teaspoon cumin seeds, or to taste
2 tablespoons curry powder

6 waxy potatoes, peeled and cut into bite-sized pieces
1 medium eggplant (aubergine), cut into bite-sized pieces
1 lb. (500 g) cooked chickpeas (garbanzos), drained (canned are fine; if using dried, you will need approx. 8 oz. (250 g) chickpeas, plus 3 to 4 hours cooking time)
1 lb. (500 g) fresh or thawed frozen green or string beans
1 lb. (500 g) fresh or canned tomatoes, diced
salt, to taste
juice of 1 lemon, or to taste

Garnishes

1 lemon, cut into wedges
3–5 scallions (spring onions), thinly sliced
1 egg, hard-boiled and diced
2–4 fresh green chili peppers, deseeded and thinly sliced
handful of fresh coriander

Make the Burmese Curry Sauce first. In a skillet or frying pan, or wok, sauté the onions, garlic, ginger, turmeric, curry powder, and lemon grass in the vegetable and sesame oils. Cover and cook over a medium-low heat until the onions and spices have lightly browned and given off much of their moisture, the oil beginning to pull away from the cooking onions and spices (about 15–20 minutes) — a typically Burmese way of preparing a dish.

Uncover the skillet or wok, and sprinkle in the chili flakes or cayenne pepper, and chickpea flour, then cook for a few moments. Stir in the coconut milk or cream, and broth. Stir well to combine all the ingredients and simmer, uncovered, until the sauce has thickened (about 20 minutes). If the sauce begins to separate or to become too thick, add a little more water. When the sauce has thickened and is flavorful, add the lemon or lime juice, stir, then set the skillet or wok to one side.

Now prepare the vegetables. Sauté the garlic in the oil until it has softened, then add the mustard and cumin seeds. Cook for a few moments until they begin to pop. Add the curry powder and potatoes. Cook until the potatoes are lightly browned and tender (about 5 minutes). About halfway through this time, add the eggplant so it browns along with the potatoes.

Add the chickpeas and beans, and cook for a few minutes longer. Add the tomatoes and cook over a medium-high heat until all the vegetables are tender and the tomatoes have reduced a little. Season with the salt and the lemon juice.

Serve the vegetables with a topping of the Burmese Curry Sauce, accompanied by the garnishes (you could choose to serve one, some, or all of them).

BRAISED TOFU, SWEETCORN, AND ZUCCHINI WITH MEXICAN FLAVORS

Serves 2–4

Puréeing the aromatics — the onion, garlic, tomatoes, and spices — into a paste, then 'frying' this in oil intensifies its flavors and condenses its liquidy consistency, which is a traditional Mexican way of cooking.

This Mexican-inspired braised tofu is typically Californian in its cross-flavoring. The sweetcorn and zucchini (courgettes) are delicious additions, but cooked kidney beans would also be good in place of the vegetables. I like this best at room temperature as the consistency of the tofu is firmer and the creamy bean curd has absorbed the flavors of its sauce more because of the cooling period.

1 onion, chopped

2 garlic cloves, chopped

1 teaspoon paprika

1 teaspoon mild chili powder

½–1 teaspoon fresh or dried thyme, to taste

1 teaspoon toasted and coarsely ground cumin seeds
  (see p. 144)

4 ripe or canned tomatoes, diced

2–3 tablespoons vegetable oil

¾–1 cup (6–8 fl. oz., 185–250 ml) vegetable stock
  (see pp. 37–8)

11 oz. (340 g) firm tofu, cut into bite-sized cubes

1 zucchini (courgette), diced

4 oz. (125 g) fresh or frozen or canned sweetcorn

2 tablespoons tomato juice or purée (passata)

salt and freshly ground black pepper, to taste

In a blender or food processor, purée the onion, garlic, paprika, chili powder, thyme, cumin seeds, and tomatoes until a smooth mixture is achieved.

Heat 2 tablespoons of the oil in a skillet or frying pan and 'fry' the purée, a ladleful at a time, letting each addition cook down and intensify before adding more. Pour in the stock and cook into a flavorful sauce (about 5 minutes) before adding the tofu, zucchini, and sweetcorn. Simmer the tofu and vegetables in the sauce without stirring it too often so that the tofu does not break up into little pieces.

When the sauce has cooked down, add the tomato juice or purée, and season with the salt and pepper. Enjoy the braise warm or leave it to cool to room temperature.

BELOW: *Braised Tofu, Sweetcorn, and Zucchini with Mexican Flavors*

Side Dishes

*T*he cuisine of California, like that of much of the Mediterranean, is often distinguished by the little plates of highly flavored foods that accompany the more sustaining main courses; the little dishes that exist to excite the palate rather than fill you up.

There are some dishes that, by their nature, are best suited to accompanying others. They may be too rich or the flavors may be too concentrated to eat whole portions of them, but in small amounts, they are pleasing.

SONOMA COUNTY CARROTS MARINATED IN GARLIC AND PARSLEY VINAIGRETTE

Serves 4–6

These tangy, garlicky morsels make a delicious accompaniment for a picnic lunch, snuggled between the covers of bread and cheese for a sandwich, or kept on hand to enrich pasta salads, hearty soups, sauces, and so on.

The recipe was given to me by an energetic, elderly Italian farmer who lives in Sonoma County with his even more energetic and elderly mother. He still makes his own cheeses, tends his own vineyard, producing a modest yearly vintage, presses his own olive oil and plays *bocce* every Sunday afternoon in the lazy summer sunshine. His mother, dressed in black even in the 100-degree-plus days of summer, looks after the garden, which includes growing a huge patch of sweet carrots.

Any leftover carrots and marinade are delicious as a salad dressing. They can even be used as a seasoning mixture for other dishes such as soups, pasta or rice salad, stews, or sandwich fillings.

2 lbs. (1 kg) carrots, cleaned and sliced
2 garlic cloves, crushed
2 tablespoons chopped fresh parsley
¼ cup (2 fl. oz., 60 ml) olive oil, or to taste
2–3 tablespoons red wine vinegar
salt and freshly ground black pepper, to taste

Steam the carrots until they are just tender, then toss them in the remaining ingredients. Season with salt and pepper. Enjoy this dish warm or leave to cool before eating.

OPPOSITE: *(from left to right) Green Beans Sautéed with Red Sweet Pepper and Onions, Sonoma County Carrots Marinated in Garlic and Parsley Vinaigrette, and Garlicky Sautéed Spinach with Sun-dried Tomatoes*

GREEN BEANS SAUTEED WITH RED SWEET PEPPER AND ONIONS

Serves 4

Red sweet peppers (capsicums) with fresh green or string beans — as lovely to look at as they are to eat — are typical of the colorful, fresh vegetables that appear daily on Californian tables.

1 lb. (500 g) fresh or frozen thawed green or string beans, cut into ¾-in. (2-cm) lengths
5 garlic cloves, coarsely chopped
2 red sweet peppers (capsicums), diced or coarsely chopped
2–3 tablespoons olive oil
salt and freshly ground black pepper, to taste

GARNISH
handful of fresh basil, chopped (optional)

Boil or steam the beans until they are just tender, then drain and set aside.

Sauté the garlic and red sweet pepper in the olive oil until they have just softened, then add the drained beans and toss them together.

Season with salt and pepper, and serve immediately, garnished with the basil (if using).

Variation

SPANISH-FLAVOR SALAD WITH GREEN OLIVES AND TARRAGON: Add a splash of sherry vinegar or red wine vinegar and a dash of Dijon-type mustard to the hot olive oil and garlic-tossed beans after you have removed them from the heat, along with a handful of sliced green or pimento-stuffed olives. Substitute tarragon for the basil, and serve on a bed of *frisée* (curly endive).

GARLICKY SAUTEED SPINACH WITH SUN-DRIED TOMATOES

Serves 4

Blanching green vegetables, then tossing them in hot, garlic-seasoned oil is a deliciously Italian–Californian way of treating them. The vegetables — in this case spinach or chard (silver beet) leaves — take on a bright green color and slick glossiness. Sun-dried tomatoes add the bright flavor accent Californians crave.

Sun-dried tomatoes, while Italian in origin, are a quintessentially Californian flavor. One finds them dried into leathery discs in farmers' markets or natural food stores, or marinated in herby olive oil in jars. This recipe uses the type in oil, for their texture is softer and pleasingly chewy, somewhat like an oil-cured olive.

1 bunch of spinach or chard (silver beet), soaked, to clean
1–2 garlic cloves, coarsely chopped
2 tablespoons oil from a jar of sun-dried tomatoes or olive oil
5–7 sun-dried tomatoes, drained then cut into strips or small pieces
freshly ground black pepper, to taste
small squeeze of lemon juice

Blanch the spinach or chard, rinse it in cold water, then squeeze dry. Cut into bite-sized pieces or strips.

Heat the garlic in the tomato or olive oil, but do not let it brown. Quickly add the spinach or chard, and toss it in the hot oil. Then add the sun-dried tomatoes and season with the pepper and lemon juice. Serve at room temperature.

Leftovers

SPINACH, SUN-DRIED TOMATO AND CHEESE PANINO: Either the recipe above or the variation below is delicious as a sandwich filling, a sort of Californian *panino*, stuffed into a chewy, tender roll, along with a few thin slices of mild, creamy mozzarella cheese.

Variation

CHARD AND GOLDEN ZUCCHINI OR SQUASH WITH SUN-DRIED TOMATOES AND SWEET BASIL: Follow the above recipe, but add 1–2 medium golden zucchini (courgettes) or squash (marrow) that have been cut into bite-sized dice, blanched, and drained. Omit the lemon juice and serve instead with a sprinkling of thinly sliced or chopped fresh basil.

OPPOSITE: *Pan-roasted Root Vegetables with Whole Garlic Cloves*

PAN-ROASTED ROOT VEGETABLES WITH WHOLE GARLIC CLOVES

Serves 4

Parboiled parsnips, carrots, and whole garlic cloves brown in a small amount of olive oil, resulting in a flavor that approaches that of roasted vegetables. Root vegetables are not as well appreciated in California as they might be. With a wealth of Mediterranean vegetables to choose from, it is no wonder that earthy roots tend to take a back seat to their more glamorous cousins. However, they do deserve greater attention as they are healthy, economical, and delicious.

Adding tender, whole garlic cloves to this recipe is typically Californian. Adding a small amount of sugar to the mixture encourages the vegetable juices to caramelize.

Serve this dish with a pasta or pilaf, Scarlet Salad Hidden under a Bed of Home-made Garlic Croûtons (see p. 4), and, for dessert, enjoy a cooling ice cream from those on pp. 163–6.

6–8 medium carrots, cut into bite-sized pieces
6–8 medium parsnips, cut into bite-sized pieces
10–15 whole garlic cloves, peeled
2 onions, thinly sliced lengthwise
1–2 tablespoons olive oil
½–1 teaspoon sugar
salt and freshly ground black pepper, to taste

Combine the carrots, parsnips, and garlic in a pan, and cover with water. Bring to the boil, reduce the heat, and simmer until the vegetables are tender. Alternatively, steam the vegetables until they are just tender. Drain them, reserving the cooking liquid for another use.

Put the drained vegetables into a skillet or frying pan (preferably a non-stick one) with the onions, olive oil, and sugar. Over a medium-high heat, cook the vegetables, tossing them every so often, until they have browned in places and the onion slices have turned to dark, crispy brown shreds. Season with salt and pepper, and enjoy immediately.

BEETS IN SPICY CORIANDER AND LEMON DRESSING

Serves 4

The sweet flavor of beet (beetroot) is enhanced by the contrast of the lemon and coriander dressing. This makes a superb appetizer as well as a side dish, and it is also a great relish-like accompaniment to grilled bread with feta cheese or pizza-like breads.

4–6 medium beets (beetroots), cooked (preferably not vinegared)*
2–3 teaspoons sugar or honey, melted
3 tablespoons Coriander and Lemon Salsa (see below)
1–2 tablespoons extra virgin olive oil
salt, to taste
lemon juice, to taste

Cut the beets into bite-sized pieces.

Toss the beet pieces in the remaining ingredients until they are all well combined.

* If using already vinegared beet, omit the lemon juice and add more sugar or honey instead, to taste.

To cook beets, either steam, boil, or bake whole in their skins until tender, about 45 minutes, depending on size of beets. Steaming takes less time, baking more. Let cool, then slip skins off and proceed with recipe.

CUMIN-ROAST POTATOES WITH CORIANDER AND LEMON SALSA

Serves 4

Cumin and olive oil enhance the earthy flavor of potatoes in an almost magical way. As with most simple dishes, it is the quality of the ingredients that is most important, so use the best highly flavored virgin olive oil you can afford.

The dish is easy to make and leaving the peel on the potatoes not only makes for quicker, simpler preparation, the skins actually bring out more of the vegetable's natural potato flavor. (Be sure to trim off any tinge of toxic green skin or flesh.)

When the potatoes come out of the oven, sizzling hot, you spoon a little of the Coriander and Lemon Salsa over them. The contrast is delicious and the little potatoes are delectable.

3 lbs. (1.5 kg) small roasting potatoes, well scrubbed and unpeeled
2–3 tablespoons extra virgin olive oil
1 tablespoon ground cumin, or to taste
salt, to taste

CORIANDER AND LEMON SALSA

2 leaves romaine (cos) or other lettuce, thinly sliced
2 garlic cloves, chopped
1/2–1 fresh red or green chili pepper, chopped
4 tablespoons fresh or bottled lemon juice
2 oz. (60 g) fresh coriander, coarsely chopped
salt, freshly ground black pepper, ground cumin, and mild chili powder, to taste

Boil the potatoes until they are just tender, just able to be pierced with a knife (about 15 to 20 minutes). Drain and leave them to cool.

Quarter the potatoes and toss them in the olive oil, cumin, and salt.

Roast in a 350°F (180°C) oven for 40 minutes, or until the potatoes are crusty and golden brown.

Meanwhile, prepare the Coriander and Lemon Salsa.* Whirl the lettuce with the garlic, chili, and lemon juice in a blender or food processor until the mixture is well puréed, then add the coriander and whirl until it becomes a smooth sauce. Season with salt, pepper, cumin, and mild chili powder.

Serve the hot roasted potatoes tossed with a few spoonfuls of the salsa and extra salsa on the side.

* This recipe makes quite a large quantity of Coriander and Lemon Salsa, but it keeps for several days chilled or for up to 2 months in the freezer, ever ready to add a spicy tang to a wide variety of dishes, from soups, pasta dishes, curries, and salad dressings to chili beans and so on. Beets in Spicy Coriander and Lemon Dressing (above) is just one example.

OPPOSITE: *Beets in Spicy Coriander and Lemon Dressing (top left) and Cumin-Roast Potatoes with Coriander and Lemon Salsa (bottom right)*

CHEESE-TOPPED THREE-ALLIUM GRATIN

Serves 4

The leeks are first cooked in broth then drained (as always, the broth is reserved for another purpose). They are then topped with cheese and chives (or a good chive-flavored cheese), and baked to a browned and melting richness. As this dish is quite rich because of the cheese, I find that a smaller portion as a side dish is more welcome than a larger, main-course portion. The whole garlic cloves cook up to tender sweetness, but may be omitted for the faint-hearted or those who are more considerate of their neighbors than myself!

1 head of garlic, cloves separated and peeled
2 cups (16 fl. oz., 500 ml) vegetable broth (see pp. 37–8)
4–6 medium leeks, cleaned, cut into 2-in. (5-cm)
* or so lengths, and halved lengthwise*
4 oz. (125 g) firm cheese (cheddar, Gloucester, etc.), thinly
* sliced or coarsely grated (see next ingredient)*
2 tablespoons finely chopped chives (or choose a chive
* or onion-flavored cheese)*

Put the garlic cloves in a saucepan with the broth. Bring to the boil, then reduce the heat and simmer for about 10 minutes, or until the garlic is half tender.

Add the leeks and continue to simmer until the leeks are just tender. Drain, saving the liquid for another use, such as soup or a sauce.

Spoon the garlic and leeks into a shallow casserole or baking dish. Top with a layer of cheese and sprinkle over the chives (if using). Bake in a hot 400°F (200°C) oven or under a broiler (grill) until the cheese is melted and lightly browned in places. Serve immediately.

TOMATO SALAD WITH BRANDY AND SWEET BASIL

Serves 4

Garden-ripened tomatoes, sleek and full of their high-season flavor, are sprinkled with a few grains of salt to bring out their juices, a few drops of brandy, and a little thinly sliced basil to echo their sweet fragrance. The untraditional addition of brandy to tomatoes and basil is one of simple brilliance, especially when the tomatoes are so delicious that they beg to be enhanced rather than drenched in a dressing (inspired by the description in Helen Brown's *West Coast Cook Book* (Little, Brown & Co., USA, 1952)).

Brandy is produced in great quantity and often excellent quality in parts of California and, hence, is used in many of the dishes of its cuisine. A dash might be added to aïoli along with a bit of diced tomato; a spoonful might be stirred into a creamy soup or used to deglaze a pan; or it might be melted with chocolate to glaze a cake.

6–8 smallish ripe summer tomatoes
salt, to taste
a sprinkling of sugar, if needed
1 tablespoon or so brandy
2 tablespoons or several sprigs fresh basil,
   cut into very thin shreds

Slice the tomatoes lengthwise, arrange them on a platter or individual plates, and sprinkle the slices with a little salt and sugar (if using).

Sprinkle the brandy over them, then the basil. Serve immediately or chill until ready to serve.

Variations

Replace the brandy with balsamic vinegar and scatter very thin slices of half a red onion over the dish.

RIPE SWEET TOMATO SALAD WITH CUMIN AND LIME VINAIGRETTE: Ripe tomatoes are given a whole new flavor when dressed with this dressing. Use the recipe for Cumin and Citrus Vinaigrette on p. 139, adding a little grated lime peel and lime juice instead of the lemon juice to bring out the slightly bitter quality of the cumin. This contrasts refreshingly with the sweet, tangy, fruity quality of the tomatoes. Serve with Garlic and Lemon Creamy Puréed White Bean Sauce (see p. 30).

OPPOSITE: *Cheese-topped Three-Allium Gratin*

DOUBLE-GARLIC MASHED POTATOES WITH ROSEMARY BUTTER

Serves 4

I love garlic passionately, yielding to its voluptuous presence even at the threat of destroying my social life! There is nothing I can think of that is not improved by a touch of this heady, aromatic bulb.

Comforting mashed potatoes, infused with masses of garlic, have, ironically, become terribly chic in recent years. Whole garlic cloves are simmered with the potatoes, becoming gentle, sweet, and tender, resulting in mashed potatoes of an ambrosial nature, scented as they are with mild and fragrant garlic, and rich with butter and cream or milk. A dab of rosemary butter, melting into a crater on top of the potatoes and running down in rivulets through the snowy potatoes . . . heaven!

I have been known to lose control and make these potatoes in vast quantities. I add just a little more butter, a drop more milk or cream, just a few more potatoes, and before I know it I have a huge potful. Luckily, the leftovers make a blissful topping for shepherd's pie, a tasty potato soup, or a bed of cheese-topped baked eggs.

2 heads of garlic, cloves separated and peeled
8 medium baking potatoes, peeled and cut into 1-in.
   (2.5-cm) cubes
2 cups (16 fl. oz., 500 ml) water
4 oz. (125 g) unsalted butter, or as required
2–3 tablespoons finely chopped fresh rosemary leaves
salt, to taste
3 garlic cloves, peeled and chopped
3–4 tablespoons milk or cream
salt and freshly ground black pepper, to taste

Put the whole garlic cloves, together with the potato and water, into a saucepan. Bring to the boil, then reduce the heat, cover, and cook over a low-medium heat, simmering, until the potatoes are tender. Drain them and keep warm (reserving the cooking water for soups, sauces, etc.).

Meanwhile, combine half the butter with the rosemary, season with salt, and set to one side.

Mash the potatoes, adding the chopped garlic, remaining butter, milk or cream, and season with salt and pepper.

Serve immediately, each portion topped with a nugget of the rosemary butter to melt into the creamy, garlicky potatoes.

Leeks Simmered with Tomato, Garlic, Thyme, and Black Olives

Serves 4

The tender, gentle leek is simmered with the strong flavors of tomatoes, garlic, herbs, and olives. Serve this as a side dish or as part of a selection of salads, accompanied by bread. Use any leftovers to fill an omelet or as the base for a zesty soup.

2 garlic cloves, finely chopped
2 tablespoons olive oil
3–4 medium leeks, cleaned, quartered lengthwise,
*   and cut into bite-sized lengths*
¼ cup (2 fl. oz., 60 ml) tomato purée (passata)
¼ cup (2 fl. oz., 60 ml) vegetable stock (see pp. 37–8)
½ teaspoon fresh or ¼–½ teaspoon dried thyme
pinch of chopped fresh rosemary (optional)

Garnish
salt and freshly ground black pepper, if needed
8–10 niçoise or kalamata olives, pitted

Lightly sauté the garlic in the olive oil until it has softened. Add the leeks and cook them over a medium-low heat for a few minutes until they have softened.

Add the tomato purée, stock, thyme, and rosemary (if using), then cover and simmer for 10 minutes or until the leeks are tender. Taste and add salt and pepper if you feel it needs them.

Cool and serve at room temperature, garnished with the olives.

BELOW: *Leeks Simmered with Tomato, Garlic, Thyme, and Black Olives (bottom left) and Fava Beans and Sweetcorn in Red Chili Sauce (top right)*

FAVA BEANS AND SWEETCORN IN RED CHILI SAUCE

Serves 4–6

This rustic dish of chili-seasoned fava (broad) beans and sweetcorn makes a delicious side dish, but try it also as a topping for tostadas, spread with hot refried beans and melted cheese, or for crusty tortas or rolled into warm, soft corn tortillas as an enchilada filling.

6 garlic cloves, chopped
2 tablespoons vegetable or olive oil
8 oz. (250 g) fresh or frozen thawed fava (broad) beans, peeled and blanched
8 oz. (250 g) fresh or frozen thawed sweetcorn, blanched
2 teaspoons mild chili powder
2 teaspoons paprika
½ teaspoon ground cumin, or to taste
pinch of cinnamon
¼ cup (2 fl. oz., 60 ml) water
squeeze of lemon juice
salt, to taste
pinch of sugar

Lightly sauté the garlic in the oil until it has softened, but not browned. Add the fava beans and cook them for a few moments, then add the sweetcorn and cook them together for another few moments, to coat the vegetables with the fragrant garlic oil.

Add the spices, stir, cooking them for a moment, then add the water, lemon juice, salt, and sugar. Cook over a medium heat for a few minutes until the vegetables are tender, the liquid is intensely red, and it has a syrup-like glaze. Season to taste and serve either hot or at room temperature.

VENICE BEACH GARLIC FRIES

Serves 4

Venice Beach, California, where life on the street is the show and, before you know it, you are also part of the strange and fascinating parade. There are roller skaters, bicycle riders, body builders, bikini wearers, dog walkers, and sun enthusiasts — all pass by in a sort of melody of motion.

Shops and cafés tend to the trendy and streetwise, with junk food and health food at times sharing the same menu, both often being very good. This recipe combines these two ends of the spectrum: fries or chips of golden, crisp potatoes are tossed with lots of chopped garlic and parsley before they are served. The trick is to be sure that the fries themselves are light, not greasy (I do them in the oven). Note that the skins are left on.

Exact amounts really do not matter here, though I have included them as a guideline. This dish is no more than a plate of hot 'fried' potatoes cloaked to near indecency with a prodigious amount of garlic.

4–6 large baking potatoes, scrubbed, unpeeled, and sliced into long fries
3 tablespoons vegetable or olive oil, or sufficient to lightly coat the potatoes
salt, to taste
4 garlic cloves, finely chopped, or to taste
2 tablespoons finely chopped fresh parsley

Lay the fries on a large, flat baking sheet and toss in the oil.

Bake in a 450°F (230°C) oven until the fries have turned golden brown and are just tender (about 20 minutes). You will need to turn them occasionally in order for them to cook evenly and to ensure that they do not stick to the bottom of the pan.

Serve immediately, tossed in the salt, garlic, and parsley.

GINGER-SCENTED PUREE OF CARROTS AND TOMATOES

Serves 4

Colored a vivid hue of red-orange, this luscious purée of carrots is fragrant with fresh ginger and tangy with pieces of tomato, all whirled together into a soft, spoonable mixture. It is not only delicious, but also strikingly unusual, as most carrot purées are overly rich with butter and cream.

This makes a splendid side dish when warm, but I like it even better cool, as a light and refreshing appetizer. For a chilled soup, thin the purée to the desired consistency with some vegetable stock.

1 lb. (500 g) carrots, sliced
³⁄₄ cup (6 fl. oz., 185 ml) water, or as required
1¹⁄₂-in. (4-cm) piece of fresh ginger root, peeled and chopped
1–2 garlic cloves, finely chopped
4–5 ripe fresh or canned tomatoes, diced
salt and freshly ground black pepper, to taste
pinch of sugar
2 tablespoons butter
3–4 tablespoons plain yogurt

Cook the carrot in the water until just tender and bright orange. Drain, reserving the cooking water.

Whirl the carrot in a blender or food processor with the ginger, garlic, and enough of the reserved cooking liquid to make a smooth purée.

Return the purée to the saucepan and add the tomatoes. Cook the mixture over a medium-high heat to reduce any excess liquid. Season with the salt, pepper, and sugar, then remove the pan from the heat and stir in the butter and yogurt, beating the ingredients together with a wooden spoon to combine them well.

FRIJOLES REFRITOS — REFRIED BEANS*

Serves 4

Ubiquitous to the Mexican table and adored in many Californian–Mexican dishes, this rich paste of mashed and fried beans is only fried once, despite its name. While in Mexico any sort of bean may be used, in California pinto beans are the most favored for down-home style fare, with black beans the choice of more contemporary restaurants and cookery books.

Canned *frijoles refritos* are readily available in most places, as they are in California, and while I

generally shy away from canned food, refried beans are delicious, available as vegetarian, and lend themselves to preparing all sorts of dishes that would be impossible if one did not have the omnipresent pot of simmering beans on the back burner.

8 oz. (250 g) pinto beans
4¹⁄₂ quarts (7 imp. pints, 4 litres) water, approximately, in total
2 onions, 1 cut into half, the other coarsely chopped
1 tablespoon bland vegetable oil
salt, to taste (beans take quite a bit)
¹⁄₃ cup (3 fl. oz., 90 ml) vegetable oil
4–8 oz. (125–250 g) cheese, grated (optional)

Put the beans in a saucepan and cover with about twice their volume of water. Leave to soak overnight or bring to the boil, remove from the heat, and leave to sit in the hot water for 1 hour.

Drain the beans, and add about half the water, as well as the halved onion. Bring to the boil.

When the skins of the beans begin to wrinkle, add the tablespoon of oil. Continue to simmer until the beans are tender, adding more water as needed.

Brown the chopped onion in the remaining oil, then remove the browned onions and reserve for another use (they are delicious), leaving behind the onion-flavored oil in the pan.

Over a medium heat, add a small amount of the beans to this oil, cooking them down as their liquid evaporates. Either mash the beans with a fork gradually as you add them to the pan, or cheat and purée about half of them in a food processor or blender before adding, leaving the rest a bit chunky. Let them cook this way until the mixture is a heavy, rather dry paste. Season with salt.

For the optional cheese, place the hot *frijoles refritos* in a casserole or shallow baking dish. Top with the cheese and bake or broil (grill) until the cheese melts and becomes bubbly.

* This recipe is adapted from *Flavours of Mexico* (Grafton/HarperCollins, UK, 1991).

OPPOSITE: *Confetti Pan 'Fries' of Mixed Multicolored Root Vegetables with Salsa*

Confetti Pan 'Fries' of Mixed Multicolored Root Vegetables with Salsa

Serves 4

It is a delicious whimsy to nibble one's way through a mound of these multicolored strands.

The carrots, yams, and parsnips taste particularly sweet; the texture of the carrots and parsnips is pleasantly leathery, a delightful contrast to the floury texture of the potatoes and yams. Beet (beetroot) 'fries' are an unexpected pleasure. The uncooked root works best, but if only cooked beet is available, cut it into strips and toss in flour before frying. Throughout the pile of crisp and tender strands, you will find our old friend, the potato. Try to use as many different colors as possible for maximum visual impact.

Salsa is a lovely dip for these 'fries'. I have also tried an assortment of sprinkles — chili powder, Cajun spices — but a shake of plain old salt still tastes best.

2–3 tablespoons olive oil, or as required, for frying
1 large baking potato, peeled and cut into julienne
1 large or 2 small to medium parsnip(s), peeled and cut into julienne
1 medium yam or sweet potato (kumara), cleaned and cut into julienne
2 medium carrots, cleaned and cut into julienne
5-in. (13-cm) or so piece of daikon radish, cleaned and cut into julienne or cassava root or celeriac, peeled and cut into fries
1 large or 2 medium beet(s) (beetroot(s)), preferably raw (see above), cut into strips (optional)
2 artichokes, thorny leaves and chokes removed, and cut into julienne or fries

Accompaniments
salt, to taste
salsa of choice (see p. 138)

Heat the oil in a wide skillet or frying pan until it is hot, but not yet smoking. Scatter in the julienne of vegetables, not adding the flour-tossed beet (if using) until the rest of the vegetables are nearly done (depending on the size of your pan, you may need to cook the vegetables in batches).

Cook over a medium-high heat, until the outsides have lightly browned, but the insides are tender. Toss several times during cooking so that they cook evenly. Push the vegetables aside when ready and add the beet, letting the flour coating on the outside brown slightly.

Remove the 'fries' from the pan and drain them on paper towels or absorbent kitchen paper. Sprinkle with a little salt and serve with the salsa of your choice.

Brunch & Supper

*T*he dishes in this chapter can be served any time of the day or night, as welcome at the beginning of the day as at the end of it. Savory waffles, crêpes, and vegetable-laden frittatas or tortillas are favored on weekends, perhaps for brunch, accompanied by mugs of steaming hot coffee and a selection of freshly baked breads, or they may be cut into small pieces and enjoyed at cool room temperature as an appetizer. My favorite time for any frittata-type dish is late at night, accompanied by an excellent film on video.

FRESH SWEETCORN WAFFLES WITH RED CHILI BUTTER
Makes 6–8

Fresh sweetcorn is wonderful in waffles, the tiny sweet kernels amplifying the earthy flavor of the cornmeal. They also give the waffle a delightful texture. Though a savory, chilied butter topping accompanies this recipe, it is equally good sweet, with honey or maple syrup.

2 cups (8 oz., 250 g) all-purpose (plain) flour
1–3 teaspoons sugar or honey
2 teaspoons baking powder
1 teaspoon baking soda (bicarbonate of soda)
³⁄₄ teaspoon salt
12 oz. (375 g) medium cornmeal
1 cup (8 fl. oz., 250 ml) milk
¹⁄₂ cup (4 fl. oz., 125 ml) plain yogurt, stirred until it is smooth
¹⁄₃ cup (3 fl. oz., 90 ml) vegetable oil
6 oz (185 g) fresh or frozen or canned sweetcorn

ACCOMPANIMENT
Red Chili Butter (see p. 145), to taste

Combine all the ingredients, except the sweetcorn and Red Chili Butter, mixing them together well. Now add the sweetcorn. Spoon the batter onto a well-heated waffle iron (see tips in the following recipe) and bake the waffle until it is golden brown.

Serve immediately with the Red Chili Butter.

Variation

SAVORY CORN PANCAKES WITH RED CHILI BUTTER: Instead of cooking the batter on a waffle iron, prepare pancakes by ladling the batter into a hot, lightly greased skillet or frying pan, cooking each pancake on one side then the other. Serve them topped with the Red Chili Butter.

TABBOULEH WAFFLES

Serves 4

Waffles are a favorite breakfast on the West Coast, as they are throughout America, and are becoming increasingly popular elsewhere, too. Whereas in the Midwest or on the East Coast, waffles will be golden, corrugated cakes awash with maple syrup, on the West Coast they might be made with blue cornmeal and served with chili butter or made with buckwheat, soy flour, oat bran, wild rice, and so on. Adding whole grains to the waffle batter gives them a delicious pop as one bites into the tender waffle.

The following waffle has leftover Tabbouleh added to it, giving it texture and a deeper taste that is savory, rather than sweet. Enjoy it for supper or midnight feasting rather than for breakfast.

3 cups (12 oz., 375 g) all-purpose (plain) flour
1 teaspoon salt
3 teaspoons baking powder
1 teaspoon sugar
2 eggs
1 cup (8 fl. oz., 250 ml) milk
⅓ cup (3 fl. oz., 90 ml) melted butter
1½ cups, approximately, Tabbouleh (see p. 8) or
  store-bought tabbouleh, well drained

GARNISH
extra melted butter or 3–4 tablespoons yogurt

Sift the flour, salt, baking powder, and sugar into a bowl.

Lightly beat the eggs, then mix them with the milk.

Stir both mixtures together, then add the melted butter and Tabbouleh (if the mixture seems too dry, add a little extra water or milk; if it is too moist, add a little more flour).

Heat the waffle iron (non-stick ones work best) until it is very hot (at least 10 minutes). Lightly oil or grease the inside, then ladle enough batter to cover only two-thirds of the iron (if too full, the batter will spill over the sides, covering everything in sight with sticky, quickly hardening goo), then close the top. After you have closed the top, do not open it again for at least a minute (a waffle takes about 90 seconds to cook) because if you open the iron too soon, the waffle separates.

Remove the waffle from the pan when it is golden brown and serve immediately, topped with melted butter or a spoonful of yogurt.

Variation

WILD RICE WAFFLES WITH SAGE BUTTER: Wild rice — long grains of nutty flavor — makes a most wonderful addition to waffles. Substitute 1 cup of cooked, well-drained wild rice or a mixture of wild rice and other brown rice for the Tabbouleh. Serve the waffles with Garlic and Olive Butter (see p. 145), substituting sage for the herbes de Provence, or with sage or wildflower honey and sweet (unsalted) butter.

SPINACH AND ROSEMARY CREPES WITH GARLIC BUTTER

Serves 4 as a snack or appetizer

Colored a deeply verdant shade of green, these tender spinach and herb crêpes make a splendid snack or delicious appetizer, accompanied by glasses of rustic red wine, such as a Zinfandel or Merlot.

While one can make perfectly good crêpes without the help of a blender or food processor, these clever little machines purée the spinach at the same time as they whip up the batter, which makes it all so easy.

Cut into wedges, the crêpes exemplify informal, sociable nibble-eating. Instead of chopped garlic and butter, you could serve the wedges of crêpes with a nugget of garlicky goat cheese.

4 oz. (125 g) cooked, squeezed dry spinach (about 1 lb.
  (500 g) fresh, raw spinach)
3 eggs
½ cup (4 fl. oz., 125 ml) milk
½ cup (4 fl. oz., 125 ml) water
1½ teaspoons chopped fresh rosemary
3 tablespoons vegetable oil
1 cup (4 oz., 125 g) all-purpose (plain) flour
½ teaspoon salt
oil and butter, as required for cooking
2–3 garlic cloves, finely chopped

ACCOMPANIMENT
butter or fresh herb or garlic-scented goat cheese

In a blender or food processor, combine the spinach, eggs, milk, water, rosemary, oil, flour, and salt. Whirl until the mixture is very green in color.

Leave to thicken and for the froth to subside (about 30–50 minutes).

Heat a small amount of oil and butter in a flat crêpe pan, pouring in enough to cover the bottom of the pan. The batter will be quite thick, producing thickish crêpes, but do not worry, they will be tender (if they are too thin they will fall apart).

Sprinkle the uncooked top of the crêpe with garlic, then, when the crêpe firms up, turn it over and cook on the other side. Toss the crêpe from the pan to the plate, and spread with a small amount of butter or top with a piece of goat cheese. Continue in this way until all the batter is used (it should make about 8 crêpes).

Serve the crêpes cut into wedges, hot or at room temperature.

PAGE 110: *Fresh Sweetcorn Waffles with Red Chili Butter*
BELOW: *Spinach and Rosemary Crêpes with Garlic Butter*

SHREDDED THREE-VEGETABLE PANCAKES

Makes 4–6

Shreds of zucchini (courgette), carrot, and potato turn this version of the traditional Eastern European potato pancake, which has been transplanted to West Coast shores by means of the turn-of-the-century immigration, into a fresh vegetable dish. Serve with a simple herbed tomato sauce or with a sprinkling of toasted and crushed cumin seeds (see p. 144) and a bowl of yogurt.

3 medium zucchini (courgettes), coarsely grated

1–2 small to medium carrots, coarsely grated

2 medium to large potatoes, peeled and coarsely grated

1 onion, coarsely grated

2 garlic cloves, coarsely chopped

generous shake of salt, freshly ground black pepper, and sugar

2 eggs, lightly beaten

¾–1 cup (3–4 oz., 90–125 g) all-purpose (plain) flour, or as needed to thicken the batter

fresh sweet basil or mild red chili powder or ground cumin, to taste (optional)

¼–½ cup (2-4 fl. oz., 60–125 ml) olive oil, for frying

Combine the zucchini, carrot, potato, onion, garlic, salt, pepper, sugar, and eggs. Stir in enough flour to make a thick batter, then season with basil or chili powder or cumin (if using).

Heat a few tablespoons of the olive oil in a heavy skillet or frying pan. Spoon in several tablespoons of the batter for each pancake and fry over a medium-high heat until the pancake is cooked on one side, then flip it or toss it onto the other side to cook. The pancake should be crisp and golden on the outside and cooked through on the inside.

Drain each pancake on paper towels or absorbent kitchen paper, and repeat the process until the batter has all been used. Serve immediately.

Variation

Serve each portion of crisp vegetable pancakes atop a bed of tartly dressed *mesclun* leaves, as the hot, rich pancakes and cool, tangy greens make a lovely contrast, the greens wilting slightly from the warmth of the pancakes resting on them.

ABOVE: *Potato, Broken Garlic, and Chive Frittata (top left) and Shredded Three-Vegetable Pancake (bottom right)*

FRITTATAS
AND OMELETS

Usually served for weekend brunches, Californian egg dishes cover a wide and exciting array of textures and tastes. Rather than being rich and subtle, as in French cuisine, they give themselves over eagerly to the zesty spicing that defines Californian food — garlic, chilies, tomatoes, crisp vegetables, and so on.

Rolled French omelets might be stuffed with roasted, peeled chili pepper and a handful of melting cheese, then topped with a cooling swathe of sour cream. Simple cheese omelets might have fresh herbs and young garlic beaten into the eggs or tender young asparagus might be sautéed then scrambled with eggs and diced garlic-flavored cheese, the latter to melt seductively into the creamy eggs. Sharp cheese, such as goat or feta, roasted sweet peppers (capsicums), and avocado are popular inclusions, as are ethnic flavors such as Mexican-style beans, Mediterranean ratatouille-like mixtures, and Chinese stir-fries.

Sometimes the eggs will be poached in vegetable stews rather than beaten into omelets. *Huevos rancheros*, fried or poached eggs topped with salsa and served on several corn tortillas, is a staple brunch dish and might be served with any of a myriad of accompaniments — from sautéed plantains, diced avocado, grated cheese, sour cream, black or refried beans, or Mexican-style rice to tropical fruit. Poached eggs might nestle into baked potato halves, whose insides have been scooped out and mixed with brightly flavored seasonings then returned to their earthly shell, or artichoke bottoms, topped with a smooth and rich aïoli or hollandaise-type sauce.

Flat omelets and frittatas are very contemporary, as the method of adding beaten eggs to lots of savory ingredients results in a dish that tastes less richly of egg and more of everything else. This simple technique opens the doors to culinary creativity.

POTATO, BROKEN GARLIC, AND CHIVE FRITTATA WITH SUN-DRIED TOMATO PESTO TOPPING
Serves 4

This omelet is originally based on a Spanish frittata. When the thick, flat omelet is cooked through, golden brown and scented with the olive oil, herbs, and double dose of alliums in it, it is turned out and either eaten hot or left to cool. Delicious as it is, it tastes even better when spread with a thin layer of sun-dried tomato pesto.

This makes a wonderful supper dish served warm, along with a salad of romaine (cos) lettuce in mustard vinaigrette, marinated and grilled leeks, and, perhaps, a chunk or two of delectably pungent, somewhat runny cheese, crusty bread (of course), and, for dessert, ice cream with raspberries and toasted, glazed hazelnuts.

> 1½ lbs. (750 g) potatoes, peeled and diced
> 10 garlic cloves, peeled and lightly crushed with the blade of a knife
> 3 tablespoons extra virgin olive oil
> salt and freshly ground black pepper, to taste
> bunch of chives or greens of 5–7 scallions (spring onions), thinly sliced
> 4 eggs, lightly beaten
> 2 teaspoons finely chopped fresh herbs of your choice (thyme, parsley, marjoram, and so forth)
> 3–4 tablespoons sun-dried tomato pesto, or to taste (see p. 141)

Put the potato into a hot pan with the garlic and olive oil. Cook for a few moments to lightly brown, then reduce the heat and cover the pan, letting the potato 'sweat' to a crisp tenderness. Turn occasionally, taking care not to break up the potato pieces or turn them into a mush. Season well with salt and pepper.

When the potato is just barely tender, remove from the pan to a bowl, leaving any excess olive oil in the pan. Mix the potatoes with the chives or scallions, and then leave to one side to cool.

Meanwhile, mix the eggs with the herbs, and season to taste with salt and pepper. When the potato has cooled to just warm or cooler, add the egg mixture and mix them together well.

Heat the pan with the reserved olive oil, adding a spoonful or two more if needed. When it is hot but not smoking, pour in the potato and egg mixture and reduce the heat, letting the omelet cook over a low-medium heat. Pull the edges away from the pan occasionally to let the runny, uncooked egg flow from the top to the underneath to cook.

When the omelet is mostly firm but the top is still a bit runny, cook the top. Either cook it under the broiler (grill) or invert a plate over the pan, turn the pan over so the omelet is then on the plate, and then flip the uncooked side into the bottom of the hot pan. Remove the omelet to a plate and serve hot, warm or cool with the top spread with sun-dried tomato pesto.

GARLICKY FETA CHEESE FRITTATA
Serves 2

Very Greek and reminiscent of the simple omelets I used to eat when I lived on the island of Crete. Back in my Californian kitchen, it picked up a wallop of garlic and might also have a layer of pan-fried potato or zucchini (courgette) slices, or a handful of thinly sliced stir-fried chard (silver beet) leaves. Such dishes are found throughout the state in contemporary cafés that specialize in weekend breakfasts and brunches. Champagne, orange juice, and freely refilled cups of enlivening coffee usually accompany the plates. And what plates they are! The bountiful platters are often garnished with fresh fruit and/or crusty hash-brown potatoes. Breads, muffins, and toast usually accompany the meal, often nestled into a napkin-lined basket to keep them warm and served with sweet (unsalted) butter and fruity jams or preserves.

At home, I usually serve this omelet for supper, with rustic country bread and a salad of chopped, raw vegetables, herbs, olives, and scallions (spring onions) dressed with olive oil and lots of lemon juice.

2 garlic cloves, chopped
2–3 tablespoons olive oil
4 eggs, lightly beaten
salt and freshly ground black pepper, to taste
8 oz. (250 g) feta cheese, cut into large dice
large pinch of dried oregano, crumbled

In a heavy skillet or frying pan, lightly sauté the garlic in the olive oil until it has softened but not browned.

Pour the beaten eggs into the pan, sprinkle with salt and pepper, then let the mixture cook for a few minutes. Place the feta cubes on top, spacing them evenly across the frittata.

Cook the omelet over a medium heat, pulling up the edges once or twice to let the liquid egg from the top run to the underneath to cook. When the egg is pretty firm all over and the bottom is golden brown, cook the top. Do this either by inverting the omelet onto a plate and slipping it back into the pan, uncooked side downwards, or by putting the pan under a hot broiler (grill).

Serve with the crumbled oregano sprinkled over the top as a garnish.

OPPOSITE: Green Chili and Cheese Souffléed Casserole

LEAH'S STIRRED ZUCCHINI FRITTATA
Serves 2 as a brunch, lunch, or supper dish

This simple dish of grated zucchini (courgettes), bound together with creamy eggs and melted cheese, is a soft scramble rather than an omelet or frittata. It is simplicity itself to prepare and is unpretentious, yet its flavor and fragrance are heady and its soft, yielding texture is inviting. As with so many simple dishes, it can easily be 'smartened up' by serving it spooned over garlic-rubbed toast or into a crisp tartlet case, nestled next to sliced ripe tomatoes, or stuffed into crisp, hollowed-out and baked potato skins.

Accompany this dish with pan-roasted herbed potato chunks and follow with a salad of delicate soft-leaved lettuce scattered with a few ripe blackberries and a little chopped fresh mint, splashed with a little olive oil and balsamic vinegar. For dessert, spoon sliced nectarines or sweet peaches over praline ice cream and drizzle with Frangelico liqueur.

This was my daughter Leah's favorite dish when she was quite small and spooned the mixture in with chubby, eager hands. These days the tables are turned and she is more likely to prepare it for me, with hands far more elegant and graceful than my own.

4 medium zucchini (courgettes), coarsely grated
2 teaspoons olive oil, or more if necessary
2 garlic cloves, chopped
4 eggs, lightly beaten
8 oz. (250 g) mild cheddar or mozzarella cheese, diced
½ teaspoon dried oregano
2 tablespoons fresh basil, thinly sliced or chopped
1 tablespoon grated fresh Parmesan cheese

Squeeze out any excess moisture from the grated zucchini. Quickly stir-fry or sauté the zucchini in the olive oil. Add the garlic, stir, then pour in the eggs and cheddar or mozzarella cheese.

Let the mixture set for a minute, then stir to scramble it into soft curds as it continues cooking (just a few minutes). Pour off any liquid that accumulates in the pan. Serve immediately, with the basil and Parmesan sprinkled over the top.

Variation
ZUCCHINI FRITTATA PIZZA: Make an omelet from the above mixture. Prepare as above, but do not stir. When cooked nearly all the way through, spread the top with a thinnish layer of tomato purée (passata), sprinkle extra garlic and the oregano over the top, and

a layer of grated mozzarella, fontina, or other cheese over that. Broil (grill) the top until the cheese is melted and sizzling. Serve hot, cut into pizza-like wedges.

GREEN CHILI AND CHEESE SOUFFLEED CASSEROLE
Serves 4–6

This really homely casserole is classic Californian brunch fare. The puffy chili and cheese mixture can be made ahead and reheated, or served at room temperature. The ingredients can be doubled to cater for a large party or the mixture may be baked in small soufflé dishes for individual portions. For a more contemporary accent, add several ounces of crumbled goat cheese in addition to or in place of the cottage cheese, as well as a roasted, peeled, and diced poblano chili and a sprinkling of fresh coriander.

butter, for greasing
5 eggs
¼ cup (1 oz., 30 g) self-rising flour
8 oz. (250 g) natural cottage cheese
8 oz. (250 g) white cheese (sharp cheddar, Monterey Jack, etc.), grated
2 tablespoons butter, melted
1 x 7-oz. (225-g) can mild green chili peppers, drained and diced or 1 green sweet pepper (capsicum), roasted, peeled, diced, and tossed in a little cayenne pepper and salt
salt and freshly ground black pepper, to taste
pinch of ground cumin or toasted cumin seeds (see p. 144)

Preheat the oven to 350°F (180°C) and grease a baking dish with the butter.

Beat the eggs in a bowl, then sift the flour into the bowl and mix them together well. Add the remaining ingredients, mix well, then pour the batter into the buttered baking dish.

Bake in the preheated oven for 35 minutes or so, until the casserole has puffed up and set, and a knife inserted into the center comes out clean. Only check its progress towards the end of the cooking, otherwise the blast of cooler air when you open the door could deflate it.

Breads, Tarts, & Sandwiches

BREADS AND OTHER BAKED GOODS

Really good bread is something that I grew up with. At the time I didn't fully appreciate it, though I did marvel at how on earth other people could enjoy a meal accompanied by a plate of bland, limp sliced white.

We had sourdough French bread, that gastronomic souvenir of the Gold Rush, crusty on the outside, sharp tasting and meltingly tender within. We also ate substantial rye bread studded with caraway seeds and pumpernickel the color of chocolate. Bagels for Sunday mornings, of course, eggy challah bread for Friday nights, and lovely tortillas whenever my mother had a yearning for Mexican foods. Health food enthusiasts, of which my grandfather was one,

promoted whole-wheat (wholemeal) and wholegrain (granary) bread. We hated it when we were little, but as we grew we learned to dote on the grainy, slightly nutty flavor of the wheaty bread.

The last several decades have seen a virtual bread revolution. Whole-wheat breads have gone from being made or bought by the hippie-healthy minority to being found delicious by the majority, and supermarket shelves are full of breads of all kinds. Specialty breads such as pita, bagels, and Eastern European multigrain breads have become everyday, mainstream foods. Small bakeries have cropped up,

OPPOSITE: *Three Onion and Cheese Bread (top left), Savory Oatmeal and Yogurt American Biscuits (center right), and Grated Zucchini Teabread (bottom left)*

producing French- and Italian-style breads so crisp, crusty, and deliciously yeasty that they seriously rival any of those made in their homelands. There is no excuse for buying bad bread these days, indeed, you will seldom be served it. In California, as in much of Europe, many people purchase fresh bread every day.

Baking at home is not such a tradition in California as it is in other regions of the USA, where the bakeries maybe are not so inviting and where the weather is more conducive to long afternoons spent tending the oven. I have not included recipes for basic Italian, French, or crusty-loaved breads as these are best purchased from a good source. Their bread is actually better than home-made for two reasons: the quality of the yeast and wood-burning ovens, which have higher temperatures and a specific humidity not possible with domestic ovens, create the crispiest crusts and the tenderest middles.

THREE ONION AND CHEESE BREAD

Makes two 1-lb. (500-g) loaves

Studded with onions, flavored with bits of cheese melted in, onion and cheese bread is a specialty of Solvang, a tiny re-created Danish village in the Santa Ynez Valley just outside Santa Barbara. At one point, I was regularly driving from Los Angeles to San Francisco, and I always stopped off to buy a loaf of this bread and a container of blissfully good pickled cucumbers. I find this rich, cheesy bread particularly good with White Bean Pâté (see p. 30).

This bread is very moist and heavy and, although it is very good hot from the oven, spread with butter to melt in and sprinkled with a bit of sea salt, it is even better the next day, accompanied by sharp, tangy, fresh things, such as a vinaigrette-dressed salad.

1 envelope (1 tablespoon) instant dried yeast
9 cups (2 ¼ lbs., 1.125 kg) strong bread flour
1 onion, chopped
about 6 scallions (spring onions), thinly sliced
1¼ oz. (40 g) dried onions
2 cups (16 fl. oz., 500 ml) lukewarm water
    (105°–115°F (40.5°–46°C))
2 teaspoons salt
12 oz. (375 g) sharp cheese (cheddar or Asiago), diced
2 teaspoons cumin seeds or dried basil or dried dill

Mix the yeast with the flour, then add the onions, water, and salt. Mix all these ingredients together until they are well combined, then knead on a lightly floured surface until it becomes a smooth, elastic dough (about 10 minutes).

Place the dough in a lightly oiled bowl and cover with a damp cloth (see p. 122). Leave in a warm place to rise for about an hour, or until the dough has doubled in size.

Turn the risen dough out onto a lightly floured surface, punch it in the middle, then knead in the cheese and cumin seeds or basil or dill. Divide the dough between two oiled loaf pans to rise again to double their size in the pans (about 40 minutes).

Meanwhile, preheat the oven to 400°F (200°C). Spray or lightly brush the loaves with water, which encourages the formation of a nice, crisp crust, then bake in the hot oven for 10 minutes. Now reduce the heat to 350°F (180°C) and continue baking for 30–45 minutes, or until the loaves have browned and sound hollow when they are removed from the pans and tapped on the bottom.

Variation

ONION AND BLACK OLIVE BREAD: Omit the cheese and, instead, knead in a generous handful of pitted, halved, black oil-cured olives, plus such fragrant fresh herbs as rosemary.

TWO SAVORY OATMEAL AND YOGURT AMERICAN BISCUITS

Makes 12–16

An American biscuit is not crisp and crunchy like a cracker, but soft and tender, more like a savory British scone in texture. Traditionally, they have been served with hearty stews or for breakfast, buttered and drizzled with honey. In California, biscuits are apt to be enjoyed as a weekend brunch meal and, chock-full of aromatic seasonings, they have come a long way from their homely origins.

The following biscuit has a very tender middle, due to the addition of yogurt, and the porridge oats add fiber, protein, and a more savory flavor. The basic recipe is given first below, together with two alternative flavoring mixtures for distinctive little pastries, as easy to throw together as they are to eat. Both flavors are delectable. Hot, I like the cheese and scallion (spring onion) ones best — with the rich cheese and pungent onion flavor, and crispy coating of Parmesan — but cooled, it is the sun-dried tomato and thyme ones that win hands down, especially when spread with a little tangy goat cheese.

BASIC BISCUIT RECIPE

2 oz. (60 g) porridge oats
1 cup (8 fl. oz., 250 ml) plain yogurt
3 cups (12 oz., 375 g) all-purpose (plain) flour
1 teaspoon salt
2 teaspoons baking powder
5 tablespoons vegetable oil

SAVORY CHEDDAR, PARMESAN, AND SCALLION FLAVORING

6 oz. (185 g) sharp cheddar cheese, finely diced
3–4 scallions (spring onions), thinly sliced
3–4 tablespoons grated Parmesan cheese

SUN-DRIED TOMATO AND THYME FLAVORING

8–10 sun-dried tomatoes, finely diced
5 tablespoons oil from the jar of sun-dried tomatoes instead
of the vegetable oil in the basic recipe
2–3 teaspoons coarsely chopped fresh thyme

Mix the porridge oats with the yogurt, and leave the mixture to rest for 5–10 minutes (this softens the oats).

Mix the flour, salt, and baking powder together with a fork, then mix in the oil, using a pastry cutter or your fingers to mix the ingredients together until the mixture resembles fine crumbs.

Preheat the oven to 450°F (230°C). Mix in the oat and yogurt mixture, then turn out the doughy mixture onto a floured surface. Knead it 8–10 times (the dough will be very sticky). Add whichever flavoring mixture you have chosen and knead it in. Roll the dough out to a thickness of about ¼ in. (5 mm). Cut rounds using a cookie or biscuit cutter, or a drinking glass dipped into flour, or use a knife to cut diamond shapes rather than rounds. Alternatively, do not roll the dough out, but lightly oil your hands, pull small amounts of dough from the ball, roll into balls, then pat flat.

Put the biscuits on greased or oiled baking sheets. Bake in the preheated oven for about 15 minutes or until they have risen and turned a light golden brown color. Transfer to a cooling rack to cool.

GRATED ZUCCHINI TEABREAD
*Makes two 9-in. (23-cm) loaves **or** 10–12 portions*

Grated zucchini (courgettes) give moisture to this mildly sweet teabread. It is delicious hot or at room temperature, and even better toasted and buttered. Though the wheat softens a bit as it sits with the wet ingredients, it remains whole and grainy. Fresh and hot from the oven, the grains are still a bit hard, but as the cake sits and cools, the grains soften.

Sweet teabreads made from grated vegetables and fruits may seem a bit strange to some, but such breads and muffins have enjoyed great popularity in California for at least the past 20 years. Beet (beetroot), carrot, apple, yellow summer squash, pumpkin — all are good additions to this cake in place of some or all of the zucchini.

The grated vegetable or fruit gives moisture and texture to the basic sweet batter. I remember my great grandmother making a carrot cake and I thought it was the height of delicious strangeness.

In place of the raisins, during the time when cranberries are in season, add a generous handful of these tart, piquant berries to the batter. Delicious.

4 oz. (125 g) fine-grain bulghur wheat (burghul)
2 eggs, lightly beaten
5 fl. oz. (155 ml) vegetable oil
¾ cup (6 oz., 185 g) golden demerara (raw) sugar
1 teaspoon vanilla extract (essence)
12 oz. (375 g) zucchini (courgettes), coarsely grated
*   (about 4)*
2 cups (8 oz., 250 g) all-purpose (plain) flour, sifted
½ teaspoon salt
1½ teaspoons ground cinnamon
2 teaspoons baking soda (bicarbonate of soda)
¾ cup (4 oz., 125 g) golden raisins (sultanas) or raisins

Preheat the oven to 325°F (170°C).

Place bulghur wheat in a bowl and over it pour boiling water to cover. Let stand for 30 minutes, then drain well and set aside to cool.

Beat the eggs until they are light and foamy, then add the oil, sugar, vanilla, zucchini, and bulghur wheat. Mix the remaining dry ingredients together, including the sultanas or raisins, then add them to the wet ingredients. Mix them only until they are well combined.

Pour the mixture into two oiled 9-in. (23-cm) loaf pans or one flat rectangular baking pan. Bake for 40–50 minutes, or until a sharp knife or skewer comes out clean when poked into the center.

SEEDED MULTIGRAIN BREAD

Makes two 1-lb. (500-g) loaves

A rustic, hearty loaf, studded with seeds and grains, this makes a particularly good accompaniment to a salad and cheese lunch or soup supper.

2 teaspoons dried yeast
¼ cup (2 fl. oz., 60 ml) warm water
3 tablespoons honey
2 tablespoons vegetable oil, plus extra for greasing
2–2½ cups (16–18 fl. oz., 500–560 ml) lukewarm water (85°F (29.5°C))
4½ cups (1¼ lbs., 625 g) whole-wheat (wholemeal) flour
2 cups (8 oz., 250 g) strong white bread flour
½ cup (2 oz., 60 g) oatmeal
⅓ cup (2 oz., 60 g) bulghur wheat (burghul)
3 oz. (90 g) millet
3 tablespoons poppy seeds
1 teaspoon salt
6 oz. (185 g) sunflower seeds
1 egg white beaten with 1 tablespoon water

Add the yeast to the ¼ cup (2 fl. oz., 60 ml) warm water, stirring until it has dissolved. Leave this liquid to stand until it is foamy (about 10 minutes).

In a large bowl, combine the honey, oil, and lukewarm water with the prepared yeast mixture.

Add the whole-wheat flour and mix it well with the other ingredients using a wooden spoon or in a heavy-duty mixer equipped with a dough hook. When well mixed, add the strong bread flour, oatmeal, bulghur, millet, poppy seeds, and salt. Turn the dough out onto a lightly floured board. Knead it well with floured hands for about 10 minutes, adding more flour if needed. About halfway through kneading, add half of the sunflower seeds. The dough is ready when it is smooth and elastic, and springs back when poked.

Lightly grease a large bowl with vegetable oill, then put the dough into it, turning it so that the whole of the outside of the dough is lightly oiled. Cover the bowl with a clean cloth and leave the dough to rise, or 'prove', in a warm place until it has doubled in size (1½ to 2 hours). Turn the dough out onto a floured surface, punch it in the center, and knead again for 5 minutes.

Cut the dough in half and form two equal-sized loaves. Roll them in the remaining sunflower seeds, pressing the seeds into the loaves. Leave them to rise as before until they have doubled in size again (about 45 minutes). While the loaves are rising, preheat the oven to 375°F (190°C).

Put the loaves on a lightly oiled baking sheet with a gap between them, brush the tops with the egg white mixture. Sprinkle any leftover sunflower seeds on top. Alternatively, they may be baked in loaf pans. Bake for 35–45 minutes, or until the loaves sound hollow when tapped on the bottom.

PRUNE AND GOLDEN RAISIN TEABREAD

Makes one 9-in. (23-cm) loaf or about 8 portions

California's fledgling prune industry got off to a quirky start. In 1905, when grower Mark Seely was faced with a shortage of labor for picking the fruit, he imported 500 monkeys from Central America to carry out the task. Arranged in groups of 50, each with a human director, the monkeys were a picture of efficiency; they picked each and every plum in sight — then they cleverly, greedily, ate them all.

This is a lovely teabread, not too sweet and with plenty of prunes and golden raisins (sultanas). When it is fresh from the oven, serve it hot spread with a little butter. I like it best when it is several days old, when the spices have a chance to meld in and mellow.

¾ cup (6 fl. oz., 185 ml) boiling water or hot tea
7 oz. (225 g) pitted prunes, chopped
2½ oz. (75 g) butter, plus extra for greasing
⅔ cup (5 oz., 155 g) light demerara (raw) sugar or half white sugar and half dark demerara sugar
1 egg
1½ cups (6 oz., 185 g) self-rising flour, sifted
¼ teaspoon salt
generous pinch of ground or grating of fresh nutmeg
½ teaspoon ground cinnamon
½ teaspoon vanilla extract (essence)
½ teaspoon almond extract (essence)
⅓ cup (2 oz., 60 g) golden raisins (sultanas)

Preheat the oven to 350°F (180°C) and grease and flour the loaf or cake pan. Pour the boiling water or tea over the prunes and butter, cover, and leave until the mixture has cooled to room temperature.

Beat the sugar(s) and egg into the prunes and butter, mixing until the mixture is creamy. Sift the flour, salt, nutmeg, and cinnamon together. Add to the creamed mixture with the remaining ingredients, mixing them in well.

Pour the batter into the prepared pan. Bake for 45–60 minutes, or until a knife or skewer inserted into the center comes out clean. Remove from the oven and serve hot or leave to cool.

BREAD AND SALAD

Bread and salad make a wonderful meal: simple, fresh, a balance of textures and flavors. It is a cozy, intimate meal that satisfies the senses as much as the appetite, tearing off a chunk of fresh, doughy bread and using it to pick up a colorful tomato wedge or biting into a sprig of fresh herbs that burst with flavor, and using a morsel of bread to wipe up the last bits of delicious dressing. My favorite suppers, especially in the summer, are based on a trip to farm markets — the evening's menu being influenced by what is best and freshest there. Fresh vegetables, all seasoned in varying and intriguing ways, scented with different herbs and aromatics accompanied by a crusty loaf and, perhaps, a plate of fresh goat or other local cheese. With little preparation involved and just a dash of imagination, you have a meal that takes literally minutes to put together and is likely to be just as memorable as a meal that required an all-day cooking marathon to produce it.

The things that make bread and salad meals memorable are the freshness of the salad ingredients and really good bread. Choose any of the salads in this book and pair them with your favorite loaf or choose from the following suggestions:

- leafy greens, fresh basil and chives, large crumbs of Roquefort or Spanish blue cheese, served with fresh baguette
- tomatoes, black oil-cured olives, sliced scallions (spring onions) or chives, goat cheese, and basil or marjoram in an olive oil vinaigrette, served with fresh *ciabatta*
- beets (beetroot), potatoes, green or string beans, tomato wedges, arugula (rocket), hard-boiled egg, with aïoli, served with olive bread
- tomatoes, basil, and onions, served atop slices of Three Onion and Cheese Bread (see p. 120).

ABOVE: *Prune and Golden Raisin Teabread*

SANDWICHES

Sandwiches are very popular in America. California is no exception to this passion, yet the sandwiches eaten here are a far cry from what is usually dished out in delis Coast to Coast.

Sandwiches in the rest of the country tend towards meat or cheese, but in California, *vegetable* sandwiches reign, so much so that even non-vegetarian sandwiches are rich with vegetables and most cafés offer innovative non-meat sandwiches.

Throughout this book you will find recipes suitable for sandwiching. Grilled vegetables, for example, make superb fillings (see 'Grilled foods', pp. 75–85, for several savory sandwiches), as do stir-fries (try the Many Treasure Vegetables with Pita Bread and Hoisin Sauce on p. 90). Appetizer spreads, such as hummus, make excellent fillings for pita bread sandwiches and many of the Californian sauces and relishes (see under 'Spreads and dips', pp. 25–34) transform even the simplest cheese sandwich.

Fillings, both hot and cold, breads from nearly every ethnic extraction possible, highly seasoned spreads, butters, aïolis, or vinaigrettes, and fresh herbs, together with an adventuresome spirit to try new combinations, make Californian sandwiches distinctively different from sandwiches you will find anywhere else, so stand out from the crowd and import some of the best tastes.

COLD SANDWICHES

ARUGULA, GOAT CHEESE, AND GREEN OLIVE CIABATTA OR FOCACCIA SANDWICH
Serves 1

This is especially good when prepared on a rosemary-scented Italian-style bread. The flavor of the goat cheese pairs perfectly with the fresh, nippy arugula (rocket), and briny green olives accent them both.

A rough red wine is delicious sipped alongside, and it all tastes best when eaten outdoors.

1 thick slice rosemary-flavored ciabatta or focaccia
2 oz. (60 g) goat cheese (Montrachet, Lezay, etc.)
2–3 plump green olives, pitted and halved
2–3 arugula (rocket) leaves

Spread the goat cheese over the bread and stud the top with the olives. Lay the arugula leaves on top and serve immediately.

EGG SALAD WITH SCALLIONS, WHOLEGRAIN MUSTARD, AND CAPERS OR SUN-DRIED TOMATOES
Serves 2

Finely chopped egg mixed with creamy mayonnaise, the jolt of mustard, pungent scallions (spring onions), and either the briny capers or sun-dried tomatoes make for a brightly flavored filling to go between slices of nearly any sort of bread, be it crusty French, tender rye, nutty whole-wheat (wholemeal), or whatever you have.

A handful of arugula (rocket), *mesclun* leaves, or watercress makes a crunchy contrast to the rich filling.

3 hard-boiled eggs, shelled and diced
3 tablespoons mayonnaise, or as needed, plus extra for spreading
2 teaspoons wholegrain mustard, or to taste
3 scallions (spring onions), thinly sliced
salt and freshly ground black pepper, to taste
generous pinch of fresh tarragon, chopped (optional)
1 teaspoon capers or about 5 sun-dried tomatoes, diced
4 slices bread
handful of salad leaves (watercress, lettuce, mesclun, arugula (rocket), etc.)

Combine the egg with the mayonnaise, mustard, and scallions, then season with the salt and pepper, and the tarragon (if using). Add the capers or sun-dried tomatoes.

Spread mayonnaise on each of the slices of bread, then spread the egg mixture on two of the slices. Top with the salad leaves, then the remaining slices of bread. Serve immediately or keep well-wrapped in a cool place until lunchtime.

OPPOSITE: *Arugula, Goat Cheese, and Green Olive Ciabatta or Focaccia Sandwich (top) and Egg Salad with Scallions, Wholegrain Mustard, and Capers or Sun-dried Tomatoes (bottom)*

Avocado, Tomato, and Sprouts on Whole-Wheat Bread with Ranch-style Spread

Serves 1

Ranch-style dressings and spreads, based on mayonnaise mixed with yogurt or sour cream and punchy seasonings of garlic, black pepper, and parsley, give this sandwich its particular Californian tang. It is the sort of mixture you would find at sandwich shops and street vendors throughout the Golden State.

2 slices whole-wheat (wholemeal) bread (preferably wholegrain (granary))
2 tablespoons or so Creamy Ranch-style Dressing (see p. 143) or mayonnaise
½ avocado, sliced
1–2 ripe tomatoes, thinly sliced
generous handful of alfalfa sprouts
2 oz. (60 g) or so cheddar or other firm cheese, thinly sliced or grated (optional)
handful of sunflower seeds, toasted (optional)

Spread both pieces of the bread with the Creamy Ranch-style Dressing or mayonnaise, then top one piece with the avocado slices, tomatoes, and sprouts. (If using the optional cheese, put it onto the bread before the avocado and if using the sunflower seeds, sprinkle them over the Ranch-style Dressing.)

Place the other piece of bread on top, cut into halves, and serve.

HOT SANDWICHES

Hot sandwiches are enticing and filling. I have been a devotee ever since the first bite of my first hot sandwich — the bread was crusty and the filling oozed deliciously.

Garlic-rubbed Rye Bread Topped with Melted Feta and Monterey Jack

Serves 2

Good rye bread, with caraway seeds and a cornmeal crust, is everyday fare in most of California because of the large Jewish community, especially in Los Angeles.

The following open sandwich is a delicious contrast of crunchy toasty bread, strong garlic, and tangy cheeses that is wonderful and simple. It makes a nice snack, accompanying a glass of wine or a hearty weekend breakfast.

2 slices rye bread
2 garlic cloves, whole
2 oz. (60 g) feta cheese, sliced or crumbled
3–4 oz. (90–125 g) white, melting cheese (Monterey Jack, cheddar), sliced

Lightly toast the bread under the broiler (grill) on one side only, then leave to cool a little. When cool enough to handle, rub each of the toasted sides with a clove of the garlic. The rough surface of the toast acts like a little grater, breaking off tiny bits of garlic and garlic juices, trapping its lovely strong flavor and aroma as no other technique can.

Top the untoasted side of each garlic-rubbed toast with a layer of the feta cheese, then a layer of the Monterey Jack or cheddar. Just place the cheese haphazardly on the bread so that there are areas not covered with cheese or covered with just one type for a variety of textures.

Broil (grill) until the cheese melts and sizzles, then serve immediately.

Black Bean and Cheese-stuffed Pita Breads

Serves 4

Californian dining is the epitome of the word cross-cultural: Italian sauces with Chinese noodles, French sauces with Japanese vegetables, risotto with Thai ingredients, polenta with south-of-the-border flavors. Pita bread has thus become as Californian as San Franciscan sourdough bread.

Pita bread is delicious stuffed with any sort of savory ingredient, no matter what its ethnic origin. Not limited to the Middle Eastern flavors that originally accompanied it, pita bread is apt to come stuffed with cheese, pizza-style, or with mayonnaise-based salads, vegetable burgers, crunchy vegetable salads, or a whole host of other mixtures. For example, I recently visited some Israeli friends living in San Francisco and they served take-out Chinese stir-fried vegetables tucked into pita bread, and it was very good. Equally, the hearty and spicy flavors of Mexican food blend exceptionally well with pita breads, and they make an excellent substitute if flour tortillas are unavailable. They are delicious in their own right, too, stuffed with beans, cheese, chilied salsas, and fresh vegetables.

4 pita breads, slit along the side to form a pocket
½ x recipe Black Bean Chili (see p. 94), mashed
8 oz. (250 g) cheddar cheese, thinly sliced or grated
small amount of oil, for frying

TOPPINGS
½ cup (4 fl. oz., 125 ml) or so sour cream or yogurt
½ avocado, sliced
3 ripe tomatoes, diced
2–3 fresh chili peppers, chopped
3–4 scallions (spring onions), chopped
2 tablespoons chopped fresh coriander
small handful of lettuce, shredded

Stuff some of the bean mixture into each pita pocket, together with the cheese, then press each down well to seal it and make a flattish disc.

Heat a tiny amount of oil in a skillet or frying pan so that the pitas cook without either frying or sticking. Cook over a medium-high heat until the pita is flecked with golden brown spots and the cheese has melted inside.

Serve immediately, topping each pita with the sour cream or yogurt, avocado, tomato, chili, scallion, coriander, and lettuce, to taste.

Variation
For a quick, easier-to-prepare sandwich, use canned refried beans in place of the home-cooked black beans. In California, black beans are easy to find in cans; if you find them difficult to get, look in Spanish delicatessens for them or use canned refried beans. Whichever you use, season appropriately.

BELOW: Black Bean and Cheese-stuffed Pita Breads

BAGELS AND MELTED BRIE

Serves 1

Every morning I used to begin my day by stopping off at my favorite café, a gathering place for freelance writers and artists. There, with the *San Francisco Chronicle* spread out on the table and the day spread out ahead of me, I reveled in a cup of strong, dark roast coffee, accompanied by toasted bagels topped with melted Brie.

Each time my teeth crunched through the melted, ripe cheese into the crisp and crunchy bagel underneath, I marveled at how something so simple could be so utterly delicious.

*1 really good bagel (favorites are onion, garlic,
  or pumpernickel)*
4 oz. (125 g), or to taste, ripe, runny Brie

ACCOMPANIMENT
Strong, dark roast coffee or strong tea

Slice the bagel in half and toast the cut side to a crunchy golden brown.

Slice the cheese onto the hot bagel halves and, as the cheese melts, spread it so that it covers the whole surface in a thick layer. Enjoy immediately.

POTATO, GREEN BEAN, AND CARROT TOSTADAS TOPPED WITH CORIANDER CREAM

Serves 4

Crisp, fried tortillas, known as *tostadas*, make an excellent base for a wide variety of toppings, also known as tostadas. Refried beans, any saucy dish, crunchy, fresh salady ingredients — all are heaped onto the fried tortilla, which acts as a sort of edible plate. Tostadas have been adopted, like so many Mexican dishes, into the mainstream of Californian cooking.

The following tostadas comprise a chilied vegetable mixture served on top of bean and cheese topped tortillas, embellished with a cooling mixture of coriander and sour cream.

2 tablespoons olive oil
2 medium potatoes, peeled and diced
1 carrot, diced
3 garlic cloves, coarsely chopped
1 teaspoon mild chili powder
1 teaspoon paprika
1/2 teaspoon ground cumin

*8 oz. (250 g) green or string beans, cut into
  bite-sized lengths*
4 tomatoes, diced
salt, to taste
1 x recipe or canned refried beans (see p. 108)
8 crisp, fried corn tortillas or store-bought tostada shells
6 oz. (185 g) melting cheese, sliced or grated

CORIANDER CREAM
1/2 cup (4 fl. oz., 125 ml) sour cream or yogurt
2 tablespoons chopped fresh coriander
2 tablespoons thinly sliced scallions (spring onions)

ACCOMPANIMENTS
*hot salsa or pickled chili peppers or sliced fresh chili
  peppers, to taste*

In the olive oil, sauté the potato and carrot until they have browned lightly. Add the garlic, mild chili powder, paprika, and cumin. Cook for a minute or two longer. Add the beans and tomatoes, and cook for another 5–10 minutes or until the topping has thickened a little. Season with the salt and then put to one side.

Heat the beans with 1–2 tablespoons water until the mixture is hot and spreadable, then spread it over the tostadas. Top with the cheese.

Broil (grill) the tostadas until the cheese melts.

Meanwhile, combine the sour cream with the coriander and scallions.

Top each tostada with a spoonful of the vegetable mixture, then another of the herbed sour cream. Serve immediately, with the accompaniments for people to help themselves to.

Variation
TORTAS DE LEGUMBRES: Using four crusty rolls instead of the corn tostadas makes a totally delicious Mexican street sandwich, beloved of the Hispanic neighborhoods of California as much as south of the border. Cut each roll open and spread with butter, other spread or olive oil. Lightly grill the cut surfaces until they are golden brown, then stuff each roll with the hot refried beans, cheese, and vegetables. Serve immediately with the Coriander Cream and spicy chili accompaniments.

OPPOSITE: *Potato, Green Bean, and Carrot Tostadas Topped with Coriander Cream*

MELTED CHEESE-TOPPED FLOUR TORTILLAS WITH ROASTED SWEET PEPPERS AND GREEN OLIVES

Serves 2

All sorts of tortillas are easily available in California. Even the smallest shop in the tiniest, most unpromising town is likely to have a supply (in the freezer, if not fresh). Traditional corn tortillas, blue corn tortillas, chili-seasoned tortillas, whole-wheat (wholemeal) tortillas, soft, tender white wheat tortillas (ranging in size from 'snack size' — 4 in. (10 cm) in diameter — to huge ones — about 18 in. (48 cm)).

By the way, the name *tortilla* comes from the Spanish word for 'little cake' and was given to the Indian flat breads of the New World when Spanish settlers did not know the local languages describing the wide variety of foods that formed (and still do) their diet.

Tortillas make quick, nutritious snacks and small meals simply and easily. Heated in a pan until soft and fragrant, they are delicious topped with nearly anything, from complex chili sauces, cheeses, simmered beans, and stews, to plain butter and jam.

Here, flour tortillas are topped with cheese, green olives, and roasted red sweet peppers (capsicums).

While a cheese topping might be traditionally Mexican, the olives are distinctly Mediterranean and locally produced roasted red sweet peppers have become a staple in the Californian pantry.

As tortillas are not always easy to find elsewhere, pita breads may be used in their place in this dish. Split the pita breads into two single-layer, pancake-like circles, then proceed with the recipe as for tortillas.

2 flour tortillas or pita breads (see above)
4–6 oz. (125–185 g) cheese of choice (Monterey Jack, cheddar, fontina, etc.), thinly sliced or coarsely grated
1 fresh or bottled red sweet pepper (capsicum), roasted and peeled, then cut into strips
5–8 pimento-stuffed green olives, sliced

ACCOMPANIMENTS
hot sauce (such as salsa or Tabasco), to taste
mustard, to taste

Top each tortilla or pita round with the cheese, then scatter the pepper and olive over the top.

Grill until the cheese has melted and lightly browned in places.

Serve immediately with the accompaniment of your choice.

Toasted Country Bread with Peruvian Chili, Tomato, and Cheese Topping

Serves 4–6

The spicy topping of tomatoes and cheese melts seductively onto the crusty bread for a toasted cheese sandwich that is special enough to serve to the fussiest of guests — as long as they like spicy foods, that is.

Turmeric and ginger are unexpected elements in this dish, yet it is an authentic Peruvian seasoning mixture, as a result of the various traders and voyagers who overlaid their own culture atop the native Inca one. The Eastern spicing combines with the Latin American ingredients of tomatoes, chilies, cumin, and cheese, each enhancing the other's own strong character.

2 medium onions, coarsely chopped
3 garlic cloves, chopped
1 fresh green chili pepper, more if needed
2 tablespoons olive oil
1½ teaspoons ground turmeric
1 teaspoon ground cumin
¼ teaspoon ground ginger
1 lb. (500 g) fresh or canned tomatoes, chopped
1 oz. (30 g) fresh coriander, chopped
8 oz. (250 g) mild cheddar cheese, cubed
½ cup (4 fl. oz., 125 ml) sour cream or Greek yogurt
salt and freshly ground black pepper, to taste
4–6 large slices country bread, cut on a bias,
    or 8–12 normal-sized slices

GARNISH
4 oz. (125 g) green or string beans, quickly cooked and
    cooled to room temperature
8–12 black olives (niçoise, kalamata, or oil-cured)

Lightly sauté the onions, garlic, and chili pepper in the olive oil until the onions have softened (about 5 minutes). Sprinkle in the turmeric, cumin, and ginger, stir together, and cook for another minute or two. Add the tomatoes and coriander, and cook over medium-low heat until most of the liquid has evaporated (about 10 minutes).

Stir in the cheese and sour cream or yogurt. Slowly heat until it forms a cheesy, creamy mixture. Season with salt and pepper, then leave to cool to room temperature and chill until it has become quite firm.

Spread each slice of bread thickly with the chilled cheese mixture, then broil (grill) until the edges of the bread are golden brown and the cheese has melted and is sizzling hot. Serve garnished with a handful of green beans and olives alongside.

Garlic and Pesto Bread

Serves 4–6

Incredibly garlicky and heady with the sweet fragrance of basil, this is a deliciously addictive garlic bread. The mixture of butter and olive oil seems to be the best of all worlds: butter's rich sweet flavor and olive oil's monounsaturates and strong flavor. The exact amounts do not really matter — the ones given below are a guideline only, so adjust them to suit your tastes and what you have on hand.

6 garlic cloves, finely chopped
4 oz. (125 g) unsalted butter, softened
½ cup (4 fl. oz., 125 ml) olive oil
½ teaspoon garlic granules, or to taste
salt and white pepper, to taste
3–4 tablespoons pesto, or to taste
1 French stick, sliced lengthwise, then into thick
    crosswise slices

Preheat the oven to 400°F (200°C).

In a food processor or blender, or in a bowl, mix the garlic with the butter, then blend in the olive oil until it is well mixed in and the mixture is smooth.

Season to taste with the garlic granules, salt, pepper, and pesto.

Spread the mixture thickly on the bread, taking care to coat all the cut surfaces, even the sides or the bottom that may lay on the baking sheet.

Place the bread on a baking sheet and bake in the preheated oven for about 15 minutes or until the bread has browned and is crusty on the edges. Enjoy immediately.

Leftovers

BOILED POTATOES WITH ROASTED GARLIC AND PESTO BUTTER: Combine any leftover garlic-pesto butter at warm room temperature with 5–10 cooled, whole, roasted garlic cloves. Spread this butter on boiled potatoes that are, likewise, at room temperature. Garnish with greens such as parsley, basil, or arugula (rocket).

OPPOSITE: *Two-Layer Spinach and Red Sweet Pepper Torta*

THREE SAVORY TARTS

TWO-LAYER SPINACH AND RED SWEET PEPPER TORTA

Serves 6

This crustless vegetable tart tastes richly of creamy ricotta, chopped spinach, and red sweet peppers. It is especially delicious eaten at cool room temperature, so is perfect for a picnic lunch or as an appetizer, served with a selection of other savory tidbits, such as a plate of olives, Florence fennel (finocchio) and red onion, roasted sweet peppers (capsicums) dressed in vinaigrette, or ripe tomatoes topped with shredded basil leaves and a splash of brandy.

1¼ lbs. (625 g) ricotta cheese
2 oz. (60 g) Parmesan cheese, freshly grated
3 garlic cloves, chopped
1 teaspoon fresh thyme and/or rosemary, chopped
2 eggs, lightly beaten
1–2 tablespoons butter or other spread, for greasing

1–1¼ cups (4–5 oz., 125–155 g) fine dry breadcrumbs
4 oz. (125 g) cooked spinach, squeezed dry and coarsely chopped (about 1 lb. (500 g) fresh spinach)
2 red sweet peppers (capsicums), chopped and sautéed, then left to cool

Preheat the oven to 325°F (170°C).

Combine the ricotta with the Parmesan, garlic, thyme and/or rosemary, and eggs.

Butter an 8–9-cup (3½-imp. pint, 2-litre) baking or soufflé dish, and coat the inside evenly with the breadcrumbs.

Divide the cheese mixture between two bowls. Combine one half with the spinach and pour it into the crumb-lined baking dish, smoothing the top. Combine the sautéed pepper with the remaining cheese mixture and pour it carefully over the spinach layer.

Bake the torta in the preheated oven for 40 minutes. Remove from the oven and leave to cool. Chill the torta until you are nearly ready to serve. Loosen the edges with a knife and turn out onto a plate. Let it warm to room temperature and enjoy.

GILROY GARLIC FLAN

Serves 6

A heady scent emanates from this shimmering garlic custard filling — a provocative change of pace from more traditional quiches.

The flan may be prepared either in a large tart pan or in individual tartlet pans. The baking time, however, must be adjusted accordingly. Alternatively, you could bake this purely as a custard, foregoing the pastry shell altogether. Whichever way you prepare it, it is delicious warm, but much better left to cool to room temperature.

Enjoy it as a first course, each portion garnished with a few leaves of mâche (lamb's lettuce, corn salad), arugula (rocket), chives, sprigs of fresh thyme, and/or several pale lavender-colored chive flowers.

30 large garlic cloves, unpeeled
1 tablespoon unsalted butter
1 tablespoon all-purpose (plain) flour
2 cups (16 fl. oz., 500 ml) vegetable broth (see pp. 37–8)
1 tablespoon fresh sage, chopped, or ¼ teaspoon dried
  thyme
freshly ground black pepper and/or cayenne pepper,
  to taste
3 large eggs, lightly beaten
1 cup (8 fl. oz., 250 ml) whipping (double) cream
3½ oz. (100 g) Parmesan cheese, freshly grated
2 garlic cloves, peeled and finely chopped
enough shortcrust pastry to line a 9-in. (23-cm) quiche
  or tart pan (about 12–14 oz. (375–435 g))

Blanch the whole garlic cloves in boiling water for a minute. Drain them well (reserving the cooking water for soup or another use) and leave to cool. When they are cool enough to handle, slip off their skins.

Melt the butter over a medium-low heat and add the flour, stirring and cooking until it is all a very light brown. Remove the pan from the heat and gradually add the broth, stirring until the sauce thickens slightly. Add the whole, blanched and peeled garlic cloves, and cook until the garlic is tender and the sauce has reduced by nearly half (about 10 minutes). Add the sage or thyme, and black and/or cayenne pepper.

Preheat the oven to 325°F (170°C). Whisk the eggs with the cream, Parmesan cheese, and chopped garlic. Gradually whisk in the hot whole garlic sauce until they are well combined, then pour the custard into the unbaked tart shell. Bake until the custard has set and the edges of the pastry shell are golden brown (about 15–20 minutes for tartlets, 30–40 minutes for a large tart). Serve at room temperature.

NACHO AND PAUL'S MEDITERRANEAN VEGETABLE TART TO TAKE ON A PICNIC

Makes one 9-in. (23-cm) tart

When the first warm days of summer are upon us, like all good Californians, I pack a picnic. Growing up in the Central Valley meant that the summer was one long picnic. (This is not as romantic as it sounds for it was just too hot to eat indoors.) In London, I often organize picnics in a pot luck manner, each guest bringing one course, all meeting up on a grassy knoll. On one of these occasions, this sunny tart was brought by friends writer Paul Richardson and Spanish botanist Nacho Trives. It tastes purely of well-cooked vegetables, held together by their own cooking juices and a crisp, light crust. It is even better eaten at room temperature than hot, making it perfect not only for picnics, but also for summer evenings on the terrace or in the garden.

2 medium onions, thinly sliced lengthwise
2 tablespoons olive oil
3 garlic cloves, coarsely chopped
1 red sweet pepper (capsicum), thinly sliced lengthwise
1 green sweet pepper (capsicum), thinly sliced lengthwise
1 medium zucchini (courgette), diced
½–1 teaspoon fresh thyme, crumbled
2 tablespoons tomato purée (passata) or juice
15 oil-cured black olives, pitted and halved
salt and freshly ground black pepper, to taste
pinch of sugar, if needed
9-in. (23-cm) unbaked, unsweetened shortcrust pie shell
  made from all-purpose (plain) or whole-wheat
  (wholemeal) flour (about 12–14 oz. (375–435 g))

Sauté the onions in the olive oil until they are golden brown and very soft. Add the garlic and sweet peppers, and cook until they have softened, then add the zucchini and cook until tender. Add the thyme, tomato purée or juice, and olives. Cook for a minute longer. Taste and adjust the seasoning if necessary with salt, pepper, and sugar. Allow to cool.

Roll out the pastry and line a 9-in. (23-cm) pie pan. Fill the pastry shell with the mixture, then crimp the edges of the pastry. Bake the tart in a 350°–375°F (180°–190°C) oven for 20–25 minutes, or until the edges of the pastry are golden brown and the vegetables have browned in places. Serve immediately or leave to cool and enjoy at room temperature.

OPPOSITE: *Gilroy Garlic Flans (top) and Nacho and Paul's Mediterranean Vegetable Tart to Take on a Picnic*

PIZZAS, CALZONE, PIZZETTAS, AND FOCACCIA

Pizza California-style is likely to be topped with goat cheese, garden or grilled vegetables, wild mushrooms, pestos of all types, chopped garlic, Eastern seasonings, or Mexican salsa — the list continues to include a never-ending array of flavors. This simple Neapolitan snack of tender dough smeared with rough tomato sauce and baked in a wood-burning oven has been transformed on the West Coast into a genre. Nearly anything can top a pizza and often the dough itself is flavored with herbs or spices. Unshackled by tradition, Californian pizza is as exciting as it is satisfying.

For *calzone*, put the filling to one side of the center of the flattened round of dough and fold the uncovered side over to encase the filling, turnover-style. Bake on an oiled baking sheet as for a pizza.

The best pizzas, pizzettas, and *calzoni* are baked in wood-burning ovens, but I have had good results on top of an outdoor barbecue. I made sure, though, that I had either oiled the grill well so that the dough did not stick or used foil underneath the dough.

Pizza dough topped not with sauce but with savory seasonings, perhaps with the seasonings kneaded into the dough itself, makes the Italian–Californian flat bread known as *focaccia*. While trendy *focaccia* is sold in the chicest restaurants and delis, stuffed with all manner of fillings, in days gone by *focaccia* was sold in Italian 'mama and papa' shops, the freshly baked breads piled onto the deli counter, sold within minutes of their delivery from the bakery. Prepare the dough as for pizza, spread out on a baking sheet, but top with a glistening of olive oil, a sprinkling of herbs, chopped onions, olives, and so on, then bake as you would a pizza.

BASIC DOUGH
Makes 1 large pizza or 4 pizzettas

1 level tablespoon dried yeast
1 cup (8 fl. oz., 250 ml) warm water
3 tablespoons olive oil
1 teaspoon salt
3–3½ cups (12–14 oz., 375–435 g) strong bread flour

Sprinkle the yeast over the warm water and leave it for about 10 minutes until it dissolves.

Add the oil, salt, and 2½ cups (10 oz., 310 g) of the flour. Mix until the mixture holds together well.

Knead the dough until it is smooth, elastic, and no longer sticky, on a floured surface, adding more flour if the dough still seems sticky. Place the dough in an oiled bowl and cover with a damp cloth. Leave it to rise in a warm place for about an hour.

To make pizzas, punch the dough in the center and knead a few times and then form either 1 large pizza or 4 pizzettas (individual pizzas). Pat the round(s) out until flat onto an oiled baking sheet, top with the toppings of your choice and bake in a very hot 450°F (230°C) oven until the cheese has melted and lightly browned, and the dough is cooked through.

Variations

GARLIC, GOAT CHEESE, AND MULTICOLORED TOMATO PIZZETTAS: Form 6 individual pizzas from the basic dough, then top each with several tablespoons goat cheese, ½–1 clove finely chopped garlic, diced red, yellow and orange tomatoes (if fresh, peeled and deseeded *or* use chopped canned tomatoes), a little grated mozzarella or Gruyère, and a sprinkle of Parmesan cheese. Drizzle a little olive oil over the top and bake as above. Serve as they are or accompanied by pesto, dried hot red chili flakes, or finely chopped fresh herbs mixed with a little olive oil.

GRILLED EGGPLANT AND PESTO PIZZA: Top the flat, pressed-out dough with sliced, olive oil-brushed and grilled eggplant (aubergine). Dot with several spoonfuls each of pesto and diced, deseeded, and peeled tomatoes. Top with a generous sprinkling of mozzarella and Parmesan cheese, then bake as above.

PIZZA D'ASPARAGI: Top the pressed-out dough with Asparagus Simmered in Garlic-scented Chili-spiked Tomato Sauce (see p. 88), then a layer of thinly sliced mozzarella and a sprinkle of Parmesan cheese. Bake the same as above, then serve with a sprinkling of fresh herbs over the top.

RUSSIAN-FLAVORED PIZZA: Roll the dough out very thinly, top with lots of chopped scallion (spring onion), and brush with olive oil. Bake the same as above, then serve hot, cut into squares, each portion spread with cream cheese.

GARLIC PIZZA: My fragrant favorite. Top the rolled-out dough with masses of chopped garlic, pressing it into the dough, then top with 6–8 oz. (185–250 g) or so of chopped fresh or canned tomatoes, or a smear of purée (passata), then shredded fontina or Asiago cheese, plus a sprinkling of Parmesan, olive oil, and dry crumbled oregano. Bake as above.

GOAT CHEESE AND GRILLED ARTICHOKE PIZZA:
Top the pressed-out dough with garlicky tomato
sauce, spoonfuls of fresh goat cheese, a sprinkling
of fresh herbs, and a layer of thinly sliced, grilled
artichoke hearts. Scatter with grated mild cheese,
such as Monterey Jack or mozzarella, and Parmesan,
then bake as opposite.

GARLICKY SPINACH AND SUN-DRIED TOMATO
PIZZA: Top the pressed-out dough with a smear of
zesty tomato sauce or purée (passata), then a layer of
Garlicky Sautéed Spinach with Sun-dried Tomatoes
(see p. 100). Top with mozzarella and Parmesan, then
bake as directed opposite.

PIZZERIA CALZONE: *Calzoni* can have anything in
them — they can be as trendy or as homely as you
like. Goat cheese is a very popular filling, as are wild
mushrooms, sautéed radicchio, ricotta and mozzarella
or fontina cheese, mixed with vegetables such as mild
green chili peppers, peas, chopped spinach, tomatoes,
and herbs. Our neighborhood pizzeria in San Francisco
serves the following *calzone*: tender dough stuffed
with sautéed mushrooms, black olives, green sweet
peppers (capsicums), and delicious, melting cheeses.
On top is a layer of sauce. Glutton that I am, I always
request extra sauce on the side. Any flavorful tomato
sauce will do — purée (passata) seasoned with garlic
and fresh herbs is delicious.

Divide the pizza dough into 4 to 6 portions and roll
each out thinly. Place several spoonfuls of sautéed
mushrooms to one side of each circle, top with several
pitted black olives, a handful of grated mozzarella, and
a spoonful of cottage or ricotta cheese. Fold the

uncovered half over, brush the edges of the dough with
water, then press together to seal. Place each parcel on
a greased baking sheet, top with a spoonful of purée or
seasoned tomato sauce, and a sprinkling of oregano,
garlic, Parmesan, and olive oil. Bake as opposite.

BLUE CHEESE AND BASIL-STUFFED FRIED BREAD:
Divide the dough into egg-sized chunks and press
them flat. Place a slice of blue cheese in the center,
along with several whole basil leaves, then fold them
up *calzone*-style. Fry them in hot vegetable oil until
they are golden brown, have puffed up, and are no
longer doughy inside. Serve immediately.

ROSEMARY FOCACCIA: Knead 3–6 tablespoons of
chopped, fresh rosemary into the dough. Roll it out,
put it on a greased baking sheet, and sprinkle sea salt
over the top, pressing it in a bit so that it sticks.
Bake as opposite.

ROSEMARY FOCACCIA PIZZA: Prepare the dough as
for Rosemary *Focaccia*, then follow the method for
Garlic Pizza.

ROSEMARY-SCENTED HUNGARIAN FRIED BREAD:
A Hungarian–Californian hybrid. Pat the Rosemary
Focaccia dough into individual, flat, pizzetta-like
cakes. Fry them in hot vegetable oil until they are
golden brown, puffed up, and no longer doughy
inside. Remove from the hot oil and drain on paper
towels or absorbent kitchen paper. Serve each portion
with a cut clove of garlic to rub over the bread and
some sea salt for sprinkling.

ABOVE: *Pizza d'Asparagi*

Sauces & Condiments

*P*ungent or aromatic sauces and dressings transform even the simplest plate of ingredients into a complex, interesting dish. Any vegetable can take on a completely different identity depending upon what it is dressed with.

California's sauces bear little resemblance to the subtle, long-simmered cream-enriched or butter-based ones of traditional French haute cuisine. Yet modern French sauces have made a contribution. You will often find a beurre blanc seasoned with citrus, hollandaise with cumin, aïoli with chili peppers, or mayonnaise with sesame oil.

As might be expected in a place where salad is eaten at least twice a day, vinaigrettes abound, but not just for salads. Vinaigrettes are often found accompanying a plate of steamed vegetables in place of butter, or sloshed onto a platter of grilled summer vegetables to heighten their flavors and, on crusty French bread sandwiches, they know no peer. Californian vinaigrettes, however, tend towards the tart side, using less oil than do traditional French dressings. They are also likely to be based on untraditional ingredients: ethnic flavors, such as Vietnamese, Thai, Chinese, Mexican, and with lots of fresh coriander, chili peppers, fermented black beans, chili, cumin, oregano, and so on. Equally, they might be given a piquant shock of sweetness from cranberry sauce or from any of the locally produced fruit preserves.

Mustard is a preferred condiment and Californian mustard is often prepared with local wines, honey, and herbs. The Russian presence in Northern California from the nineteenth-century whalers left behind a traditional sweet and hot mustard flavored with sesame oil.

Often, instead of a sauce, a fresh relish will accompany a dish. Based on garden herbs, garlic, and pungent ingredients such as chili peppers, sun-dried tomatoes, or olives, they swagger with high flavor and add a bright accent to whatever they partner. These uncooked relishes have evolved from the traditional Mexican salsas — savory mixtures of raw vegetables, fruits, and chili peppers — and the savory herb paste from Genoa, pesto.

The rest of the book, thus far, contains many other sauces, salsas, vinaigrettes, condiments, and seasoning pastes if you want more. Feel free to mix and match in the knowledge that you will be being very Californian.

CHUNKY AVOCADO SALSA
Serves 2–4

Salsa, a simple mixture of tomatoes, chili peppers, onion, garlic, and often coriander, is a basic on the Mexican table. Its spicy freshness is ubiquitous in Californian cuisine, a culinary legacy of Spanish/ Mexican rule. Salsa à la California, however, often strays far from the classic, adding herbs, spices, fruits, or, in this case, avocado. Serve this salsa nestled between the covers of a toasted cheese sandwich or roll up in a warm, soft tortilla along with a portion of refried beans. Try, too, a spoonful stirred at the last minute into a zesty broth.

> 2 ripe fresh tomatoes, diced
> 1 avocado, preferably a black- or dark-green skinned one, diced
> juice of ½ lime
> ½ onion, finely chopped and/or 2 garlic cloves, finely chopped
> 1–4 fresh green chili peppers, chopped
> salt, to taste
> ¼–½ teaspoon ground cumin or toasted cumin seeds (see p. 144), lightly crushed
> 2 tablespoons chopped fresh coriander leaves

Combine all the ingredients and serve.

PAGE 136: *Chunky Avocado Salsa (top left), Curried Green Coriander Hot Sauce (bottom left), and Oil-less Thai-inspired Sweet Red Chili Dressing (bottom right)*

CURRIED GREEN CORIANDER HOT SAUCE
Makes about ¾ cup (6 fl. oz., 185 ml)

This sauce is delicious with beets (beetroot) and boiled potatoes that have been tossed with a little cumin-scented oil or spooned onto melted cheese-topped corn or flour tortillas or lightly fried eggs and sautéed fresh tomatoes.

> 3 garlic cloves, finely chopped
> 2 fresh green chili peppers, or to taste, finely chopped
> 2 tablespoons vinegar
> ½ teaspoon ground cumin, or to taste
> pinch of ground turmeric
> 1 oz. (30 g) fresh coriander, coarsely chopped
> 2 tablespoons tomato paste (purée) or purée (passata)
> salt and freshly ground pepper, to taste

In a blender or food processor, whirl the garlic, chilies, and vinegar together to form a smooth paste. Add the remaining ingredients, whirl until smooth, then season with salt and pepper.

Variation
CORIANDER SALSA: Lessen the amount of vinegar used to about a tablespoon, or to taste, and omit the turmeric.

Oil-less Thai-inspired Sweet Red Chili Dressing

Makes about 1 1/2 cups (12 fl. oz., 375 ml)

I was inspired by the sweet and spicy dressings that are used over the platters of raw vegetables and fruit of which Thais are so fond. Thai cuisine has become enormously popular in California in recent years, especially in the San Francisco area. Not only are restaurants numerous and excellent, the ingredients are to be found in the myriad of well-stocked stores. Thai cuisine is popular elsewhere, too, and the ingredients used here are widely available.

A great bonus of this dressing is that it uses no fat whatsoever, and so can be used knowing that it will provide you with negligible calories and will not contribute to hardening of the arteries.

A few spoonfuls are delicious on a salad of nippy green leaves, such as watercress, and satsuma (mandarin) or orange segments. The recipe makes a large amount, as leftovers are good in mustards and salads. The dressing lasts in the refrigerator for up to 2 weeks and freezes very well.

> *1 cup (8 fl. oz., 250 ml) water*
> *2 tablespoons mild chili powder*
> *2 tablespoons paprika*
> *1 1/2 tablespoons honey*
> *1-in. (2.5-cm) piece of fresh ginger root, freshly grated*
>   *(use large holes of grater)*
> *1/3 cup (3 fl. oz., 90 ml) white wine vinegar*
>   *or rice vinegar*
> *salt, to taste*

In a saucepan, combine a small amount of the water with the chili powder, paprika, and honey, enough to form a smooth paste. Gradually add the remaining water, then bring to the boil and simmer for about 5 minutes.

Remove the pan from the heat and add the ginger, vinegar, and salt. Leave the dressing to cool and use as desired.

Variation

TANGY CHILLED MUSTARD: Add 2 teaspoons or so of the above dressing to 2 tablespoons Dijon-type mustard. Increase the amounts proportionately for greater quantities.

Sun-dried Tomato Vinaigrette

Makes about 1/2 cup (4 fl. oz., 125 ml)

This tangy vinaigrette with bits of sun-dried tomato in it is particularly delicious splashed onto a salad of greens, basil, and feta cheese, or spooned onto roasted eggplant (aubergine). It is also good as a dressing on cooled, cooked *kasha* or buckwheat groats, making a hearty grain salad.

> *8–10 sun-dried tomatoes, cut into small pieces*
> *3 garlic cloves, finely chopped*
> *1/2 cup (4 fl. oz., 125 ml) extra virgin olive oil*
> *2 tablespoons red wine vinegar*
> *generous pinch of fresh or dried thyme or basil*
> *salt and freshly ground black pepper, to taste*

In a blender or food processor, whirl the sun-dried tomatoes and garlic until a chunky mixture results, then add the oil, vinegar, and herbs.

Whirl until it is well-mixed, then season with salt and pepper.

Cumin and Citrus Vinaigrette

Makes about 1/4 cup (2 fl. oz., 60 ml)

The unexpected jolt of toasted cumin combined with olive oil and lemon juice makes a lively, out-of-the-ordinary vinaigrette.

> *2 tablespoons olive oil*
> *2 teaspoons lemon juice*
> *1/2 teaspoon toasted cumin seeds (see p. 144), coarsely*
>   *crushed, or 1/4 teaspoon ground cumin*
> *salt and freshly ground black pepper, to taste*

Combine all the ingredients, mixing them together well (this is easily done by shaking them in a jar with a tightly fitting screw-top lid).

GAZPACHO VINAIGRETTE

Serves 4

Light and tasting of freshly puréed vegetables in a bath of olive oil and vinegar, spiked with cumin, garlic, and oregano, this makes a lovely dip for fresh vegetables, especially romaine (cos) lettuce leaves, or spooned onto slices of creamy avocado.

1 garlic clove, chopped
⅛ cucumber, diced
½–1 small chili pepper, chopped
¼ red or yellow sweet pepper (capsicum), diced
¼ green sweet pepper (capsicum), diced
1 scallion (spring onion) or 2 golden shallots, chopped
3 tablespoons lemon juice or sherry vinegar
5 tablespoons olive oil
½ teaspoon ground cumin
large pinch of dried oregano, crumbled
salt and cayenne or freshly ground black pepper, to taste
2–3 tablespoons finely chopped fresh or canned tomatoes

In a blender or food processor, whirl the garlic, cucumber, chili pepper, sweet peppers, and scallion or golden shallot with the lemon juice or vinegar. When you have a smooth mixture, add the oil, whirling it in and letting it emulsify with the puréed vegetables and lemon juice.

Season with the cumin, oregano, salt, and cayenne or black pepper. Add the tomato, give it all a quick whirl, then serve. The vinaigrette will separate if it sits for a while, but simply shake, whirl or stir to recombine the ingredients.

BELOW: *Gazpacho Vinaigrette*

PESTO
Makes about 1½ cups (12 fl. oz., 375 ml)

Pesto, that pungent green balm of basil, garlic, and olive oil, may have originated in Genoa, but, over the past several decades, it has become indispensable in California and a great number of homes elsewhere, too. In season, markets in California sell great bunches of basil, at nearly give-away prices. Home-made pesto then becomes not only an epicurean project, but a delicious economy since it keeps extremely well in the freezer. There is nothing so delicious as home-made pesto.

The first time I ever set foot in any part of Europe was in Genoa, and I did so for no other reason than its fame for pesto. For three weeks I wandered through the labyrinthine cobbled streets of the old area of town, eating pesto-spread everything in tiny trattorias until I thought I would turn green myself.

I have never overcome my passion for this green substance. My windowsill has a basil plant growing on it perennially, my refrigerator always has a bottle of pesto in it, and in the freezer are several containers of home-made pesto.

Pesto is, to my taste, at its best when absolutely stinking with garlic, and its fragrant basil flavor is undiluted by too much in the way of nuts and cheese. (I actually prefer not to include pine nuts or walnuts at all in the puréed mixture, but toss just a few over any pesto-sauced dish for flavor and crunchy texture.)

Whereas in Genoa you will find pesto served in a wide variety of traditional dishes, in California you never know where you will find it. It is used in salad dressings, dips, soups, casseroles . . . Pesto is also likely to be prepared with extra ingredients such as coriander, oregano, marjoram, spinach, and sun-dried tomatoes. I recently tasted a tarragon and goat cheese pesto! Pesto — of one sort or another — is so much a part of Californian cuisine, one food correspondent recently jokingly referred to pesto as 'a basic food group, like vegetables, legumes, and grains'.

4 garlic cloves, chopped
4 oz. (125 g) fresh basil leaves, coarsely chopped
¾ cup (6 fl. oz., 185 ml) extra virgin olive oil, as required
4 oz. (125 g), approximately, or to taste, fresh Parmesan cheese, grated
salt, to taste

In a blender or food processor, chop the garlic and basil, then slowly add the oil until it forms a smooth purée. Add the cheese and whirl everything together, adding extra oil if needed for texture and consistency, and extra cheese, if needed, for flavor. Keep the pesto in a clean screw-top jar in the refrigerator until needed (use within several days or freeze).

Variation

CALIFORNIAN CORIANDER PESTO: This pesto is delicious atop a plate of hot pepper-spiked, tomato-sauced pasta or *pasta arrabbiata*. Follow the above recipe, but substitute fresh coriander for the basil and decrease the amount of cheese, to taste, using sharp cheddar, Asiago, aged Jack, or other freshly grated cheese in place of the Parmesan. Season generously with a good hot pepper sauce, such as Tabasco.

SUN-DRIED TOMATO PESTO
Makes about 1½ cups (12 fl. oz., 375 ml)

This pesto captures the sun-drenched flavors so beloved by Californians: sun-dried tomatoes, garlic, olive oil, and basil. It is delicious as a condiment, topping for *bruschetta*, pasta sauce, sandwich spread, or licked from your fingers when no one is looking.

4 garlic cloves, finely chopped
10–15 sun-dried tomatoes, diced
6–8 ripe tomatoes, blanched, peeled, and deseeded, or canned tomatoes, peeled and deseeded, both diced
⅓ cup (3 fl. oz., 90 ml) oil from the jar of the sun-dried tomatoes, or as needed, plus extra virgin olive oil, if necessary
½–1 oz. (15–30 g) fresh basil, coarsely chopped

In a blender or food processor, whirl the garlic and sun-dried tomatoes until they are finely chopped. Add the tomatoes and oil and whirl until the mixture is the consistency of a sauce, then add the basil and continue to whirl, until the basil is finely chopped into the sauce. Keep the pesto in a clean screw-top jar in the refrigerator until needed (use within several days or freeze).

Variation

TWO-MINUTE TRIPLE-TOMATO APPETIZER: The combination of cooked tomatoes, sun-dried tomatoes, and fresh, sweet, ripe, raw tomatoes is fantastic. Nothing could be simpler to prepare once you have the pesto. Simply combine 4 diced ripe, raw tomatoes (no need to peel or deseed) with 3 tablespoons Sun-dried Tomato Pesto. Serve with garlic-rubbed croûtons or baguette slices, and a sprig or two of fresh sweet basil.

OLIVADA AND SWEET BASIL PESTO
Makes about 1½ cups (12 fl. oz., 375 ml)

This chunky relish tastes of pungent, salty black olives and the sweet flavor of fresh basil, and has the Mediterranean scents of olive oil and garlic. It makes a delicious sauce for pasta, marinated and grilled vegetables, or addition to tomatoey vegetable soups. Try it spooned onto pizza or tucked into a toasted cheese sandwich. It is best, however, spooned on top of a hearth-roasted potato.

6–8 oz. (185–250 g) kalamata or similar black olives,
  pitted and halved
2–3 oz. (60–90 g) fresh sweet basil leaves
1 garlic clove, chopped
⅓ cup (3 fl. oz., 90 ml) extra virgin olive oil

In a food processor or by hand, coarsely chop the olives and basil. Combine with the garlic and olive oil until you have a chunky, relish-like consistency. Use as desired, within a day or two as the basil loses its fresh texture rapidly.

Variation
OLIVE AND FRESH ROSEMARY PESTO: In place of the basil, use 1–2 oz. (30–60 g) chopped fresh rosemary. Serve as you would any pesto. It is especially good spooned onto pasta with creamy goat cheese.

PACIFIC RIM PESTO
Makes about 1 cup (8 fl. oz., 250 ml)

Fragrant with sweet mint and the distinctive coriander, crunchy with peanuts and hot from the fire of fresh chilies, this makes a delicious sauce for pasta, grilled eggplant (aubergine), dumplings, tofu, even pita bread.

3 garlic cloves, chopped
3 fresh green chili peppers, chopped
2 oz. (60 g) roasted peanuts, coarsely chopped, or
  crunchy peanut butter
1 oz. (30 g) fresh mint, coarsely chopped
2 oz. (60 g) fresh coriander, coarsely chopped
juice of ½ lemon
salt, to taste

Combine the garlic, chili peppers, peanuts or peanut butter, mint, coriander, sugar, lemon juice, and salt, if needed, in a blender or food processor. Keep the pesto in a clean screw-top jar in the refrigerator until needed (use within several days or freeze).

RED CHILI AIOLI
Makes about ½ cup (4 fl. oz., 125 ml)

Aïoli, like pesto, has become an adopted Californian sauce and, also like pesto, it often bears little resemblance to the original recipe. In California, when the word aïoli appears, you will find the requisite garlic and mayonnaise, yes, but one never knows what else one will find. Regularly added ingredients include herbs, sun-dried tomatoes, olives, and chili peppers, among others. It may not be recognized by a native of Provence, but it is delicious.

I have been experimenting, using store-bought mayonnaise as a base for a variety of highly flavored aïoli-like sauces and have been deliciously rewarded for my efforts. Garlic, chili peppers, herbs, citrus juices, flavored oils — all add their savor to a base of creamy store-bought mayonnaise.

This Red Chili Aïoli is an absolutely delicious example. Serve it with pan-browned or grilled eggplant (aubergine), crusty bread sandwiches filled with squeezed dry spinach and sliced mozzarella, or make little nouvelle tacos by wrapping a radicchio leaf around an asparagus spear, a slice or two of red sweet pepper (capsicum), and a julienne of smoked tofu or a handful of cooked pasta, all held together with a dab of the Red Chili Aïoli. It is just spicy enough to thrill, and can be fired up further by adding a bit of chopped fresh red chili pepper.

1 garlic clove, chopped
2 teaspoons mild chili powder
1 teaspoon paprika
4 tablespoons mayonnaise
2 tablespoons extra virgin olive oil
⅛–¼ teaspoon ground cumin or cumin seeds
dash of lemon or lime juice
salt and freshly ground black pepper, to taste

Combine all the ingredients in a blender or food processor. Season with salt and pepper, and chill until needed. Chilling will firm and thicken it somewhat.

OLIVE AND PESTO AIOLI
Makes about ¾ cup (6 fl. oz., 185 ml)

This aïoli is one of the best possible things to spread on bread. It transforms any sandwich, regardless of what tops it, whether it be roasted sweet peppers (capsicums), thinly sliced cheese or firm tofu, sliced hard-boiled eggs and *mesclun* greens, grilled eggplant (aubergine) . . .

2 tablespoons good, strong home-made or
  store-bought pesto
3 tablespoons mayonnaise
8–10 flavorful black olives, pitted and chopped,
  or olive paste (olivada)
1–2 teaspoons extra virgin olive oil

Whirl all the ingredients together in a blender or
food processor until smooth and well combined. If
you make the aïoli by hand, however, use olive paste
instead of chopped olives and gradually work in the
pesto, then the mayonnaise, then the olive oil.

SESAME AND GINGER MAYONNAISE
Makes about ½ cup (4 fl. oz., 125 ml)

Sesame oil and ginger add an Oriental scent to plain
mayonnaise. At one time I prepared this using home-
made mayonnaise, but I have adapted it to store-
bought and it tastes just as good. It is delicious served
on a sandwich of watercress and smoked tofu, or
with grilled soy sauce-seasoned vegetables.

3 tablespoons mayonnaise
4 teaspoons sesame oil
¼–½ teaspoon ground ginger

Stir the mayonnaise until it is smooth, then slowly
add the sesame oil and ginger. Taste to check the
seasoning and chill until needed (it keeps for up to
2 weeks in the refrigerator).

FIFTIES' DINER BURGER DRESSING
Makes enough for 3–4 vegetarian burgers

I adore vegetarian burgers, stuffed into a seeded bun,
topped with this dressing. It is sloppily delicious, far
more than you would think given the prosaic
ingredients. It originally hails from a hamburger diner
I frequented in my childhood. There, the air was
scented with the unmistakable aroma of frying onions,
the countertops were Formica, and it was an ordinary
place selling good, honest food.

½ cup (4 fl. oz., 125 ml) mayonnaise
3 tablespoons Dijon-type mustard, or to taste
½ head of round or iceberg or romaine (cos) lettuce,
  very thinly sliced

Stir the mayonnaise until it is smooth, then stir in the
mustard. Shortly before serving, fold in the lettuce,
mixing as you do so to combine it well with the
mayonnaise.

CREAMY RANCH-STYLE DRESSING OR DIP
Makes about 1¼ cups (10 fl. oz., 310 ml)

Creamy and flavorful, redolent of garlic and flecked
with parsley, ranch-style dressings and dips are
enormously popular. You will find them spooned
onto a crisp romaine (cos) lettuce salad or dipped into
with crunchy raw crudités.

This recipe is the basic mixture, but by preparing it
with cream cheese instead of sour cream or yogurt,
the dressing becomes a spread for such classic
Californian sandwiches as avocado with bean or
alfalfa sprouts, and cheese or sunflower seeds.

As a dip, it may be lightened with any number of
chopped vegetables, my favorite being the variation
given below, Californian Spinach Dip.

BASIC DRESSING
½ cup (4 fl. oz., 125 ml) mayonnaise
½ cup (4 fl. oz., 125 ml) sour cream or rich yogurt
½ vegetable bouillon (stock) cube, or to taste, crumbled or
  dissolved in a spoonful of hot water
2–3 garlic cloves, finely chopped or crushed
freshly ground black pepper, to taste
3–4 tablespoons finely chopped fresh parsley
2 tablespoons milk, or as required
dash of lemon juice, if necessary

Stir the mayonnaise until it is smooth. Do the same
with the sour cream or yogurt, and then stir them
together until the mixture is smooth.

Stir in the bouillon cube or bouillon cube and
water, garlic, black pepper, and parsley. Mix them
together well, then thin with the milk until it is a
creamy, spoonable consistency.

Check that the seasoning is to your taste, adjust if
necessary, adding a dash of lemon juice if extra tang
is needed.

Variation
If you are using this recipe as a dip, omit the milk as
the mixture will need to be of a thicker consistency.

CALIFORNIAN SPINACH DIP: Prepare as above,
omitting the milk, and add 1 lb. (500 g) spinach,
cooked, squeezed, and chopped, 2–4 thinly sliced
scallions (spring onions) and ¼–½ teaspoon dried or
1–2 teaspoons fresh dill, or more or less of either
according to taste. Chill the dip to meld the flavors.
A typically Californian way of presenting this dip is
to serve it in a hollowed-out red cabbage, surrounded
by fresh vegetables for dipping.

FRAGRANT LIME MUSTARD
Makes about 3 tablespoons

Sharp citrus flavors such as lime, or sweetly tangy ones such as orange, flavor pungent mustard with a particularly Gallic–Californian accent.

3 tablespoons mustard of choice (such as Dijon)
¼ teaspoon grated lime rind
1 teaspoon lime juice

Combine all the ingredients and mix together well.

Variation

MIXED CITRUS MUSTARD: Substitute orange rind for the lime and/or orange juice for the lime juice. You can use any combination you like. Lemon is very nice as well.

GARLIC AND PARSLEY WHOLEGRAIN MUSTARD
Makes about ½ cup (4 fl. oz., 125 ml)

Nearly equal amounts of finely chopped parsley and prepared wholegrain mustard make the basis for a fresh-tasting mustard, able to transform sandwiches in a single spread.

1 garlic clove, finely chopped
2 tablespoons finely chopped fresh parsley
2 tablespoons wholegrain mustard
dash of lemon juice or red wine vinegar
pinch of dried tarragon or herbes de Provence

Combine all the ingredients and mix together well.

NORTH COUNTRY MUSTARD
Makes about ⅓ cup (3 fl. oz., 90 ml)

Mendocino, Napa and Sonoma Counties, in addition to being known for their vineyards and wines, are also known for the mustards made using those wines. Often scented with sweet local honey and fragrant mountainside herbs, they add sophisticated savor to the simplest sandwich. A streamlined recipe for such a mustard follows.

⅓ cup (3 fl. oz., 90 ml) Dijon-type mustard,
*   prepared with wine*
3 tablespoons strongly-flavored honey, or to taste
pinch of dried thyme

Combine all the ingredients and mix together well.

TOASTED CUMIN SEEDS

Toasted cumin seeds can be used whole or crushed using a pestle and mortar, or a spice grinder. Store as you would any other spice, in a tightly sealed jar.

generous handful of cumin seeds

Toast the cumin seeds in an ungreased, heavy skillet or frying pan over a low-medium heat, tossing and turning the seeds as they cook. They will darken and smell fragrant as they toast, but they burn very easily, so take great care. The whole process will take about 3–5 minutes.

HERB AND CHIVE FLOWER BUTTER
Makes about 6 oz. (185 g)

Sweet, fresh, and unsalted butter smoothed into little individual molds, garnished with the petals of edible flowers, is enchanting. Nasturtium petals are visually exciting, their yellow, red, and orange colors fresh and bright, their flavors fresh and peppery rather than sweet, as flowers such as roses are.

They all look lovely, but do not taste as oniony delicious as pale lavender chive flowers and chopped green chives mixed with the butter.

As with any flowers for eating, be sure that they are indeed edible and that they have not been sprayed with any chemicals. Purchasing them from a source specifically for eating should circumvent any problems (see also p. 6).

When preparing any seasoned butters, be sure to enjoy them within a few days as they can absorb other flavors and aromas very easily in the refrigerator.

about a handful of chive flowers
4 oz. (125 g) sweet (unsalted) butter, at room temperature
2–3 tablespoons chopped chives
pinch of salt

Pull the petals from some of the flowers and chop them up coarsely, saving enough flowers to garnish each pot.

Mix the chopped blossoms with the butter, chives, and salt, then pack into little pots, smooth the tops, and chill until ready to enjoy. Garnish each pot with a reserved flower.

OPPOSITE: *North Country Mustard (top left) and Red Chili Butter (bottom right)*

GARLIC AND OLIVE BUTTER

Makes about 4 oz. (125 g)

This highly flavored butter makes a delicious spread on sliced baguettes for antipasti or a fragrant, yet simple, mixture to toss fresh pasta in. You could use it also to spread onto succulent grilled vegetables, or as a seasoning, adding a spoonful to puréed vegetable soups, such as potato, asparagus, green or string bean, tomato, etc.

> 2–3 garlic cloves, finely chopped
> 2 tablespoons finely chopped black olives (kalamata)
>   or olive paste (olivada)
> 2–3 oz. (60–90 g) sweet (unsalted) butter, at room
>   temperature
> pinch of herbes de Provence (optional)

Combine the garlic with the olives or olive paste, and mix this in well with the butter. Season with the *herbes de Provence* (if using). Pack the flavored butter into a small dish and enjoy as desired.

Variations

CANAPE: Spread the butter thickly over slices of baguette. Top each 'tartine' with a whole basil leaf.

PASTA WITH GARLIC AND OLIVE BUTTER AND SAGE: Toss cooked, flat, delicate fettucine pasta with spoonfuls of the seasoned butter and coarsely chopped leaves of fresh sage.

RED CHILI BUTTER

Makes about 4 oz. (125 g)

Sweet butter, seasoned with garlic and chili, is a delicious spread for nearly anything: melting atop grilled corn, spread onto bread and baked, garlic-bread style, or nestled into a hot, roasted yam. Place in an attractive small bowl to serve at the table.

> 3 oz. (90 g) sweet (unsalted) butter, at room temperature
> 2 garlic cloves, finely chopped
> 1 teaspoon paprika
> 1 teaspoon mild chili powder
> pinch to 1/4 teaspoon ground cumin, or to taste
> pinch of dried oregano
> 1 tablespoon olive oil
> 1 teaspoon chopped fresh coriander
> salt, to taste

Combine all the ingredients, mixing them together well.

Sweet Things

*D*espite the constant talk of fitness and health clubs, Californians do like to indulge their collective sweet tooth — rich ice creams, crunchy sweet cookies (including chocolate chip and chocolate chunk), brownies, fruit-filled pies, and creamy cheesecakes seem to be everywhere. Low-fat frozen yogurts are doted on, available in a dizzying variety of flavors and often topped with fruit, sundae fashion. They may be eaten with a feeling of self-righteousness, for they are indeed healthy and lean, but they are delicious, too.

Fresh fruit is abundant all year long and served generously, lavishly. At its worst, it is like supermarket fruit anywhere — a pale phantom of the real thing — but from the garden or farmers' markets, Californian fruit bursts with the sort of flavorful vitality usually associated with Mediterranean-grown fruit.

Desserts made of fruit are often simple in preparation, but lavish in flavor: strawberries dipped into melted chocolate for tangy fresh bonbons, sliced oranges drizzled with honey and garnished with edible flower petals, ripe nectarines plopped into a glass of red wine, or fragrant and tropical fruit puréed and frozen into sorbets and Mexican-style ice confections.

OPPOSITE: *Basket of Strawberries with Lime Yogurt Dipping Sauce*

BASKET OF STRAWBERRIES WITH LIME YOGURT DIPPING SAUCE

Serves 2–4

What could be more inviting than a basket of strawberries, tipped on its side with its luscious scarlet fruit spilling out. A prim bowl of dipping sauce stops you getting carried away. The dipping sauce, lightly sweetened plain yogurt flavored with lime juice and grated zest, is healthy and light. This is the perfect dessert for a summery afternoon lunch.

½ cup (4 fl. oz., 125 ml) plain yogurt
2½ tablespoons sugar, or to taste
grated rind and juice of ½ lime
1 carton (punnet) strawberries (preferably large ones), unhulled

Combine the yogurt with the sugar, lime rind, and juice. Cover tightly and chill, preferably overnight, to blend the flavors together.

Serve the Lime Yogurt Dipping Sauce in a bowl alongside a basket of the strawberries.

Variation

BASKET OF STRAWBERRIES WITH MELTED CHOCOLATE DIPPING SAUCE: If you veer towards the path of wanton indulgence, instead of the Lime Yogurt Dipping Sauce, try a bowlful of warm, melted chocolate, thinned with a little whipping (double) cream, and flavored with a few drops of vanilla extract (essence) or fruit liqueur.

NEO-FAUVIST FRUIT PLATE

Serves 4–6

Fresh fruit is so easily available for much of the year that it is easy to take it for granted. In just such a jaded state of mind, I created the following dessert. The idea may be Abstract Expressionism, but the colors are pure Fauvist. Puddles of brightly colored fruit purées decorate each plate — forget careful, artful presentation, this is passion. Save a few pieces of each fruit to strew over each plate and serve with crisp *biscotti* or sweet *bruschetta* (stale baguette slices buttered and sprinkled with sugar, then toasted in a low oven until crunchy and lightly caramelized).

1 carton (punnet) strawberries, cleaned
4 kiwi fruit, peeled and diced
1 mango, peeled and diced
1 carton (punnet) blackberries or blueberries (bilberries), cleaned
1 carton (punnet) raspberries, cleaned (optional)
sugar, to taste
brandy, fruit brandy, liqueurs, balsamic vinegar, and lemon juice, to taste (try raspberries with fraise de bois, mango with tequila, strawberries with balsamic vinegar, blackberries with brandy, etc.)
4–8 biscotti or other hard, sweet Continental biscuits (cookies)

Prepare the fruit purées by whirling each fruit separately in a blender or food processor. Reserve a slice or two of each fruit and a handful of each berry. Season each purée with sugar and a dash of either brandy, fruit brandy, liqueur, balsamic vinegar, or lemon juice. Chill until ready to use.

Arrange puddles of the purées on each serving plate, taking care so that they do not all run together. On top of the by now brightly colored plate, arrange the extra fruits and berries. For a crisper presentation, squeeze the fruit purées from plastic dispenser bottles (the type that tomato ketchup comes in), drawing big squiggles on the plate or decorations on a background of one-color fruit purée. Serve immediately, each portion accompanied by one or two of the *biscotti*.

RUBY ORANGES WITH ROSE PETAL SAUCE

Serves 4

Ruby red oranges lying in a pink pool of fragrant rose petal sauce are nothing less than stunning. This dessert looks like a sunset and has the scent of an exotic garden in bloom.

3 tablespoons rose petal jam
2 teaspoons water
rose water, to taste
4 ruby (blood) oranges, peeled and thickly sliced across the segments

Put the rose petal jam and water in a small saucepan, and stir to combine them well. Bring to the boil, then reduce the heat and simmer for a few minutes until the consistency is like a sauce rather than a jam. Stir in the rose water and then leave to cool.

Spoon a little of the sauce onto each plate then top with the slices of orange. Serve immediately.

OPPOSITE: *Neo-Fauvist Fruit Plate*

NECTARINE, STRAWBERRY, AND RASPBERRY FRUIT SALAD WITH INFORMAL BERRY ICE

Serves 4

Nectarines, strawberries, and raspberries all come into freshness at about the same time. All three are sweet and fragrant, and utterly irresistible *au naturel* or sliced and accompanied by cream or yogurt. Together in one bowl, they are the most delicious fruit salad imaginable. I like to serve the mixed fruit topped with chunks of fresh raspberry ice, sort of a sundae in reverse. Sometimes I drizzle it all with brandy or fruit liqueur. If you do not feel terribly ambitious, however, the fruit salad is lovely on its own, *sans* ice or liqueur.

As to the curious title, 'Informal Berry Ice'. It is just easily and informally thrown together — there is nothing more behind it than that. A good-quality store-bought sorbet or frozen yogurt is even more informal still, of course.

3 ripe nectarines, sliced
½ carton (punnet) strawberries, trimmed and sliced
handful of raspberries
several teaspoons sugar, to taste
dash of lemon juice
1 carton (punnet) raspberries (extra)

2 tablespoons confectioners' (icing) sugar, or to taste
2 egg whites
brandy or fruit liqueur or fruit brandy, to taste (optional)

Combine the nectarines, strawberries, and the handful of raspberries, sweeten with the sugar and add a dash of lemon juice if needed, then chill.

Meanwhile, mash the extra raspberries with a fork. Sweeten with the confectioners' sugar. Whip the egg whites until they are almost stiff, then take a spoonful and fold it into the berry mixture in an ice cream maker according to its instructions or in an ice cube tray (without the dividers) in a freezer, taking the mixture out and scraping the tray occasionally. Alternatively, you could freeze it in a shallow pan to a depth of say ½ in. (1 cm), then break the ice into bite-sized pieces and strew them atop the mixed fruit. Serve immediately, drizzled with the brandy or liqueur, if using.

Leftovers

TUTTI FRUTTI SOFT ICE CREAM: Freeze any leftover fruit mixture and whirl it, along with some of the berry ice, in a blender or food processor, along with ½–1 cup (4–8 fl. oz., 125–250 ml) whipping (double) cream, lightly whipped, and several tablespoons confectioners' (icing) sugar to sweeten. Serve right away as the frozen fruit whips the cream to form a soft, fluffy ice cream that begins to melt immediately.

CARAMELIZED PEARS BAKED WITH CREAM

Serves 4

Pears baked in a cloak of caramelizing sugar, cream added to smooth the edges, this cozy, bistro-like sweet is perfect for chilly fall (autumn) evenings.

2 tablespoons unsalted butter

2 tablespoons sugar

2 ripe pears, halved and cored, but unpeeled

½ teaspoon almond or vanilla extract (essence)

½ cup (4 fl. oz., 125 ml) light (single) cream

Preheat the oven to 400°F (200°C). Grease a baking dish with half the butter, then sprinkle half the sugar over it. Place the pears cut side down in the dish, then sprinkle with the remaining sugar and spread the rest of the butter over the pears.

Bake for 10 minutes, then sprinkle the almond or vanilla extract over them and the cream over the top. Return to the oven for another 20 minutes, then serve.

OPPOSITE: *Nectarine, Strawberry, and Raspberry Fruit Salad with Informal Berry Ice*

BELOW: *Caramelized Pears Baked with Cream (left) and Central Valley Winter Fruit Compote with Scented Tea and Brandy-soaked Golden Raisins*

Central Valley Winter Fruit Compote with Scented Tea and Brandy-soaked Golden Raisins

Serves 4

This recipe stems from my grandmother's Russian–Jewish way of stewing fruit, pouring hot tea over the dried fruit, then leaving it to soak overnight and plump up. As the fruit steeps rather than stews, it keeps its fresh flavor. I like to use lightly flavored teas such as jasmine or apricot for added aroma. Soaking the golden raisins (sultanas) in brandy turns the dessert away from wholesome towards indulgent. Ordinary raisins may be used in place of the golden ones. The California raisin, interestingly enough, came about as a result of a natural disaster. In 1873, a terrible heat wave devastated the Muscat grapevines, leaving in its wake shriveled, wrinkled fruit. The sun-dried grapes made superlative raisins.

Prunes, too, are one of California's largest crops. Of the 2,000 or so varieties of plums, about 200 are grown in California. When I was growing up, each summer my Russian grandfather took us on an annual holiday drive down the coast of Central California. We children always clamored for beach picnics, swimming, and sunbathing, but my grandfather had other ideas. We meandered down the coast in our old Chevrolet, stopping at the tiny towns whose claims to fame read: Gilroy, the garlic capital; Half-Moon Bay, the pumpkin capital; Castroville, the artichoke capital; Watsonville, the prune capital. At each stop, we climbed out of the big car and lolloped into the fields, picking the fruits or vegetables on offer and filling up a big bag of the cherished produce, then off we went again. Little Philistines that we children were, we couldn't figure out why anyone would want to shop like this; what was wrong with the supermarket? And why on earth would anyone go out of their way to buy prunes?

Yet, no doubt, each of us children cherishes the same memory: sitting in the back of the car as the temperature approached the 90s, a cool breeze blowing through the window, sticky hands swiping at each other in that childishly cranky fashion, nibbling our way through the fruits of Papa's grand farm tour, even the prunes. As an adult I love prunes.

7 oz. (225 g) dried mixed fruit (apricots, pears, apples, prunes)
hot, freshly brewed tea, to cover (apricot tea, Earl Grey, jasmine, etc.)
1½ tablespoons sugar, or to taste
1–2 slices lemon
3 oz. (90 g) golden raisins (sultanas) or raisins
¼ cup (2 fl. oz., 60 ml) brandy

Put the mixed fruit into a bowl, cutting larger pieces into bite-sized ones. Pour the hot tea over the fruit, the level of the tea being about 1 in. (2.5 cm) higher than the fruit, add the sugar and lemon. Cover and leave to cool to room temperature.

When it has cooled, chill overnight.

Several hours before serving, pour the raisins or sultanas into a bowl, pour the brandy over them and cover. Leave to soak up the brandy and become plump.

Serve each portion of sweet, juicy fruit topped with a spoonful of the brandy-soaked raisins or sultanas.

Peach or Nectarine Fromage Frais and Yogurt Mousse

Serves 4

Blending fruit with flavored fromage frais and yogurt, a billow of whipped cream added for good measure, then serving it with a topping of crumbled cookies (biscuits), is one of those very straightforward desserts that seems too good to be true. Mousse-like in consistency, it is more interesting in flavor, as well as being lighter and more easily prepared.

Nectarines, by the way, are not a cross between the peach and the plum as is so often thought. Originally bred in England (where for many years its rarity made it a fruit for the aristocracy only), California currently grows over 150 varieties of nectarines, most of which have been developed since the Second World War.

Because of their similar flavor — aromatic, almost flower sweet, and slightly tangy — nectarines and peaches can be used pretty much interchangeably.

2 ripe peaches or nectarines, peeled and coarsely mashed
½ cup (4 fl. oz., 125 ml) peach- or strawberry-flavored fromage frais
½ cup (4 fl. oz., 125 ml) peach- or strawberry-flavored yogurt
½ cup (4 fl. oz., 125 ml) whipping (double) cream
superfine (caster) or confectioners' (icing) sugar, to taste, if needed
a few drops of almond or vanilla extract (essence) (optional)
6 or so oatmeal and whole-wheat (wholemeal) cookies (biscuits) or amaretti, crumbled

Combine the peaches or nectarines with the fromage frais and yogurt. Whip the cream until it is quite firm, but stop before it becomes buttery. Combine it with the fruit, fromage frais, and yogurt mixture, adding a little superfine or confectioners' sugar if it is not sweet enough, and the almond or vanilla extract (if using).

Chill until firm (at least 2 hours), then serve topped with lots of crumbled cookies or *amaretti*.

PLUMP DATES STUFFED WITH MASCARPONE IN A POOL OF CARAMEL, TOPPED WITH PISTACHIOS

Serves 4

Dates thrive in California's desert regions where hot, dry conditions are much like those in the Middle East. The Cochella Valley, southeast of Los Angeles, produces 95 percent of the US date supply. Indio, a tiny town nestled in that sun-parched valley, is the date capital. There, one can cool off with a frosty date shake that is incredibly rich — a frothy whirl of sweet dates and ice cream. There are date breads, date cakes iced with cream cheese, chocolate-covered date sweetmeats, or date ice cream scooped into crisp cones and eaten in the sweltering heat out-of-doors.

This is a rather more elegant sweet than the ones just mentioned, however. I like the contrast of flavors and textures — tangy soft cheese, sweet earthy dates, a pool of rich caramel sauce, and a scattering of crunchy pistachio nuts. Pistachio nuts, by the way, have in recent years become a big crop in California. They are sold in their natural color, rather than the dyed red hue of the imported Iranian nuts.

⅓ cup (3 oz., 90 g) light demerara (raw) sugar
2 oz. (60 g) unsalted butter, chopped
⅓ cup (3 fl. oz., 90 ml) light (single) cream
tiny pinch of salt
¼ teaspoon vanilla extract (essence)
12 plump, moist, sweet dates
4 oz. (125 g) or so mascarpone or cream cheese
3–4 tablespoons coarsely chopped raw pistachio nuts

In a heavy-bottomed saucepan, gently heat the sugar until it melts and caramelizes, then turns brownish, but take care not to let it burn.

Remove the pan from the heat and add the butter gradually, stirring, then add the cream and stir well to combine. Add the salt and vanilla extract, then return the pan to the heat and bring it to the boil. Cook the mixture for a minute or two longer, then leave it to cool. It should now be of a creamy consistency.

Meanwhile, pit the dates and stuff each with a nugget of cheese. Chill until ready to serve.

Spoon a little of the caramel sauce onto each plate, then top each with 3 cheese-stuffed dates. Sprinkle the pistachio nuts over the plates, then serve immediately.

BELOW: *Plump Dates Stuffed with* Mascarpone *in a Pool of Caramel, Topped with Pistachios*

PHYLLO PASTRY GOODIE BAGS FILLED WITH MARZIPAN AND SERVED WITH FRESH FIG ICE CREAM

Serves 4

Phyllo dough is such a good friend: crisp and airily light, good-naturedly eager to combine with either savory or sweet fillings.

You can serve these almond paste-filled delicacies on their own or, for a more elaborate presentation, with fresh figs and ice cream, combined or separate as you wish. For the ambitious, prepare your own ice cream; for the lazy, of which I include myself, a good store-bought one is fine.

8 oz. (250 g) marzipan, broken or cut into small pieces
1 egg
sugar, to taste
½–1 teaspoon almond extract (essence), or to taste
2 tablespoons orange flower water, or to taste
½–1 teaspoon ground cinnamon
4 oz. (125 g) phyllo pastry sheets

2 oz. (60 g), approximately, unsalted butter, melted
confectioners' (icing) sugar and ground cinnamon, for sprinkling
8 fresh figs, sliced
2½ cups (1 imp. pint, 625 ml) vanilla ice cream

Combine the marzipan with the egg, sugar, almond extract, orange flower water, and cinnamon. Mix well in the food processor until it is smooth.

Working one phyllo sheet at a time, brush each one with melted butter, then fold it into quarters. Place 3 tablespoonfuls or so of the marzipan mixture in the center and gather the edges up together, parcel-like. Place the finished 'bags' on a large greased baking sheet.

Bake the bags in a 350°–375°F (180°–190°C) oven until they have turned golden brown (about 10–15 minutes).

Remove from the oven and sprinkle with the confectioners' sugar and cinnamon.

Serve the parcels warm, surrounded by the figs and a small scoop of vanilla ice cream or fig ice cream (dice fresh figs and combine them with lightly softened ice cream and refreeze until just firm).

LEAH'S APPLE FLAN
Serves 6

This is my daughter's favorite pie. Foolproof, it is made whenever a situation calls for desperate measures: such as exams to study for. (This recipe appears in *From Pantry to Table*, Aris/Addison-Wesley, US, 1991.)

Apples have been grown commercially in California since the 1820s. These days Northern California produces an ever-increasing variety of apples, from the standard Golden Delicious, Granny Smith and red to the pink-fleshed Fuji, with its delicate, distinctive flavor and aroma, the crisp and fragrant gala, and a wide variety of apples grown for their flavor, bouquet, and crunch rather than for keeping and storing.

enough shortcrust pastry for a 9–10-in. (23–25-cm)
* pie pan or flan dish*
2 large or 3 small to medium tart, green apples,
* peeled and thinly sliced*

2 oz. (60 g) unsalted butter
2 eggs, beaten
3 tablespoons sugar
½ teaspoon vanilla extract (essence)
1 tablespoon fruit brandy
1 teaspoon ground cinnamon
Line the pan with the pastry.

Layer the apples into the pastry shell and bake at 375°F (190°C) for 30 minutes, or until the apples are becoming tender and the pastry is turning golden brown. Leave the oven on.

Mix the remaining ingredients together and pour the liquid over the apples in the pie.

Return the pie to the oven and continue baking for another 15 minutes. Serve warm or cool.

OPPOSITE: *Phyllo Pastry Goodie Bags Filled with Marzipan and Served with Fresh Fig Ice Cream*
BELOW: *Leah's Apple Flan*

Fresh Nectarine or Peach and Apricot Tart in Almond-scented Oatmeal Crust

Serves 6–8

A lovely almond-scented oatmeal crust, filled with a compote of half-cooked, half-raw fruit. Cooked nectarines or peaches and diced, raw apricots are used in the following recipe, but the order could be reversed, or you could use only one type of fruit.

ALMOND-SCENTED OATMEAL CRUST

1½ cups (6 oz., 185 g) all-purpose (plain) flour
½ cup (3 fl. oz., 90 ml) vegetable oil
½ cup (4 oz., 125 g) golden demerara (raw) sugar
1 teaspoon almond or vanilla extract (essence)
3 tablespoons cold water
4 oz. (125 g) porridge oats

FILLING

5 medium nectarines or peaches, diced and lightly mashed
    with a fork
3 tablespoons cornstarch (cornflour)
¾–1 cup (6–8 oz., 185–250 g) golden demerara (raw)
    sugar, or to taste
2 tablespoons lemon juice
½–1 teaspoon almond or vanilla extract (essence)
8–10 ripe apricots or 5 additional nectarines or
    peaches, diced

GARNISH

¾–1 cup (6–8 fl. oz., 185–250 ml) sour cream or
    whipping (double) cream, lightly whipped
sprinkling of confectioners' (icing) sugar

Preheat the oven to 350°F (180°C).

First, make the pastry shell. Combine the flour and oil until the mixture is smooth, then add the sugar, almond or vanilla extract, cold water, and oats. Combine well to form a ball of dough.

Roll the dough out on a floured surface, then press into a 9-in. (23-cm) pie dish or pan, and bake for 25–30 minutes, or until it is golden brown in places, like shortbread. About 15 minutes into the cooking time, open the oven and you will see that it has puffed up. Pierce it in a few places with a fork, press it down, and continue baking. When baked through, remove the pastry shell from the oven and leave to cool.

Prepare the filling. Combine the mashed nectarines or peaches with the cornstarch, sugar according to the sweetness or otherwise of the fruit, and the lemon juice. Pour the mixture into a saucepan and cook over a low–medium heat, stirring all the time, until the mixture is translucent and thick. Remove from the heat and stir in the almond or vanilla extract. When the fruit mixture has cooled, stir in the diced apricots or nectarines or peaches. Chill until ready to serve.

To serve, simply fill the pastry shell with the fruit mixture and serve topped with a couple of tablespoons of the sour or lightly whipped cream and a sprinkling of confectioners' sugar.

Variation

Add 6 oz. (185 g) or so of sliced strawberries or whole raspberries, tayberries, blueberries (bilberries), or blackberries to the cooled fruit mixture when you add the diced apricots. If you have a large quantity of berries, decrease the amount of diced apricots.

Exotic Fruit Compote with Sweet–Tart Dried Cherries

Serves 4

Dried cherries are a recent entry into the dried fruit market. They are tart and sweet, lightly scented with almond, and make a scrumptious addition to a variety of savory dishes as well as sweet ones — fruity vinaigrettes and salads, particularly.

As with most fruit salads, amounts do not really matter — sweet orchard flavor and fragrance does — but here is a guideline.

large handful of dried cherries
hot, but not boiling, water, to cover
¼–⅓ cup (2–3 fl. oz., 60–90 ml) brandy
selection of diced fruit (ripe pears, kiwi fruit, apricot,
    guava, banana, pineapple, orange or ruby (blood)
    orange, whatever is ripe and in season)
honey, to taste

Put the dried cherries into a bowl and pour the hot water over them, along with the brandy. Cover and leave to soak overnight to plump up.

Combine the cherries and their soaking liquid with the remaining fruit, and sweeten to taste with the honey. Chill until ready to serve.

Leftovers

EXOTIC FRUIT AND DRIED CHERRY CRUMBLE: Use any leftover fruit salad, drained of its excess liquid, as the basis for a tasty fruit crumble.

OPPOSITE: *Fresh Nectarine or Peach and Apricot Tart in Almond-scented Oatmeal Crust*

BERKELEY CHOCOLATE FUDGE PIE

Serves 6–8

This chocolate fudge pie was legendary in the late sixties. The restaurant where it was made would serve the great brown wedges topped with billows of soft, sweet, whipped cream. Too rich to eat as an after-dinner pudding, we frequently succumbed to it as a late-night munch and ordered a portion or two to take away, trying desperately to get home with the pie intact so that we could enjoy it properly, in a dignified manner, with a cup of coffee sipped alongside. We seldom did. Usually by the time we reached home, the pieces of pie were devoured, leaving behind no more than cream-smeared paper and the faint aroma of the chocolate fudge.

The restaurant burned down mysteriously one night. I always jested that it had been set alight by a crazed slimmer who could no longer stand the constant temptation! For years afterwards, conversations with anyone who had lived in the area might turn wistfully towards the remembrance of that chocolate pie and speculations on what exactly the recipe might be.

This recipe is my version. It is intensely chocolatey, much like the flourless chocolate cakes doted on in France and known in California as 'decadence', but here the chocolate mixture is poured into a crust before baking, turning this dish into a lusciously delicious pie.

> *enough shortcrust pastry for a 9–10-in, (23–25-cm) pie pan or flan dish*
> *8 oz. (250 g) bittersweet dark chocolate, broken into small pieces*
> *1 cup (8 fl. oz., 250 ml) hot, strong coffee*
> *4 oz. (125 g) unsalted butter, softened and cut into small pieces*
> *¼–⅓ cup (2–3 oz., 60–90 g) sugar, or to taste*
> *3 tablespoons cocoa powder*
> *pinch of salt*
> *3 eggs, lightly beaten*
> *1 teaspoon vanilla extract (essence)*

GARNISH
> *1 cup (8 fl. oz., 250 ml) whipping (double) cream*
> *vanilla extract (essence), to taste*
> *superfine (caster) sugar, to taste*

Bake the pastry shell blind, filled with baking parchment and beans or ceramic baking beans or metal weights designed for the purpose, at 350°F (180°C) for 20 minutes, then remove the shell from the oven and leave it to cool before using. Turn the oven up to 375°F (190°C).

Meanwhile, put the chocolate into a bowl and pour the hot coffee over it. Cover and leave it to stand for 10 minutes or until the chocolate has melted (do not stir it, as you want the heat of the coffee to melt the chocolate but not dilute it).

Pour the coffee carefully off the chocolate, leaving behind a little of the coffee directly on the melted chocolate. (Keep the poured-off coffee to heat through with milk for a fragrant coffee-break cupful).

Stir the softened butter into the melted chocolate quickly so that the chocolate does not stiffen. Add the sugar, cocoa, salt, egg, and vanilla extract, mixing everything well, then pour the mixture into the cooled pastry shell.

Bake the pie in the heated oven for 30 minutes. The top will crack and become a bit crusty, but this is the way it should be.

When it is done, remove the pie from the oven and leave it to cool. Chill until you are about to serve.

When you are ready to serve, whip the cream and flavor it with the vanilla extract and sweeten with the superfine sugar. Serve the pie chilled, cut into wedges, each portion topped with a generous spoonful of the sweet whipped cream.

OPPOSITE: *Berkeley Chocolate Fudge Pie*

Very Lemony Cheesecake

Serves 8–10

Cheesecake is to Californians, especially Californians who have spent time in New York, a necessary food. Often, however, in inimitable West-Coast style, the cheesecake will be flavored, layered, garnished, or otherwise embellished with any of a wide array of ingredients — the more adventurous the better. The espresso café near my home boasts a daily selection of about 20 different cheesecakes so the task of making a decision is never easy. Should I have the one studded with plump raisins and grated citrus rind, or the one glazed and with sugared berries, apricots or cherries, or the one marbled with dark chocolate, or the one flavored with coffee liqueur or topped with almond praline? Some are high and grand, others flat and tart-like. There are even savory cheesecakes, the creamy cheese custard seasoned with green chili peppers, onions, and crumbled feta cheese.

The following sweet cheesecake is, as its name states, a very lemony one, the pleasantly sharp lemon flavor offsetting the richness of the cheese.

Fresh blueberries (bilberries), blackberries, raspberries, strawberries, or sweet, ripe cherries are all blissful with cheesecake.

Crumb Base

3 oz. (90 g) butter
8 oz. (250 g) graham crackers or digestive biscuits,
    crushed into crumbs
⅓ cup (3 oz., 90 g) sugar

Filling

3 large lemons, plus extra juice as needed
12 oz. (375 g) cream cheese, softened
¾ cup (6 oz., 185 g), plus 2 heaped tablespoons sugar
2 eggs
2½ tablespoons all-purpose (plain) flour

Topping

¾–1 cup (6–8 fl. oz., 185–250 ml) lightly sweetened
    whipped cream or ½ cup (4 fl. oz., 125 ml) sour cream
    with sugar and vanilla extract (essence), to taste

Prepare the crumb base first. Gently melt the butter in a saucepan, then pour in the crushed cookie crumbs and sugar. Mix the butter into them well. Press the mixture into a soufflé dish or a 9 x 3 in. (23 x 7.5 cm) or so pie pan or flan dish.

For the filling, grate the zest from the lemons and put it to one side. Squeeze the juice from the lemons and make up to ⅓–½ cup (3–4 fl. oz., 90–125 ml)

with the extra juice, according to taste. (I like mine rather tart and so use the larger amount.)

Preheat the oven to 325°F (170°C). Beat the cream cheese until it is smooth, then gradually add all but 2 tablespoons of the sugar and mix it in until the mixture is light and fluffy. Separate the eggs and beat the yolks into the cream cheese mixture, together with the flour, reserved lemon rind, and lemon juice. Whip until a smooth mixture results.

Beat the egg whites until soft peaks form, then slowly add the 2 tablespoons sugar and continue to whip until the whites form stiff peaks.

Fold the whites into the lemony cream cheese mixture (it will be quite runny).

Pour the mixture into the crumb-lined dish and place it in a larger baking pan filled with hot water (enough to come 1–2 in. (2.5–5 cm) up the side of the pan), then bake the cheesecake in the preheated oven until the cheese mixture has set and is golden brown (about an hour). If using the second topping listed in the ingredients, spread the sweetened, vanilla-scented sour cream over the hot cheesecake 10 minutes before the end of the cooking time and return it to the oven to finish cooking.

Remove from the oven, leave to cool, then chill for at least 4 hours. If using the first topping, serve with a large spoonful of the lightly whipped cream.

Variation

FROZEN LEMON CHEESECAKE: Simply freeze the above finished cheesecake and serve it frozen, thawing it just long enough to allow you to cut through the crust and serve the wedges. Frozen, this cheesecake takes on a refreshing sorbet-type quality.

OPPOSITE: *Very Lemony Cheesecake*

BLONDIES
Makes 12 bars

Blondies are dense, cake-like confections, much like chocolate brownies, but a golden blonde color, hence the name. They are filled with chocolate chips or chunks, and have a crunchy exterior that gives way to a slightly chewy center. Cookies made from the same dough are sold on the street, freshly baked, their sweet aromas enticing and beckoning you shamelessly.

4 oz. (125 g) butter, softened
⅔ cup (5 oz., 155 g) dark or medium demerara
 (raw) sugar
¾ cup (6 oz., 185 g) superfine (caster) sugar
1½ teaspoons vanilla extract (essence)
1 egg, lightly beaten
3 cups (12 oz., 375 g) self-rising flour
½ teaspoon salt
4 oz. (125 g), approximately, semisweet (dark plain)
 chocolate, broken into small pieces
2 oz. (60 g) walnut halves or pieces (optional)

Preheat the oven to 350°F (180°C).

Cream the butter then add the sugars, vanilla extract, and egg. Mix until you have a creamy consistency.

Mix in the flour, salt, chocolate, and walnuts (if using), until all the ingredients are well combined. Spoon the mixture into a greased non-stick pan, about

9 in. (23 cm) wide or a similar size rectangular shape, and smooth the top.

Bake in the preheated oven for 50–60 minutes. The mixture will puff up somewhat, like a soufflé at first. When it comes back down and goes all crusty on top, and it is not too runny inside, it is done. Leave to cool in the pan before cutting into bars. Make the first cut across, halfway along the long side of the tin, then cut parallel with the long side at 1½-in. (4-cm) intervals.

Variations

MILK CHOCOLATE CHUNK BLONDIES: Use milk chocolate instead of the semisweet chocolate.

RICH AND CRISP CHOCOLATE CHUNK COOKIES: Drop spoonfuls of the mixture onto an ungreased, non-stick baking sheet. Bake for 10–15 minutes for old-fashioned American chocolate chunk cookies.

WHITE CHOCOLATE AND MACADAMIA NUT COOKIES: Use white chocolate and macadamia nuts instead of the semisweet chocolate and walnuts.

COCONUT AND MACADAMIA NUT COOKIES: Omit the chocolate and instead add ⅔–1 cup (2–3 oz., 60–90 g) desiccated coconut and use double the amount of macadamia nuts instead of the walnuts.

ABOVE: *Blondies*

OPPOSITE: *Lemon and Basil Granita (left) and Kiwi Sorbet (right)*

ICE CREAM AND OTHER FROZEN DELIGHTS

Californians are ice cream mad. Not only ice cream, however, also frozen yogurt, sorbets, frozen fruit mousses, and so on. It is a phenomenon that is a constant independent of the weather, as ice cream and frozen yogurt shops are nearly as busy in the middle of a miserable, wintry day as they are during the warm and sultry days of summer. One shop I can think of has a continual line (queue), rain or shine.

Californians have this delicious frozen dessert readily available in a dizzying array, with independent creameries plying their wares throughout the state. Sometimes it seems as if eating ice cream is a regional pastime. Following is a mere sampling of some of the more unusual and best-tasting offerings one can prepare at home, with suggestions for making store-bought ice cream a bit more interesting.

LEMON AND BASIL GRANITA

Serves 4

This is absolute refreshment, with its citrus grove flavor. It is not such a surprise to find basil in a dessert rather than in the savory pesto, pasta, pizza, and other places where it is usually found, as basil is a member of the mint family and, as such, is sweetly fragrant. As an example, try the delicious simplicity of a bowl of sweet cherries — the golden type with a gentle pink-red blush — surrounded by fresh basil, alternating a bite of each.

While freshly squeezed lemon juice is, as always, preferable, bottled lemon juice is an almost indistinguishable alternative.

¾ cup (4 oz., 125 g) confectioners' (icing) sugar
1 cup (8 fl. oz., 250 ml) water
½ cup (4 fl. oz., 125 ml) lemon juice
1–2 teaspoons or 2–3 sprigs thinly sliced fresh basil

Dissolve the confectioners' sugar in a small amount of the water, then add the rest of the water and the lemon juice, and stir to mix well. Add the basil and pour the mixture into an ice cube tray or other flat, freezerproof pan, then put it into a freezer.

Freeze until ice crystals form around the edge of the mixture, then stir them in and refreeze. Repeat, using a fork to break up the ice into tiny granular bits, making a smoothish mixture, but more grainy than sorbet.

When it is nearly fluffy, serve. Granita is fragile, beginning to defrost immediately upon serving, so it has to be served and eaten straight away.

ORANGE AND ROSEMARY OR PINEAPPLE AND MINT GRANITA: Substitute half orange or pineapple juice/half water for the plain water, decrease the lemon juice by half, and substitute $\frac{1}{2}$–1 teaspoon fresh rosemary or 1–2 tablespoons fresh spearmint for the basil.

LEMON AND ROSEMARY GRANITA: Follow the Lemon and Basil Granita recipe, but substitute $\frac{1}{2}$–1 teaspoon fresh chopped rosemary for the basil.

KIWI SORBET
Makes 4–6 servings

The kiwi fruit is a native of China, indeed it is sometimes known as the Chinese gooseberry. It first traveled to New Zealand at the turn of the century and, in the 1930s, was introduced into California where it has flourished. Now California grows all the kiwi fruit produced in the USA.

The emerald-fleshed fruit, with its tiny black ring of seeds and white heart, was much maligned as the darling of nouvelle cuisine when it was tossed onto and into all manner of dishes, indiscriminately and thoughtlessly. Luckily, however, its gentle flavor of both tropics and orchard has withstood the judgments of fickle fashion. Peel and slice them into fruit salads, ice cream, cakes, and other confections, or purée them into a coulis or, as in the following recipe, freeze them into a sorbet. Campari adds a bittersweet edge. Try adding a tablespoon as does Margaret Fox, whose Café Beaujolais in Mendocino is not to be missed if you ever happen to be in the vicinity.

In California, kiwi fruit juice mixed with mineral water is sold in stores, lightly sweet and refreshing. If you should find a bottle of this, pour it into a freezer tray or ice cream maker, and freeze for an impromptu and cooling sorbet.

$\frac{1}{2}$ *cup (4 oz., 125 g) sugar*
$\frac{1}{3}$ *cup (3 fl. oz., 90 ml) water*
6 large or 8 small to medium kiwi fruit, peeled and cut up
$\frac{1}{4}$ *cup (2 fl. oz., 60 ml) lemon juice*

Combine the sugar with the water in a pan, and bring it to the boil. Leave to cool, then chill.

Meanwhile, purée the kiwi fruit. Strain out seeds at this stage if you wish. Add the purée to the sugar syrup, along with the lemon juice. Freeze the mixture in an ice cream maker or in an ice tray (see the following method for Grapefruit and Tequila Sorbet).

GRAPEFRUIT AND TEQUILA SORBET
Makes slightly over 2 $\frac{1}{2}$ cups (1 imp. pint, 625 ml)

Tart and tangy grapefruit paired with strong tequila makes a surprisingly brilliant combination. I often serve the mixture for Sunday brunch, as it is light and refreshing, but delightfully potent.

Here the two are combined in a sorbet — a perfect ending for any spicy meal. If you can get pink grapefruit juice, this will make the sorbet a lovely pale pink.

2 cups (16 fl. oz., 500 ml) grapefruit juice, preferably pink
$\frac{1}{4}$ *cup (2 fl. oz., 60 ml) tequila*
3–4 tablespoons superfine (caster) sugar

Stir together all the ingredients until the sugar has dissolved, then pour it into an ice cream maker or ice cube tray to freeze. Freeze until ice crystals form around the edge of the mixture, then beat it well to break them up and combine until the mixture is smooth. Return to the freezer and freeze until it is almost solid, and beat again to form a smooth mixture. Repeat this two or three times more, or until the sorbet is very thick when you have finished beating. Freeze until you are about ready to serve it, then let the sorbet soften in the refrigerator for about 15 minutes or so.

COOKIES AND CREAM ICE CREAM
Serves 4–6

Dark chocolate 'cookies' or Bourbon biscuits are folded into vanilla ice cream, then it is refrozen to produce this ice cream. The bits of cookie become slightly softened and chewy, their dark shock of flavor a delicious combination with the cold, creamy, vanilla ice cream.

Be sure to use a good quality ice cream that tastes of vanilla rather than some of the store-bought ice creams that taste of coconut oil or other ingredients that have no place in a good, honest vanilla ice cream.

1 pack dark chocolate cookies (biscuits) or chocolate cream cookies (Bourbon biscuits), crumbled into uneven bits, some chunks, some small crumb-like bits
1 quart (1 $\frac{3}{4}$ imp. pints, 1 litre) good-quality vanilla ice cream, slightly softened

Combine the crumbled biscuits with the softened ice cream.

Return the ice cream to the freezer, and freeze until it is firm and you are ready to serve.

Variations

Adding bits of crunchy, sweet, interestingly-textured ingredients to rich ice cream appeals deliciously to anyone who likes decadence. Here are just a few suggestions, made by softening store-bought ice cream and mixing in the extra, chopped ingredients:

- choc chip
- cookie ice cream
- crushed pecan or walnut pralines in caramel swirl ice cream
- diced brandy-soaked dark cherries and semisweet (dark plain) chocolate chip in vanilla or chocolate ice cream
- after-dinner mint chip chocolate ice cream or semisweet (plain) chocolate sorbet
- vanilla and chocolate and toffee chip ice cream
- white chocolate and semisweet (plain) chocolate chips in chocolate ice cream
- peach or pineapple chunks, white chocolate chip, and macadamia nut in vanilla ice cream.

BELOW: *Orange and Vanilla Ice with Drunken Blackberries*

ORANGE AND VANILLA ICE WITH DRUNKEN BLACKBERRIES
Serves 4

Orange sorbet swirled into vanilla ice cream is definitely refreshing. Serve scoops of it topped with blackberries that have macerated in a little crème de cassis or Grand Marnier.

1 carton (punnet) blackberries, picked over and cleaned
crème de cassis or Grand Marnier, to taste, plus sugar,
*   if needed*
2 cups (16 fl. oz., 500 ml) vanilla ice cream
²⁄₃ cup (5 fl. oz., 155 ml) orange sorbet

Mix the blackberries with the liqueur and add sugar to taste, according to the sweetness or tartness of the fruit. Leave to marinate, chilled, for 30 minutes or so.

Meanwhile, leave the ice cream and sorbet out of the freezer to soften for 20–30 minutes. Then, spoon the ice cream into a freezerproof container, spoon the sorbet over it, and stir just until the sorbet marbles the ice cream as attractively and as evenly as possible with lines of sorbet. Return to the freezer and freeze until it is firm.

Serve the Drunken Blackberries spooned over scoops of the Orange and Vanilla Ice.

CHEWY CHOCOLATE ICE CREAM WITH DOUBLE CHOCOLATE CHUNKS AND TOASTED NUTS

Makes 5 cups (2 imp. pints, 1.25 litres)

In true California excessiveness, this chewy, deeply chocolate ice cream is studded with chunks of dark and white chocolate, and bits of crunchy nuts.

2½ cups (1 imp. pint, 625 ml) whipping (double) cream
2 cups (16 fl. oz., 500 ml) milk
⅔ cup (5 oz., 155 g) sugar
9 oz. (280 g) semisweet (dark plain) chocolate
4 egg yolks, beaten
⅓ cup (1½ oz., 45 g) unsweetened cocoa powder
1 teaspoon vanilla extract (essence)
2 oz. (60 g) white chocolate, broken into chunks
½ oz. (15 g) toasted, chopped almonds or walnuts or pecans or hazelnuts

In a heavy-bottomed saucepan, combine the whipping cream, milk, and sugar. Cook over a medium heat until the sugar has dissolved and the mixture is quite hot, stirring it every so often, then remove the pan from the heat.

Break up 8 oz. (250 g) of the chocolate and add the chunks to the hot cream mixture (break the remaining chocolate into smallish chunks and reserve). Leave the pan covered for about 5 minutes or until the chocolate has melted.

Stir or beat the chocolate to mix and dissolve it well into the cream, but do not worry if bits of chocolate still remain, they will eventually disappear.

Gradually add 1 cup (8 fl. oz., 250 ml) of this hot chocolate mixture to the egg yolks, beating them together well, then stir the egg mixture into the rest of the hot chocolate mixture.

Make a paste from the cocoa powder by adding a very little of the hot chocolate mixture to it, then add the paste back to the hot chocolate mixture. Cook the mixture gently over a low heat, stirring occasionally. When the mixture is hot and has thickened slightly, enough to coat the back of a spoon, remove the pan from the heat and add the vanilla extract.

Leave to cool, then freeze it either in an ice cream maker or baking tray, forking it up or stirring it every 30–45 minutes to break up the ice crystals.

When the ice cream is solid and creamy, remove it from the freezer and let it melt for a few minutes. Spoon in the remaining dark chocolate, the white chocolate, and the nuts. Return the ice cream to the freezer for 30 minutes to firm up, then serve as desired.

Variation

CHEWY CHOCOLATE ICE CREAM WITH ESPRESSO BEANS: Omit the chocolate chunks and nuts, adding instead 2 tablespoons instant coffee powder or espresso powder to the cocoa paste and toss a handful of chocolate espresso beans into the ice-cream just before serving.

DRUNKEN DRIED FRUITS OVER ICE CREAM

Rum and raisin is the most famous combination, but apricots steeped in Cognac and Sauternes are yummy as well, as are brandy-soaked figs and brandy-soaked prunes over coffee ice cream. Nearly any type of dried fruit may be macerated in nearly any sort of spirit.

Put the fruit into a bowl, cutting it into bite-sized pieces first if you want to, then pour the chosen spirit over them, covering the bowl tightly and leaving them to steep for 2 hours at least or, preferably, overnight until they have plumped up.

FROZEN CRANBERRY FOOL

Serves 4

Tangy and sweet, with the distinctive bitter edge that characterizes the cranberry, this frothy whip of fruit and cream is one of the reasons that seeing the first cranberries of the season triggers feelings of excitement within me.

12 oz. (375 g) frozen cranberries, frozen
1½ tablespoons sugar, or to taste
1 satsuma (mandarin), peeled, deseeded, and diced
½ cup (4 fl. oz., 125 ml) sour cream or Greek yogurt
2 cups (16 fl. oz., 500 ml) whipping (double) cream

Let the cranberries partially defrost so that they are slushy and still somewhat icy. In a blender or food processor, whirl the cranberries with the sugar and satsuma, then add the sour cream or yogurt. Whip the cream until it forms firm peaks, then fold it into the cranberry mixture. Serve immediately.

Variation

Use frozen and unsweetened strawberries or raspberries in place of the cranberries. Follow the same method as above.

OPPOSITE: *Chewy Chocolate Ice Cream with Double Chocolate Chunks and Toasted Nuts*

Beverages

With so many sun-filled days and an active lifestyle, Californians are devotees of light, cooling, and refreshing drinks. Regional bottled waters are a favored drink, not only au naturel, but carbonated and/or scented with fruit and herbal essences. Iced rather than hot teas are popular, especially the herbal and fruit-flavored ones.

Juices abound, too, sweet and freshly pressed, from orchard and tropical fruits to garden vegetables: sweet cherry, fragrant apple, papaya (pawpaw), mango, pineapple, kiwi fruit, banana, carrot, wheat grass, and all manner of combinations.

While alcoholic drinks are rather frowned upon in these days of neo-prohibition, meals are often accompanied by several glasses of any of California's excellent wines, often served half and half, spritzer-style, with mineral water. When something stronger is called for, it is usually a local brandy or tequila from south of the border whirled into an icy margarita.

'Smoothies' — drinks made from frozen fruit whirled together with yogurt — might be served in place of breakfast or lunch, or drunk on the run from a street stand or natural foods store. Diner-style frothy milk shakes, based on ice cream, will never disappear, no matter how health-conscious people become — they are just too delicious.

Whereas coffee drinking is down across the USA, specialty coffee consumption is at an all-time high, and California leads the nation in the consumption of cappuccino and espresso drinks. The 'ssssss' of the espresso, the 'whoosh' of the steaming milk are background noises that accompany life in the Golden State. Decaffeinated coffee and espresso are often the choices of the health-conscious, as is hot herbal tea in any of hundreds of flavors.

OPPOSITE: *Strawberry Lime Frappé (left), Peach and Ginger Sparkler (center), and Vanilla-scented Winter Fruit and Muesli Smoothie (right)*

FRUIT SELTZER
Serves 1

We drank gallons of this during the endless days of 100°F- or 38°C-plus summers in my Central Valley childhood. Nothing seemed to quench our burning thirst or revive our flagging spirits in quite the way that this refreshing drink did. I have always suspected it had Russian origins as my Kiev-born grandfather was the man who poured the refreshing glassfuls (the grown-ups, by the way, had vodka in theirs).

handful of ice cubes
½ cup (4 fl. oz., 125 ml) fruit juice of choice (orange, cherry, pineapple, kiwi, cranberry, or tropical mixtures)
¼–½ cup (2–4 fl. oz., 60–125 ml) fizzy mineral water or soda water

Put the ice cubes into a glass and pour the fruit juice over them. Then, fill the glass to the brim with fizzy mineral water or soda water, and drink immediately.

VANILLA-SCENTED WINTER FRUIT AND MUESLI SMOOTHIE
Serves 2–4

Winter fruits — such as apples, oranges or satsumas (mandarins), and bananas — and a handful of muesli blended with milk and yogurt make a delicious snack or breakfast drink. The thing about smoothies is that they taste so good, yet they are very, very easy to make (if you have a blender, that is).

4–6 ice cubes, lightly crushed
1 apple, cored and diced, but unpeeled
1¼ cups (12 fl. oz., 375 ml) milk
2 satsumas (mandarins), peeled, deseeded, and diced
1 medium or 2 small banana(s), diced
honey, to taste
2 tablespoons muesli of choice (preferably untoasted)
dash of vanilla extract (essence)
2 tablespoons or so plain unsweetened yogurt
other fruits, as desired (optional)

Whirl the ice and apple together in a blender or food processor, then add the milk and whirl until smoothish and with grains of ice.

Add the satsumas, banana, honey, muesli, vanilla extract, yogurt, and the other fruits of your choice. Whirl until the mixture is relatively smooth and thick, then serve immediately.

PEACH AND GINGER SPARKLER
Serves 1

The combination of spicy ginger and sweet–tart peach is classically good. Here it is combined in an embarrassingly simple-to-prepare drink that is, none the less, the definition of refreshment.

This beverage is particularly good served alongside Mexican food.

1 ripe peach, peeled and sliced, or diced, and lightly mashed
ice cubes
ginger ale, American-style, or ginger beer, British-style

Into each glass, place half the mashed peach and ice cubes. Fill each glass with the ginger ale or ginger beer, and drink immediately.

TROPICAL FRUIT YOGURT SMOOTHIE
Serves 2

Adding a carton of flavored yogurt gives more fruit flavor to this drink, as well as sweetening it. Try, too, adding frozen fruit for a frozen-yogurt-like consistency.

3–5 ice cubes, lightly crushed
1 kiwi fruit, peeled and diced
10 or so strawberries, hulled and halved
½–1 mango, peeled and diced
1 medium or 2 small, ripe banana(s), diced
1 individual carton fruit-flavored yogurt of choice
1–1½ cups (8–12 fl. oz., 250–375 ml) milk
honey, to taste

Whirl the ice cubes in a blender or food processor until they have broken into small pieces. Add the fruit and whirl so that it is puréed with the ice.

Add the yogurt, 1 cup (8 fl. oz., 250 ml) of the milk, and honey, to taste depending on the sweetness or tartness of the fruit. Whirl the mixture to a froth, adding more milk or ice if needed. Serve immediately, or the ice begins to melt and the drink loses its icy, refreshing qualities.

STRAWBERRY LIME FRAPPE
Serves 4

A shot of tequila, rum, or vodka adds a refreshing punch to this delicious drink.

2 cartons (punnets) strawberries, cleaned, hulled and sliced
juice of 1 large lime, plus a little of the finely grated zest
3 tablespoons sugar or honey, dissolved in a little hot
*   water, then left to cool*
8–10 ice cubes, lightly crushed

Whirl all the ingredients in a blender or food processor, and serve immediately.

FRESH FRUIT FROSTY
Serves 2

This makes an icy, sweet, spoonable drink, and uses no dairy products. It is light and consummately refreshing.

2 nectarines, sliced (leave peeled or unpeeled, as preferred)
1 banana, sliced
2 tablespoons frozen, slightly defrosted, sweetened berries
*   (if unsweetened, add sugar or honey, to taste)*
1 satsuma (mandarin) or small orange, peeled, deseeded,
*   and diced*
dash of lemon juice
6–8 ice cubes, lightly crushed

Whirl all the fruit and the lemon juice together in a blender or food processor, then add the ice cubes and continue whirling until it is smoothish, frosty, and icy. Enjoy immediately.

JAVA CITY CAPPUCCINO MILK SHAKE
Serves 1

Cappuccino is California's favorite coffee, brought over by Italian immigrants during the Gold Rush days. Walking down nearly any street, one can often catch the aroma of the strong, dark-roasted beans as they are ground in any of the numerous tiny coffee-roasting businesses or cafés that punctuate the major urban regions — San Francisco Bay Area, Los Angeles, Sacramento.

While San Franciscans tend to stick with the original hot, frothy drink, encouraged no doubt by the chilling summer fogs, in the warmer areas summer coffee drinks tend to be iced. Take, for instance, California's Central Valley. The valley swelters in the sultry summer when the thermometer climbs to over 100°F or 38°C, then refuses to budge downwards. The capital city, Sacramento, lies in this valley and, when summer hits the town, coffee bars switch from that hot cup of 'java' to infinitely more cooling, chilled coffee drinks.

Java City is the name of the Sacramento-based chain of café bars that are the brainchild of a couple of fellow caffeine addicts who also happen to be my cousins. This recipe is theirs.

1 serving espresso, cooled
¹⁄₃–¹⁄₂ cup (3–4 fl. oz., 90–125 ml) cold milk
1 generous scoop rich ice cream, cut into several pieces
*   (preferably Italian-style gelato in chocolate, coffee,*
*   vanilla, hazelnut, or other coffee-compatible flavor)*

In a blender or food processor, combine all the ingredients and whirl until it is all a smooth, icy froth.

ICED ESPRESSO
Serves 1

This is made from strong, strong coffee that has been left to cool and is then poured over a glassful of ice cubes and chilled to icy refreshment. Iced coffee is on every café menu in California as soon as the 'dog days' of summer are upon us.

When preparing iced coffee, I use espresso coffee, which is dark and intense, as it holds up best against the melting ice cubes and still has good, strong flavor once the ice has diluted it somewhat. Milk may be added, for a more cappuccino than espresso flavor, but I find it more refreshing without.

¹⁄₂ cup (4 fl. oz., 125 ml) strong espresso coffee, cooled
a glass full of ice
sugar, to taste
milk (optional)

Pour the espresso into the glass of ice and sweeten to taste. Add milk, if using, and enjoy immediately.

Variation
Iced coffee is extremely good with a floating scoop of ice cream. Chill the espresso over ice, then strain it to remove any remaining ice cubes. Serve immediately with the ice cream on top.

ICED CHOCOLATE

Serves 1

During a heat wave, a frosty glass of iced chocolate is a lovely indulgence. Milk may be used in place of water for a richer, creamier drink. Or, for a classic East Coast cum West Coast drink, combine the chocolate syrup with a half-glass of milk, then fill the glass with fizzy water.

> 2 tablespoons unsweetened cocoa powder
> sugar, to taste
> 2 tablespoons hot water
> dash of vanilla extract (essence)
> ¾ cup (6 fl. oz., 185 ml) water
> ice cubes

Mix the cocoa powder with the sugar, then add the hot water and mix to form a paste.

Stir in the vanilla extract, then the water, and pour it over ice in a tall glass.

Variations

FROZEN CAFE MOCHA: In place of the water, use cold, strong coffee or cold espresso mixed with milk.

ICED CAFE AMORE: Omit the ice and the cold chocolate and espresso mixture of the first variation, and float a scoop of vanilla ice cream on top.

TEQUILA AND PINEAPPLE WITH FRESH MINT

Serves 1

Tequila is, without doubt, California's favorite spirit. Its somewhat vegetal, somewhat saline flavor pairs brilliantly with the cooling, bittersweet juices adored on the West Coast. Plus, it gives you a heady slap of alcoholic potency.

> 1 measure tequila (preferably the golden aged variety)
> 1 teaspoon or so fresh mint, thinly sliced or crushed
> ¾ cup (6 fl. oz., 185 ml) unsweetened, pure
>   pineapple juice

Combine all the ingredients in a glass with lots of ice cubes, and enjoy immediately.

BELOW: *Java City Cappuccino Milkshake (left) and Tequila and Pineapple with Fresh Mint (right)*

Index

Numbers in *italics* refer to illustrations

Index